# If You Really Loved Me

JASON EVERT

# If You Really Loved Me

## 100 Questions on Dating, Relationships, and Sexual Purity

REVISED AND EXPANDED

Totus Tuus
—PRESS—

DENVER
2013

Published by Totus Tuus Press, LLC
P.O. Box 280021
Lakewood, CO 80228
totustuuspress.com

Cover photo by Howard Decruyenaere
Cover design by Chris Gilbert, DesignWorks
Typesetting by Loyola Graphics

Printed in the United States of America
ISBN 978-0-9830923-7-7

# Dedication

*For Mary*

# Contents

It is Jesus that you seek when you dream of happiness; He is waiting for you when nothing else you find satisfies you; He is the beauty to which you are so attracted; it is He who provokes you with that thirst for fullness that will not let you settle for compromise; it is He who urges you to shed the masks of a false life; it is He who reads in your hearts your most genuine choices, the choices that others try to stifle. It is Jesus who stirs in you the desire to do something great with your lives, the will to follow an ideal, the refusal to allow yourselves to be ground down by mediocrity, the courage to commit yourselves humbly and patiently to improving yourselves and society, making the world more human and more fraternal.[1]

～

Dear young people, have the sacred ambition to become holy like He is holy! Young people of every continent, do not be afraid to be the saints of the new millennium! May the gospel become your most precious treasure . . . may most holy Mary give you the strength and wisdom to be able to speak to God and of God.[2]

—Pope John Paul II

# Introduction

Planned Parenthood recommends that to have a healthier sex life, you should "be selective when you choose a sex partner. . . . Be sure you know your partner's name *and* phone number."[1] *Newsweek* magazine reported that since female chimpanzees, grasshoppers, hyenas, dung flies, and penguins are sexually promiscuous, this may be evidence that such behavior is beneficial for women as well.[2]

I have been to the zoo on several occasions, but since I cannot recall seeing any hyenas that felt used after a broken sexual relationship, I would not recommend that you make any life-changing decisions based on *Newsweek*'s findings. The same is true for the advice of Planned Parenthood.

Our generation is ready for a better kind of love than the world typically offers. The reason we hunger for direction in relationships becomes obvious when we consider the quality of advice the world gives. Medical professionals tell us how to avoid venereal infections, and *Cosmopolitan* magazine offers "lust lessons,"[3] but what we really want to know is how to find authentic, lasting love.

To find a different kind of advice, I read through the Bible as well as the writings of saints, physicians, philosophers, theologians, and marriage counselors. Based on that collective wisdom, and through the lens of Pope John Paul II's brilliant "Theology of the Body," this book addresses the one hundred most common questions we have on dating, love, and the meaning of sex. I speak to about fifteen thousand high school and college students per month, and the following questions are a collection of the best ones they have asked me.

In researching this book, I discovered that the one key that seems to unlock the mystery of sexuality is reverence—purity of heart. When we become irreverent toward sex, we are blind to a reality that would take the world's breath away. As Christ said, "Blessed are the pure in heart, for *they shall see God*" (Matt. 5:8). Through purity of heart, a man is able to see God's image in a woman, and a woman is able to see God's image in a man. We catch a glimpse of what Adam and Eve originally saw in each other, and we discover our vocation to love one another as God loves us. Since God created us to love as He does, *to love with purity is to rediscover the meaning of life*.

As Pope John Paul II said, "Man cannot live without love. He remains a being that is incomprehensible for himself, his life is senseless, if love is not revealed to him, if he does not encounter love, if he does not experience it and make it his own, if he does not participate intimately in it. This is why Christ the Redeemer 'fully reveals man to Himself.'"[4]

Christ crucified teaches us what it means to be human: that we will find ourselves only in the fullest giving of ourselves. For each person, this fullest giving of one's self will come in a unique way. For one, it may be the giving of one's self in marriage; for others, in the religious or the single life. All are called to make a sincere gift of themselves and in this way fulfill the very meaning of their existence.

I have not always lived with this mentality. At more times than I would like to admit, I have tried to keep God's nose out of my business: "If only I can live this part of my life without Him, then I'll have some freedom. How am I supposed to have a life otherwise?" If we harbor this thought, we have bought the biggest lie on earth: "God is holding out on us, and when it comes down to it, He does not want us to be happy and have love. If we want fulfillment, we need to forget God and the Church and grab it ourselves!" Essentially we are saying, "If only I can keep the Author of love out of my love life!"

To let God into our love lives, we must have the courage to listen to our conscience. This is an echo of the voice of God in our hearts, directing us to authentic love and telling us when we are selling ourselves short. At times we might suppress our conscience, seeing it as the enemy of freedom and love. But if we have the courage to follow it, we will have life and have it abundantly. It is ironic that we find the freedom and love we long for in the place we least expect—in obedience to God's laws.

Even those who click onto a pornographic Web site are yearning for what only God's plan for love can fulfill. Everyone who gets drunk at a party and the next morning cannot remember who he slept with is on the same quest. Though such people might seem uninterested in God, they are actually longing for Him, because behind every sexual desire and even every addiction is a yearning for God, a hunger to experience love in all its intensity. We all long for the kind of love for which we were made. The good news that Christ bears is that this love is possible (regardless of our past), and He is waiting for us to come to Him so that we might receive it.

If we truly desire love, we must have the courage to take a deep look into the motives of our hearts and a deep look at the meaning of sex. Do we *really* want to know the truth about sex? Are we willing to hear the demands that authentic love places upon us? Part of the truth is the bad news: all of us are tempted to use others for our emotional or physical gratification. A battle exists in the heart between love and lust; those who experience true love will be the ones who wage war against the counterfeits we are all prone to embrace.

So what is the cost of following God's way? What is God asking of me when it comes to purity? Is it simply that I avoid adultery and X-rated movies? If I have the courage to listen to Christ, will He ask me to give Him something that I am not ready to surrender? If we retreat from the challenge of looking honestly at our hearts, if we act as if there is no fault in us that needs correction, we deceive ourselves. We will always make the frustrating mistake of confusing lust with love.

If you wish to find love and be free, hear the good news: the truth will set you free. God's plan for life and love is so profound that when we understand it, we will never look the same way at the relationship between a man and a woman. *When we see God's plan for love, lust looks boring.* When we see the truth about our bodies and sex, we change our lives, but not out of guilt, or fear of pregnancy, or disease. We change our lives because God's view of love is everything the human heart longs for. But as Pope John Paul II remarked in a letter to a friend, "It is not enough simply to want to accept such love. One must know how to give it."[5]

Therefore, let us offer our sexuality to God so that every action, word, glance, and desire will be lifted to Him. Then He will guide our hearts toward the truth of human love. It is our turn for a sexual revolution, and those who lead our generation to victory will be those who have conquered lust by surrendering to the God of love. If we do not rise to this challenge of building a culture of life and a civilization of love, we have wasted that heroic enthusiasm, courage, and fortitude that our youth affords us.

It is my prayer that all who read this book will find guidance where there is uncertainty, encouragement where there is despair, healing where there are wounds, and a deep sense of the joy and peace that come from offering to God everything we are, and everything we do. As you read this, be assured that I have already been praying for you. Please keep all those to whom I speak about chastity, all those reading this book, and myself in your prayers as well.

*"The Lord bless you and keep you. The Lord make His face to shine upon you, and be gracious to you. The Lord lift up His countenance upon you, and give you peace"* (Num. 6:24–26).

Jason Evert

# I

# Chastity and the Meaning of Sex

## 1

### *Is chastity the same thing as abstinence?*

Abstinence means that a person is not sexually active. If I heard that a guy was abstinent, that would not tell me much about him. Maybe he is a man with courage and character and is saving himself for his bride. Maybe he just cannot find a date. Either way, abstinence is defined as what a person is *not* doing—in other words, no sex.

Chastity is different because it is defined by what a person *is* doing with his or her sexuality. It means having the strength to use your sexuality according to God's plan, whether you are single or married. Living this virtue purifies your heart, heals your memories, strengthens your will, and glorifies God with your body. For an unmarried person it means saving marital intimacies for marriage. As one woman said, "It is sexuality dedicated to hope." [1]

For the married and the unmarried, it means having reverence for the gift of sex. Chastity is a virtue that defends love from selfishness and frees us from using others as objects. It makes us capable of authentic love. In short, abstinence ends in marriage but chastity holds marriage together.

## 2

### *Is chastity the same thing as virginity?*

Some people think that chastity and virginity are synonymous, but they are not. Not all chaste people are virgins, and not all virgins are chaste. For example, before their conversions, Saint Augustine fathered a child out of marriage, Saint Margaret of Cortona lived with her boyfriend, and Saint Pelagia was a prostitute. While they may not have been virgins, they became chaste—and became saints.

On the other hand, some people are technically virgins, but they compromise their purity in countless ways. Many virgins assume, "As long as I retain my virginity, I'm being good. Therefore, everything short of intercourse is OK." They may give parts of themselves to people they know they will never marry and assume that they are still pure because they are not having intercourse. Slowly they begin to believe that sexual intimacy is not a big deal. By the time they meet the person they truly deserve, they need a lot of healing for all they have given away.

But chastity is not something that can be lost forever because something shameful happened in your past. Virginity concerns our sexual history, but chastity is *not* concerned with the past. Chastity is a virtue that exists only in the present. People often think that because they have lost their virginity, purity will always be out of their reach. It is not. Just as a person who has led a pure life can fall into immorality, a person who has sinned can return to purity. To be pure it is necessary that your heart be directed to God. In His eyes, the repentant prostitute is purer than the lustful virgin. We need to remember that our worth lies in how God sees us, not in how others see us or even in how we sometimes see ourselves.

### 3

*Doesn't chastity ruin the spontaneity and excitement of romance?*

It depends upon what you consider romantic. Real romance is not what you find in a grocery store novel with Fabio on the cover. Giving in to one's hormones at the drop of a hat is not romance. This is lust, and while it may be spontaneous and temporarily exciting, using another person is not romantic. In fact, too many good romantic relationships have been ruined by lust.

Only humans are capable of romance because romance is where imagination and love meet. Sometimes a person's actions may appear romantic because they are so imaginative and thoughtful, but the actions may be done for the sake of seducing another. This is not romance, because love is absent. Only when purity is present can one tell the difference between loving romance and selfish seduction.

In fact, romantic moments do not require physical intimacy —and the most romantic couples are the ones who realize this. They know that romance requires respect. You can have lust and passion without respect (as in prostitution), but you cannot have romance without respect. When that loving respect for the other person is present, a man stirs up his romantic creativity not for the sake of getting something from a woman but for the sake of expressing his love to her.

Lust, on the other hand, is boring, because it allows no room for mystery and anticipation. Everything secret is given away. The pure have more passion than the lustful, and it is precisely their passion that gives them the ability to build a greater kind of love. They exercise self-control not because of an absence of passion but because of the presence of love.

A twenty-three-year-old woman pointed out that there is something exciting in restraint, something that makes a chaste couple seem to glow in their wedding pictures. She proposed that chastity "may be the proof of God, because it means that we have been designed in such a way that when we humans act like animals, without any restraint and without any rules, we just don't have as much fun." [2] In fact, people who have misused their sexuality are longing for enduring love. They know that being loved is much more exciting than being used.

We need to remember that God is the author of romance. The Bible is His love story, and He is all in favor of human romances that reflect His love for us. For example, one of the most important ingredients for romance is thoughtful creativity. Psalm 139:17 says that the designs of the Lord are precious, and the book of Proverbs adds that God has glory in what He conceals.[3] For proof that God is not the rival to love, consider this:

I recently met a young man named Kevin who was married not long ago. When he and his fiancée visited their priest in preparation for the wedding, the pastor thumbed through their baptism and confirmation certificates. Pausing for a moment, the priest looked closer at one of the documents and said, "Did you two know that you were baptized on the same day when you were babies?" The couple looked at each other and enjoyed a sense of peace that God's hand was upon them. The priest interrupted their moment to add one more detail: "Wait a minute. You two were baptized in the same church . . . and at the same Mass!"

After their meeting Kevin and his bride-to-be called their parents and asked them to dig through the old photo albums. Sure enough, they discovered a photo of the two babies celebrating their first sacrament together, decades before God would reunite them to receive the sacrament of marriage.

You have to wonder how often God intervenes like this in our lives. But when we distance ourselves from Him, we sell ourselves short and settle for poor substitutes for the great love He wants to give us.

When it comes to the topic of sexuality, the media tell us that the most exciting sex is outside marriage. In reality the opposite is true. In 1999 *USA Today* published an article titled "Aha! Call It the Revenge of the Church Ladies."[4] This report summarized the findings of the most "comprehensive and methodologically sound" sex survey ever conducted in the United States. The first three sentences of the report say it all:

Sigmund Freud said they suffer from an "obsessional neurosis" accompanied by guilt, suppressed emotions and repressed sexuality. Former *Saturday Night Live* comedian Dana Carvey satirized them as uptight prudes who believe sex is downright dirty. But several major research studies show that church ladies (and the men who sleep with them) are among the most sexually satisfied people on the face of the Earth.

Now isn't that special?

The article concluded by saying that the Bible's teaching on sex would "come as a shock to those who believe that God is a cosmic killjoy when it comes to sexuality." The world constantly tells us that when it comes to sex, everyone is doing it, and the people having the most fun are the wild singles depicted on television sitcoms, while married life is dull and unromantic. However, according to the researchers who published the sex survey just mentioned, *"The public image of sex in America bears virtually no relationship to the truth."* [5]

Of those having sex, researchers found that the least satisfied were unmarried people. [6] Those who had sex outside of marriage were aware that while it felt good during the act, that did not mean they felt good about themselves afterward. The guilt coupled with the anxious fear of being used, becoming pregnant, or contracting a disease lessened the sexual satisfaction of those who were promiscuous.

On the other hand, research showed that those who were married to a faithful partner had the highest reports of sexual enjoyment on both a physical and emotional level, and they were most likely to feel "satisfied," "loved," "thrilled," "wanted," and "taken care of." [7] Contrary to what the world incessantly says, research shows that marriages benefit from a *lack* of premarital sexual experience. [8] In other words, great sex is not the result of sexual experience and technique. If anything, sexual joy is the result of a happy marriage, not the cause of it.

Lastly, it has also been discovered that "married couples who pray together are 90 percent more likely to report higher satisfaction with their sex life than couples who do not pray together." [9] So if we are only interested in doing what gives the most pleasure (which we should not be), the facts point back to God's original plan: "A man leaves his father and his mother and clings to his wife, and they become one flesh" (Gen. 2:24).

4

*Isn't being chaste the same thing as being a prude?*

The world looks at chastity and sees repression: a dull and frigid
lifestyle that is probably the result of fear or not being able to find
a date. "Those poor people living chaste lives. They don't have
a clue what they're missing. If only someone could liberate them
from their prudishness." Sound familiar?

This may come as a surprise to those who think that chastity
and prudery are synonymous, but chastity has nothing to do with
having a negative idea of sex. In fact, only the pure of heart are
capable of seeing the depth and mystery of sex. For the person
who is pure, sex is a sacred gift and the body is a temple of the
Holy Spirit. Therefore, the foundation of chastity is the dignity
of every person and the greatness of sex.

Sure, chastity says no to sex before marriage. This is not because sex or the body is bad but, on the contrary, because sex is a
holy mystery and a person's body is a holy temple. Holy things are
not open to all; they are only for those who meet the requirement,
who pass the test.

Think of the Holy of Holies in the Jewish temple, into which
no Israelite dared enter except the high priest once a year. The
doors were closed to other good and pious Jews not because the
Holy of Holies was dirty or because the Jews were embarrassed
about it. On the contrary, it was restricted because it was so holy,
so special, that it was appropriate only for the one priest pledged
to the temple's service to enter.

A human body likewise is holy and special, and access to this
temple is only for the one pledged forever to it in the sacrament of
matrimony. If we understood chastity for what it is, we would see
that nothing testifies to the goodness of the body and sex as much
as chastity does. *Just as humility is the proper attitude toward greatness,
purity is the proper attitude toward sex.* Purity guards the secret of sex
because of its greatness. Those who treat sex as if it were a fair
exchange for a nice dinner or six months of commitment are the

ones who have yet to discover its real value. As writer Elisabeth Elliot said, "There is dullness, monotony, sheer boredom in all of life when virginity and purity are no longer protected and prized. By trying to grab fulfillment everywhere, we find it nowhere." [10] We constantly look for what we can get out of someone, how we can please ourselves and "live in the moment."

This is why the impure are never satisfied or free. They have yet to learn that they cannot be filled unless they empty themselves. Ironically, the satisfaction and freedom they yearn for is waiting for them in the place they least expect it—chastity. It trains us in self-control so that we can become truly free. "The alternative is clear," the *Catechism of the Catholic Church* tells us, "either man governs his passions and finds peace, or he lets himself be dominated by them and becomes unhappy." [11]

Chastity has a bad reputation because it involves dying to ourselves. But this death serves a purpose. In the words of Christ, "Unless a grain of wheat falls into the earth and dies, it remains alone; but if it dies, it bears much fruit" (John 12:24). The world sees chastity as death because it does not have the patience to see the life and love that spring forth from the sacrifice. It is not repression or guilt that motivates the chaste man or woman; it is the desire for real love. Because of this the virtue of purity is wildly attractive. Freed from selfish sexual aggressiveness, the pure are empowered to love as we were created to love.

I travel around the country frequently to give talks about chastity, and I often end up in conversations aboard airplanes about my line of work. Inevitably people ask if I practice what I preach. After I explain that I waited for marriage before having sex, the person—without fail—looks bewildered. Then comes the universal question: "So . . . you just didn't have the desires then?" I have pondered all sorts of amusing ways to answer this, but the bottom line is that the world cannot fathom a young person who has sexual desires and does not surrender to them.

Working toward God's plan for love does not eliminate sexual desires, it orders them. The chaste person experiences sexual attractions in all their intensity but places love for the other above the temptation to lust. On the other hand, lust reduces men and women to the flesh, as illustrated in the song "Mambo Number 5." The lyrics state that all the singer needs is a little bit of several women—a little bit of Rita, Tina, Sandra, Mary, Jessica—concluding that having a little bit of each woman makes him their man. Why only a little bit? Because the singer is not man enough to handle an entire woman. Lust allows us to reduce others to "bits."

The problem with lust is not that the desires are too strong; they are too weak, lukewarm, and self-absorbed. Prudishness is fittingly represented as cold and frigid, but purity is white hot. Purity burns with a passionate love that puts lust in the freezer.

## 5

*How do I know when I am ready to have sex?*

The easiest way to know if you are ready to have sex is to look at your left hand. If you do not see a wedding ring, you are not ready for sex. This may seem like a simplistic answer, but look at the logic behind it. What does it mean to be *ready* for sex?

Sex cannot be reduced to a biological act. Every aspect of the person is affected: the body, heart, mind, soul, and future. Therefore, a person is physically able to have sex long before he or she is ready for its consequences. One woman said, "It took losing my virginity at a very young age, losing my self-respect and possibly my fertility, helping to ruin another person's marriage and family life, acquiring a non-curable virus, not getting the fulfillment that sex should provide in marriage, and living with the guilt that Satan always tries to make me feel . . . for me to realize how detrimental sex before marriage can really be."[12]

But instead of zeroing in on the negative consequences, it is more important for a person to understand the meaning of sex. Then it becomes clear when we are "ready" for it.

We arc commonly told with regard to sex, "Just say no." Why?

"Because sex before marriage is bad." But what kind of answer is that? Most people have never been told *why*—why sex *within* marriage is so good and beautiful and why sex *outside* of marriage is a counterfeit of the love that we have been created to give and receive. Instead of fear tactics, we need to hear the truth about the goodness and beauty of sex and God's plan for love.

To help us understand the gift of our sexuality, Pope John Paul II gave the Church a series of teachings known as the "Theology of the Body." In it he explained that when we accept the demands of love and live according to the truth of our sexuality, *we make visible in our bodies the invisible reality of God—that He is love*. If we don't understand this deeper meaning of sex, marriage may seem like nothing more than a piece of paper that legalizes intercourse.

Once we are aware of the greatness of the gift of sex, we will have an attitude of reverence toward it, and only with God's permission will we lift the veil of its mystery. This demands faithfulness to Him while we are waiting to find our spouse. And we can start preparing for a good marriage right now by avoiding anything that could harm a relationship with a future spouse.

If a person does not understand the meaning of sex, he or she may give it away to the first bidder. Some say that they want to save the gift of sex for the "right" person, someone they really love. But strong feelings of love do not make a person ready for sex. This is clear in sexually active couples who are afraid of what sex means. They fear that their lovemaking could bring forth life. They also hide what they are doing from those who love them, such as their parents, and they fear that the incredible bond they have created might not be permanent.

Within marriage no such fears exist. Instead a husband and wife are ready to give and receive each other without reservation. They understand that sex is like saying wedding vows with your body. It is making a complete gift of yourself to another person.

When you understand this meaning of sex, it is obvious that premarital sex is dishonest: it is a lie in the language of the body.

With your body you are saying, "I give myself to you entirely. There is nothing more of me that I could give you," but in reality there is no such commitment and gift of self. There is a total physical gift but no total gift of the person. The gift is reduced to a loan or a lease, because the body is given to the other temporarily.

In other words, you are ready to have sex when your body speaks the truth: "I am entirely yours. Forever." Therefore, only in marriage can one be "ready" for sex.

## 6

*Why is premarital sex bad? My friend just started high school, and she is trying to tell me that it is good and she is going to do it.*

It might help to know that your friend is *not* on a quest for sex. Perhaps your friend has some hurt or loneliness in her life, and she figures that if she has sex, it will feel like love and security, and she will be happy. Or perhaps she's just curious and too immature to realize the consequences of sex. Either way, if you look into her heart you will see that she is not longing for a series of physical relationships with random guys. She is looking for enduring love and for intimacy, to be accepted by a man and cared for by him.

Your friend deserves these things, but she needs to be careful and courageous so that she does not fall for a counterfeit. There are plenty of boys out there who will tell her how beautiful her eyes are and how much they love her and will "always" be there. They will give her "love" for the sake of getting sex, and she may want to give them sex for the sake of feeling loved. Her heart is made for something better than this, and so she needs to realize that she is worth the wait. She cannot find happiness otherwise. As the Bible says, "She who is self-indulgent is dead even while she lives" (1 Tim. 5:6).

The following are some of the bad effects of premarital sex; do not dwell on them any longer than is necessary to give her a reality check. What she needs more than the bad news about premarital sex is the good news about what she is worth and what plans

God has in store for her. She needs to be encouraged to wait not because sex is bad but because real love is so good. The negative consequences of premarital sex can be seen from the relational, physical, emotional, and spiritual points of view.

Consider how premarital sex can affect *relationships*. One high school girl wrote, "I am sixteen and have already lost my virginity. I truly regret that my first time was with a guy that I didn't care that much about. Since that first night he expects sex on every date. When I don't feel like it, we end up in an argument. I don't think this guy is in love with me, and I know deep down that I am not in love with him either. This makes me feel cheap. I realize now that this is a very big step in a girl's life. After you have done it, things are never the same. It changes everything."[13] Another young person said, "I slept with many, many people trying to find love, to find self-worth. And the more people I slept with, the less self-worth I had."[14]

Some people may argue, "Well, what if I really care about him or her? I think sex will bring us closer together." Indeed, sex creates a bond. However, 80 percent of the time, the physical intimacy of a teen's first sexual relationship won't last more than six months.[15] Couples who want what is best for their relationship or future marriage will have the patience to wait.

Beyond one's relationship, premarital sex frequently causes tension within families because of the dishonesty that usually accompanies the hidden intimacies. Relationships with friends are often strained, and when things turn sour, the gossip and social problems often become unbearable. Everyone talks about how hard it is to say no to sex, but no one tells you how hard it is when you say yes.

In regard to the *physiological* side of things, it is dangerous for a young single woman to be sexually active. Because a teenage girl's reproductive system is still immature, she is very susceptible to sexually transmitted diseases (STDs).[16] In fact, early sexual activity is the number one risk factor for cervical cancer, and the second is multiple sexual partners.[17] A girl's body, like her heart, is not designed to handle multiple sexual partners.

While your friend might plan on sleeping with only one guy, she could be exposing herself to the STDs of hundreds of people through a single act of intercourse. Here's how: Scientists studied the sexual activity of a public high school of about one thousand students.[18] About half (573) of the students had been sexually active, and most of them had only been with one partner. However, when the scientists tracked the web of sexual activity among the students, it was discovered that more than half of the sexually active teens—without knowing it—were linked together in a network of 288 partners within the school! So if your friend slept with a guy from this school, theoretically she could be in bed with one-fourth of the entire student body.

The *emotional* side effects of premarital sex are also damaging to a young woman. One of the most common consequences of teenage sexual activity is depression. Girls who are sexually active are more than three times as likely to be depressed as girls who are abstinent.[19] In fact, the condition has become so predictable that the *American Journal of Preventive Medicine* recommends to doctors: "[Girls who are engaging in] sexual intercourse should be screened for depression, and provided with anticipatory guidance about the mental health risks of these behaviors."[20] Even if a girl experiments with sex once, research shows an increased risk of depression.[21] Also, consider the fact that the rate of suicide attempts for sexually active girls (aged twelve to sixteen) is six times higher than the rate for virgins.[22] Tragically, these girls do not realize the purity, hope, and forgiveness that they can find in Christ.

Unfortunately, many young women search for meaning only in relationships with guys, instead of with God. It is not uncommon for a girl to have sex in order to make a guy like her more or to encourage him to stay with her. She may compromise her standards because she is afraid of never being loved. Once he leaves her, though, an emotional divorce takes place. A person's heart is not made to be that close to a person and then separated.

Since teenage sexual relationships rarely last, the girl's sense of self-worth is often damaged. She may conclude that if she looked better, he would have stayed longer. This mentality can lead to harmful practices, such as eating disorders. Or the disappointment she feels may drive her into a state of self-hatred. Some young women even begin to hurt their own bodies in an attempt to numb the emotional pain. Such practices never solve the problems, though. If she wants to be loved, she needs to begin by loving herself.

In her heart, a girl who has been used knows it. However, she may immediately jump into another sexual relationship to escape the hurt. If she tries to boost her self-esteem by giving guys what they want, then her self-worth often ends up depending upon those kinds of relationships. Her development as a woman is stunted because without chastity she does not know how to express affection, appreciation, or attraction for a guy without implying something sexual. She may even conclude that a guy does not love her unless he makes sexual advances toward her. She knows that sex exists without intimacy, but she may forget that intimacy can exist without sex. A girl on this track usually feels accepted initially, but that acceptance lasts only as long as the physical pleasure.

Such a lifestyle will also take its toll on her ability to bond. Here's why: Sharing the gift of sex is like putting a piece of tape on another person's arm. The first bond is strong, and it hurts to remove it. Shift the tape to another person's arm, and the bond will still work, but it will be easier to remove. Each time this is done, part of each person remains with the tape. Soon it is easy to remove because the residue from the various arms interferes with the tape's ability to stick.

The same is true in relationships, where previous sexual experiences interfere with the ability to bond. This does not mean that if a person is not a virgin on the wedding night, he or she will be unable to bond with a spouse. It simply means that when we follow God's plan, we have the most abundant life possible. But when we turn from his designs and break his commandments, often we are the ones who feel broken afterward.

*Spiritually* sin cuts us off from God, and this is the most serious consequence of premarital sex. After going too far, many of us know all too well the cloud of guilt that weighs on our hearts. The solution is not to kill our conscience but to follow it to freedom. It is calling us, not condemning us. Provided we repent, God will be there to welcome us home and let us start over (see John 8 and Luke 15).

What this all means is that our bodies, our hearts, our relationships, and our souls are not made for premarital sex. We are made for enduring love.

7

*I heard that the Bible does not say anything about premarital sex. Is that right?*

Anyone who says that the Bible is silent on premarital sex has not spent much time reading the Bible. The phrase *premarital sex* does not appear in the Bible, because Scripture uses the term *fornication* instead. This term is used in passages such as 1 Corinthians 6, where the apostle Paul says:

> Do not be deceived; neither fornicators nor idolators nor adulterers . . . will inherit the kingdom of God. . . . The body, however, is not for immorality, but for the Lord, and the Lord is for the body. . . . Avoid immorality. Every other sin a person commits is outside the body, but the immoral person sins against his own body. Do you not know that your body is a temple of the Holy Spirit within you, whom you have from God, and that you are not your own. For you have been purchased at a price. Therefore glorify God in your body. (1 Cor. 6:9–10, 15, 18–20, *NAB*)

In 1 Thessalonians 4 Saint Paul says, "This is the will of God, your holiness: that you refrain from immorality, that each of you know how to acquire a wife for himself in holiness and honor, not in lustful passion as do the Gentiles who do not know God. . . . For God did not call us to impurity but to holiness. Therefore, whoever disregards this, disregards not a human being but God, who [also] gives His holy Spirit to you." (1 Thess. 4:3–5, 7–8, *NAB*). Elsewhere the Bible exhorts us, "Immorality or any impurity . . . must not even be mentioned among you, as is fitting among holy ones" (Eph. 5:3).[23]

This provides biblical support, but it hardly answers the real issue. A person who claims that the Bible says nothing about premarital sex is often a person who is trying to suppress his conscience. Impurity erodes our faith. When we live an immoral lifestyle and go to church, we have to grapple with the tension between how we are living and what we believe. If our behavior does not match our religious doctrine, one of them has to go.

As this tension mounts, we search for moral loopholes, such as "The Bible doesn't say it's wrong." When no loopholes are left, we grope for some reason to leave the faith altogether. "I think the faith is unreasonable," we argue. Or "I don't care for organized religion." "I have doubts about the reliability of the biblical manuscripts." "I won't obey the Church because Church leaders don't always live up to its teachings." There is always something to divert us and keep us from studying and confronting the truth. We may claim to be "spiritual" but not "religious." The words of Saint Paul are a challenge to us all: "They profess to know God, but they deny Him by their deeds" (Titus 1:16). If we love God, we will obey Him. If we do not obey Him, we cannot claim to love Him.[24] Or in the words of Saint Augustine, "If you believe what you like in the gospel, and reject what you don't like, it is not the gospel you believe, but yourself."[25]

People in this situation need to turn to Christ and allow themselves to be transformed. God's laws are not burdens. He is not a taskmaster who overwhelms us with rules so that we will blindly conform and live miserable lives to satisfy Him. He wants to raise us up as His sons and daughters, training us in discipline so that we can become free to love. His laws exist because He loves us and wants us to share in that love.

"Jesus loves you." We hear that often, but do we ever let the message sink in? Could it be that the God of love is not out to ruin our lives? Could it be that God has an interest in our love lives beyond making sure that we do not go too far? And could it be that He has established a Church to guide us to the truth? If we come to God with sincere and humble hearts, we will know the truth and be set free. We will not be bound by the illusion that God and His Church are out to rob us of our freedom.

8

*Can't we accept that people have different values when it comes to sex? We need to be realistic: times have changed since the Bible was written.*

A poll in Rhode Island asked seventeen hundred students in grades six through nine if it is OK for a guy to force a young woman to have sex if the two of them have dated for six months or more. Two-thirds of the guys said that this was acceptable—and half of the girls did as well! 86 percent of the young men said that it was OK to rape your wife, and 24 percent said that it was OK to rape a date if you spent "a lot of money" on her.[26] Modern culture tells us that if something feels good and we want it, we should have it. Go ahead. Gorge yourself. But when this mentality seeps into the minds of the youth, we end up with grade-schoolers who don't see a problem with rape.

Are you willing to "accept" those students' responses as those of "people having different values"? There is no doubt that times have changed since the Bible was written, but does the morality of an act depend upon where you live, when you live, or how many people agree with you? For example, if you created a time machine, how far into the future would you need to go in order for child abuse to become moral? If you went back in time and took a poll of Nazi guards, and the majority said that killing Jews was good, would that mean that we should be open-minded and accept their different values? Even today, if I were taken to court for shooting a clerk and shoplifting, do you think that the judge would be convinced of my innocence because I "just have different values"?

I hope you agree that no matter how times change, these acts will always be immoral. Why is it then that when we get to the sixth and ninth commandments (the ones regarding sexuality), people feel that morality is subjective and the Ten Commandments are multiple choice? Morality is objective, and a properly formed conscience can see this. No one likes to be told that what he wants to do is wrong, but we are not the authors of right and wrong. We need to overcome the temptation to judge God's laws by our standards and begin measuring our standards by His laws.

We cannot construct our own private system of values. As Pope John Paul II said during the 1993 World Youth Day in Denver, Colorado: "Do not give in to this widespread false morality! Do not stifle your conscience." Saint Paul also warned us that "the time is coming when people will not endure sound teaching, but having itching ears they will accumulate for themselves teachers to suit their own likings, and will turn away from listening to the truth and wander into myths. As for you, always be steady, endure suffering, do the work of an evangelist, fulfil your ministry" (2 Tim. 4:3-5).

Although our civilization has lost the sense of sin, God still takes sin seriously. Look at a crucifix. There on the cross is our answer. Sin is still sin, and for this reason Christ's call to holiness applies for all times to every person on the globe. Christ makes demands on us precisely in the arena of sexual values. He asks much because He knows we can give much. We cannot dismiss our responsibilities by saying, "I gotta be me," or, "Boys will be boys." We will either glorify God or offend Him by how we use the gift of our sexuality.

Ask yourself, "Do I *really* desire union with God?" If so, the quickest route is simple and humble honesty. Since God is truth, our union with Him depends on whether or not we are willing to submit our lives to the truth. We must love the truth and desire it with every fiber of our being, regardless of how inconvenient it may be. In the words of Scripture, we must, "even to the death, fight for truth" (Sir. 4:28, *NAB*). This is the sincerity of heart that God longs to find in us.

One man noted, "There are few better tests for whether or not someone lives a life in submission to God than what he or she does with their sexuality. Sex is such a powerful and meaningful desire that to give it up and obey God in that area is a true sign of worship."[27] As Jesus said in His agony in the garden, "Not my will, but yours, be done" (Luke 22:42). If we say that we love God but we still want to make up the rules when it comes to sexual desire, we have made pleasure our god. We should ask ourselves, "Am I willing to disregard God's will in order to pursue mine, or am I willing to disregard my own will in order to pursue God?"

## 9

### What authority does the Church have to tell me not to have sex?

This question is really asking, "What authority does the Church have in my life at all?" Since some of God's commandments involve sex, and Christ ordered His Church to teach all that He commands (Matt. 28:20), the Church has the duty and authority to pass on to us what God has revealed about sexual morality. Scripture is clear that Jesus instituted His Church with such a mission. It would be unfaithful to Christ if it did not pursue this aspect of its mission.

Consider some of the ways Jesus made it clear that He was investing the Church with His authority. In commissioning individuals to go and preach His message, Jesus emphasized: "He who hears you hears me, and he who rejects you rejects me" (Luke 10:16). At the Last Supper Jesus told the apostles that He was conferring a kingdom upon them (Luke 22:29). He previously had promised them that whatever they "bind on earth shall be bound in heaven, and whatever [they] loose on earth shall be loosed in heaven" (Matt. 18:18).

Jesus stated that the gates of hell would not prevail against this one Church (Matt. 16:18), which was to be the pillar and foundation of truth (1 Tim. 3:15). He invested the Church with His own teaching authority because He knew that He would not be with the apostles on earth forever. He established a Church with "bishops" who "give instruction in sound doctrine" (Titus 1:7, 9). The faithful are to submit to these spiritual leaders and defer to their authority in order not to be led away by strange and diverse teachings (Heb. 13:17). The authority of the apostles has been passed on to bishops from age to age through prayer accompanied by the imposition of hands (Deut. 34:9; 1 Tim. 4:14; 2 Tim. 1:6). Through the bishops of the Church, we are able to trace this "laying on of hands" in an unbroken line back to the apostles. The Holy Spirit guides the Church (John 16:13) so that it teaches what God entrusted to it. The Church guards its children as a mother watches over her young. The children may not always understand the mother's reasons for her rules, but they would do well to trust that her commands come from a loving heart and not a dictator's whims.

## 10

*If premarital sex is so bad, why does it feel so good?*

We cannot determine the morality of an action based upon how good it feels. Rapists and child molesters feel pleasure, but no one would doubt that their actions are immoral. Likewise, things that cause tremendous pain can be acts of great love, as when one person gives his life for someone else. If we measured the goodness of an act by the pleasure received, then adulterers would be virtuous and war heroes would be scoundrels.

If you want to know the morality of an act, "Do not conform yourself to this age, but be transformed by the renewal of your mind, that you may discern what is the will of God, what is good and pleasing and perfect" (Rom. 12:2, *NAB*).

## I I

*If sex is good and natural, why shouldn't we have it whenever we want?*

Just because a thing is good, this does not mean that it is without boundaries. For example, because sleep is good, imagine that you decide to sleep until one in the afternoon on a school day. You walk into school with the creases from your pillow still embedded in your face. When your teacher asks where you have been, you yawn, wipe the drool from your chin, and remind him that sleep is good and so you were enjoying sleep. You add that when you go home you will probably eat thirty pounds of Girl Scout cookies because eating is good, too.

Needless to say, while sleep and food are good, they do have their limits. Similarly, the good gift of sex has its boundaries as well—and the boundary for sex is marriage. When we take sex outside of marriage, it is like taking fire out of the fireplace. The beautiful gift can quickly become destructive.

But what about the fact that sex feels so natural? Suppose that one day at work I decide to have an affair with my secretary. When I come home, my wife Crystalina asks how my day was. I tell her that work went well, the drive home was pleasant, and that I cheated on her. Upon hearing this, she throws my belongings onto the front lawn. To ease her pain, I point out how "natural" the affair was. Needless to say, she would not be comforted. She is well aware that the fact that sex is natural is not a sufficient reason to engage in it.

Although pleasure is a natural result of sex, it is not the purpose of sex. If you confuse the purpose of sex (babies and bonding) with the additional benefit of pleasure, you abandon love and use the other person as an object of lust.

When people argue that couples should be free to have sex outside of marriage, they do not realize what they are asking for. "Liberating" sex from the confines of marriage is like liberating a goldfish from its bowl—not a great idea. In the same way, the intimacy of sex was never meant to be separated from the total intimacy that makes up married life. It was not meant to be "free." One woman explained, "So-called sexual freedom is really just proclaiming oneself to be available for free, and therefore without value. To 'choose' such freedom is tantamount to saying that one is worth nothing."[28]

When we divorce sex from marriage, we inevitably meet with disappointment. We are trying to grab the privileges of marriage without accepting the commitment and sacrifice that must accompany the gift of total intimacy.

12

### Isn't it hard to say no all the time?

As I see it, there are two ways to live and to love. One sees temptations as obstacles to virtue, demanding a constant need to say "no!" in order to obey all God's seemingly burdensome laws. It is a life that is based upon "Thou shalt nots." Every day is an exhausting struggle to avoid offending God. If we live like that, then it will be pretty hard to say no all the time.

Here is the alternative: Instead of living life trying not to offend God, live life trying to glorify Him. Live each moment as an act of worship to God. Instead of seeing temptations of lust as obstacles to holiness, see overcoming them as the very means to holiness. Certainly this involves avoiding temptation and saying no to sin, but the motivation is the yes of true love.

As Mother Teresa said, "Intense love does not measure . . . it just gives."[29] Or in the words of Pope John Paul II, a young heart feels "a desire for greater generosity, more commitment, greater love. This desire for more is a characteristic of youth; a heart that is in love does not calculate, does not begrudge, it wants to give of itself without measure."[30] "There is no place for selfishness— and no place for fear! Do not be afraid, then, when love makes demands. Do not be afraid when love requires sacrifice."[31] "Real love is demanding. I would fail in my mission if I did not tell you so. Love demands a personal commitment to the will of God."[32]

Therefore, the virtue of purity is not first a no to illicit sex but a yes to authentic love. It is not a prolonged series of noes but a continual yes to Jesus. Since we receive more grace each time we say yes to God, we soon see how possible and joyful this life really is. The Blessed Mother offers us the perfect example of how to live this when, in the Gospel of Luke, she gives us the recipe for holiness: "Let it be to me according to your word" (Luke 1:38). The more we are able to imitate her yes, the more joy and peace we will find in our lives. When asked how we could become saints, Mother Teresa replied: "Whenever Jesus asks something of you, say yes."

Living the virtue of chastity now means that you cherish your future marriage more than passing pleasures. It also prepares you to be a better wife or husband because you will learn how to express intimacy without always needing to be physical. It has been said that when a couple has healthy intimacy, the closer the two become, the more they become themselves. When a couple is experiencing unhealthy intimacy, they usually feel as if they are losing their identity.

The yes I have spoken of is possible with God, because the love of God has been poured into our hearts through the Holy Spirit (Rom. 5:5). Tap into that, and ask God for the grace to be pure. Have confidence, because with God's grace *anyone* can achieve sexual purity.

As you work toward the virtue of chastity, know that the desire to become pure is not something that comes from your body. There is no chastity gland located near your spleen, secreting abstinence hormones. Chastity arises from the will and is awakened and made possible by love. Granted, there will always be a tension between the desire to please God and the desire to act on our impulses. In the words of Christopher West, "Winning this battle takes faith in Christ, dedication, commitment, honesty with ourselves and others, and a willingness to make sacrifices and deny our own selfish desires. But love is not afraid of those things; love *is* those things."[33]

One practical note: Take a look at what surrounds you. If you constantly have to say no to various temptations, this implies that you end up in tempting situations on a regular basis. There will always be temptations, but we should work to avoid the occasion of sin. If you listen to music with sexually explicit lyrics, watch MTV, spend time in risqué chat room conversations, look through swimsuit or *Cosmopolitan* magazines and so forth, you are pouring lighter fluid on the fire that you are trying to extinguish. As the Bible says, "Who will pity a snake charmer bitten by a serpent, or any who go near wild beasts? So no one will pity a man who associates with a sinner and becomes involved in his sins. . . . Flee from sin as from a snake; for if you approach sin, it will bite you" (Sir. 12:13–14; 21:2). If there are bad influences in your life, replace them. Find better music and decent books to read. Also, increase your time in personal prayer, Scripture reading, and other devotions, and you will be surprised at how much easier chastity becomes. Never forget that purity is a gift from God; you have to ask for it.

## 13

*How should I respond when people in my high school say, "Everyone is doing it"?*

You could respond to this in any number of ways. For one, you could ask the person, "If I can prove that the majority of high school students are virgins, will you be abstinent?" The most authoritative research on the sexual activity rates of high school students is the Youth Risk Behavior Survey conducted by the Centers for Disease Control. According to this nationwide survey of more than 150 high schools, only about a third of all students are currently sexually active.[34] Since 1991 teen sexual activity rates have been dropping, and now the majority of high school students are virgins.[35] In fact, between 1991 and 2005 the sexual activity rate of high school boys dropped twice as quickly as that of high school girls![36] Among teens who have already lost their virginity, two-thirds of them wish they had waited longer to have sex (77 percent of girls and 60 percent of guys).[37]

The trend toward chastity is well underway, even if you haven't noticed it on your campus. The National Campaign to Prevent Teen Pregnancy surveyed teens from around the country, asking them if it was embarrassing for teens to admit that they are virgins. Surprisingly, 87 percent of teens said *no*, it's not embarrassing.[38] Most of those who said it was embarrassing were under the age of fifteen. Only 5 percent of older teens (fifteen to seventeen years of age) thought virginity was an embarrassing admission.

Despite the fact that these teens said virginity wasn't something to be ashamed of, you don't hear much about it because the sexually active students do all the talking. For some reason chastity gossip just doesn't seem to spread as quickly. This gives the impression that "everyone is doing it," when in reality the majority are not.

You could also point out that the "everyone" who is "doing it" is also getting STDs, that "everyone" is breaking up three weeks after they have sex, and "everyone" ends up getting divorced if they stay together long enough to get married. You are in no rush to join any of these crowds. We all have a fear of not being accepted or of being a loner if we do not conform to the world. But you must hold out for the higher standard of love.

The bottom line is this: What is your motivation? Is it to please God or to conform to the world and make life-changing decisions based on the opinions of classmates, most of whom you will probably never see again after graduation? Stay strong. You are well worth the wait. Besides, the world needs to see young people who are not scared out of their minds to be chaste. This is something to be proud of, and if enough people on your campus realize this and have the courage to stand up, I would bet the saying "everyone is doing it" will soon refer to chastity.

# 2

# Dating and Courtship

## 14

*How do you know if you really love a girl?*

What is love? I used to think of it as a warm, fuzzy feeling. When you see *her*, the world seems beautiful, the birds are singing, and everything reminds you of *her*. Your heart races whenever *she* walks into the room.

That is "being in love." This spontaneous emotional reaction is a lot of fun, but we should not confuse these feelings with love itself. Some people think that they can tell how long a relationship will last based upon how powerful the feelings of attraction are. They spend massive amounts of time trying to decide whether or not they are in love.

What they are overlooking is the fact that love is a decision to do what is best for another person, even if the warm fuzzies are long gone. But it is not enough to *want* to do what is good for the other. We must form our minds according to the truth that God has revealed so that we *know* what is good for the other, and we are not just doing whatever feels good. Once we know what is good for the other, all that remains is to follow through and live out that love in our actions.

Love does not "happen" to couples—it is something they *do*. It is a task. If the initial excitement of a relationship tapers off and we conclude from this that love is gone, we can be sure that love was never there to begin with. After all, if love is simply about having romantic feelings, how could a bride and groom promise each other that their marriage will last "until death do us part"? More likely it would last "until boredom do us part." Therefore, you cannot determine the worth of a relationship by measuring the intensity of emotions.

Suppose you are married and your pregnant wife has food cravings. It is four in the morning, and she wants you to go to the grocery store to get her fudge brownie ice cream and pickle juice. You roll over and look at your bride, and she does not seem to be glowing the way she did on your wedding day. At four in the morning, your world is not looking beautiful and the singing birds have gone mute. But after kissing her fevered forehead, you walk out the door and drive to the store. Has love gone away? Actually, it is more real than ever.

So how do you know if you love a woman? Pope John Paul II has answered this question perfectly in saying that "*the greater the feeling of responsibility for the [beloved] the more true love there is.*"[1] The greatest example of this love is Christ. He alone perfectly reveals how to love a woman. If we ever need to know how to properly love a woman, all we need to do is look at a crucifix.

## 15

### *How do you know if a guy loves you or if he wants to use you?*

If you ever want to know if a guy loves you, apply the love test. Here is how it works. I know a young woman who applied this love test on a first (and last) date with a particular guy. He made certain suggestions as to his intentions for the evening, but she informed him that she practiced chastity. He responded, "That's OK. We can do other stuff" (implying everything short of intercourse). She proceeded to give him a crash course in the definition of chastity, and he responded, "So you mean that I'm not going to get *anything?*"

He sounded like an eight-year-old boy having a tantrum because his mother would not buy him a toy. His request coupled with the childish reaction shows that he had no idea of the value of what he was requesting. He assumed that buying her dinner should more than suffice to gain him access to the priceless treasure of her body. This is the blindness that comes with an irreverent attitude toward sex.

What this young woman did was not easy, but it was much easier than dating the guy for six months before realizing that he loved pleasure more than he loved her. Because she practiced the virtue of chastity, she saw through the manipulation that he would have used to get her into bed. She knew that if a guy pressured her to give him her body, then he did not love her. Because of a woman's great dignity—she is made in the image and likeness of God—she deserves authentic love. She must never allow herself to be used or treated as a thing. Her body is priceless in the sight of God, and her heart is to be treasured.

Although this love test will weed out a lot of immature guys, only time will reveal a man's intentions. One man said, "If I sensed there was a moral dilemma in her mind, I would play any role necessary to reach the point where sex became inevitable."[2] There are many good guys out there, but there are also plenty of predators who will tell a girl whatever she wants to hear. Therefore a girl needs to proceed slowly, develop the skill of listening to her heart, and have the courage to follow it. Otherwise a young woman may be left feeling like this fifteen-year-old did: "I felt strange, and in a sense, used. It was like we were both caring for the same person—him. I felt left out of it."[3]

## 16

*I am a junior in high school, and I have never had a girlfriend. Is that bad, and when should I begin dating?*

This is not bad at all. In fact, it has some great advantages. For example, let's say you meet a girl whom you would love to marry, but marriage is still a decade away. What do you think would be more likely to last ten years: a high school relationship or a solid friendship? The friendship is more easily maintained, and will serve as a foundation for any lasting love that does unfold. Besides, what is the point of committing to someone when you know you're probably going to break up when you go to college in two years? What many people do not realize is that you don't need to date in high school in order to get to know the opposite sex or to have a successful relationship in college.

Do not worry that love will elude you if you do not rush into romance now. Take this time to be free from distractions, and ask yourself what God wants of you during these years. With all of your vigor and life, unreservedly give your youth to Him. Try to outdo Him in generosity, and watch what happens.

There is wisdom in taking your time before beginning a committed relationship. For example, a study of over eight hundred high school students was conducted to determine how their dating age impacted their sexual behavior. Here's what the study found: Among the teens who began dating in seventh grade, only 29 percent of boys and 10 percent of girls were still virgins. However, of those who waited until they were sixteen years old to date, 84 percent of boys and 82 percent of girls were still virgins.[4] This does not mean that if you started dating early you will inevitably be sexually active in high school. I started dating in the fifth grade, which I now realize was pointless, and I still saved my virginity for my bride.

Taking your time will not only safeguard your virginity; it will also give you a better foundation for future relationships. For example, some people spend their high school years running around trying to find a date, frantic because everyone else seems to have one. Others always need to be dating someone new. As soon as one relationship ends, they jump into another because they feel incomplete without a date. They practically develop ulcers searching for their worth and their identity in relationships. Still others spend all four years staring into the eyes of a boyfriend or girlfriend. Their relationship consumes them, and by the time high school is over they are not sure of their identity or dreams. The high school years are not meant for intense relationships that leave you feeling as if you would die without the other. This is a time to find out who you are, discover the world, and set the course for your life.

Everyone wants the love of another person, but there is a season for everything. Right now draw near to God so that you understand your worth in His eyes. Many people leap into relationships where their self-worth depends upon how the other treats them. Knowing what God thinks of you decreases your chances of falling into this trap.

So come to Him, listen to His voice, and do whatever He tells you. As one woman said, "Inviting God to write the chapters of our love story involves work on our part—not just a scattered prayer here and there, not merely a feeble attempt to find some insight by flopping open the Bible every now and then. It is seeking Him on a daily basis, putting Him in first place at all times, discovering His heart."[5] He is the best guide when it comes to relationships, so stay close to him.

Lastly, your question presupposes that dating is the only option. It is not. Currently there is a resurgence of young people leaving behind the modern concept of dating in favor of courtship.

## 17

*What is the difference between dating and courtship?*

The concept of dating is about as old as the automobile. Nowadays we are so used to it that we might not be able to imagine any other approach to relationships. But back before the car, the purpose of investing time with a young man or woman was to see if he or she was a potential marriage partner. The reason you expressed romantic interest was to woo the person toward that lifelong commitment. This process usually took place within the context of family activities.

When the car was invented, this courting could be divorced from spending time with family because the couple could leave the family behind. Soon, the whole point of spending time together shifted from discernment of marriage to wooing for the sake of wooing. Many people would begin a relationship simply because they found the other to be cute and fun.

This put a new spin on the focus of relationships, and short-term relationships became commonplace. With this mentality a person who dates successfully breaks up with everyone in his life except for one person (and this is supposed to be good preparation for a successful marriage). Of course, the majority of relationships do not end in marriage, but some become so intimate and intense that the couple seem emotionally married. If a breakup occurs, then they experience a sort of emotional divorce. It is not uncommon that by the time a person is married, he feels as if he has already been divorced several times.

You may ask, "Well, what is the alternative? Am I supposed to shelter myself, put walls around my heart, and forget having a social life?" Not at all. The alternative is to rethink the way we approach relationships. Whether we admit it or not, the world has molded our views of preparing for marriage. We need to seriously ask ourselves, "What is the godly approach to relationships?" What would God have us do? Perhaps his ways are a 180-degree change from everything you have experienced. Perhaps you are burned out from the dating scene anyway and could use a breath of fresh air.

Either way, I suggest a return to the principles of courtship. When I first heard of the resurgence of Christian courtship, I was skeptical. I remember thinking, "Oh, courtship. So if I want to spend time with a girl, I have to arrange for our families to go to a pumpkin patch together, followed by an exciting evening of board games, and then go home by seven. Woo hoo—real practical for a guy just out of college, living in southern California." I had heard a great deal about courtship, but when I began reading books on the subject I ended up liking the idea more than I hoped I would. There was a great deal of wisdom I had never tapped into.

Many books propose different forms of biblical dating, but the fact is that no one ever dated in the Bible. In some passages the parents arranged the marriage, and in other places we read of men going to foreign countries to capture their wives. Although the idea of traveling overseas and capturing a spouse may seem appealing, the Bible also provides guidelines that are more practical.

Just because the concept of dating was unknown to those before the twentieth century does not mean that Scripture cannot help us understand the mind of God on the matter. In Psalm 78:8 we read of a generation that had no firm purpose and whose hearts were not fixed steadfastly on God. If that is a good description of our relationships, they need some reworking. We should be intent on finding out if it is the Lord's will for us to be with a certain person, and until we are ready to move in the direction of marriage, what is the point of committing to another?

Some may argue that this is all too serious, but should we be giving our hearts away to people who are in no position to make a real commitment? I am not proposing that you build an impenetrable wall around your heart but that you guard it with prudence. We can wrestle over the terms *courtship* and *dating*, but the essential thing is to glorify God and act wisely. The time spent prior to marriage must be a school of love in which two young people learn the art of forgetting themselves for the good of the other.

While it's important to become friends and spend time with members of the opposite sex, committed relationships should be entered into for the sake of discerning marriage. When we do enter into relationships, we should allow wisdom to chaperone romance. This involves having the humility to become accountable to others. Find a member of the same sex whom you look up to, and go to him or her for guidance in your relationships. As Proverbs says, "Without counsel plans go wrong, but with many advisers they succeed" (Prov. 15:22).

There is also a great deal of wisdom in spending time together with the other person's family. Not only does it honor the parents, it also helps you get to know the family that you may join one day. Finally—and this may be a real eye-opener—how this person treats his or her family will likely be how he or she treats you when the feelings taper off. For example, if you are a young woman dating a guy who is disrespectful toward his mother and sisters but is a perfect gentleman around you, guess what you have to look forward to if you settle down with him.

The type of time a guy and girl spend together determines how well they ground their relationship in reality. If they spend every waking hour tucked away in private gazing into one another's eyes, they will never find out who they are. Spending time in service, with family, and even playing sports will help reveal who the other person really is.

These are some of the principles of courtship: ask God's blessing at the beginning of a relationship; enter it with direction, toward discerning marriage; involve the families; be accountable to others; pace yourselves as you spend time together; and always listen for the Lord's guidance.

## 18

*Where can I find a good guy? All the boys at school are interested in only one thing.*

All women deserve a man who has one thing on his mind: doing God's will. Therefore, wait for a guy whose intention is to love you purely and lead you to God. Do not settle for less. You may be thinking, "Yeah, right. Where am I going to find a guy like that? I'll be in a nursing home by the time he shows up."

Put the matter in God's hands. Take this time to give yourself unreservedly to the Lord to build up His kingdom. Let Him worry about building up yours. Too often people are so concerned with finding Mr. or Miss Right that they miss the opportunity to serve God in their singleness. Your job is to give your singleness to Christ. Keep your eyes on Him instead of on potential future spouses.

I firmly believe that the strongest marriages are those in which both the man and the woman, prior to marriage, embraced the gift of singleness. Often we do not accept this gift because we are waiting for the gift of marriage or exhausting ourselves maintaining passing relationships. Saint Paul said, "I have learned, in whatever state I am, to be content" (Phil. 4:11). If a woman does not learn to be content now, then when she is married she may wish she were still single. After all, marriage does not change you internally; you are still the same person.

Besides, if a woman is happy and content in her present situation, she is more attractive. In fact, the ideal wife spoken of in the Bible "laughs at the time to come" (Prov. 31:25). She anticipates the future with joy, trusting in the goodness of God. Before we can be happily married, we need to learn to be happily single. That way our happiness is not dependent upon outside events but upon an inner joy. In the words of Thérèse of Lisieux, "The happier they are to be as He wills, the more perfect they are."[6] I once asked a Missionary of Charity if she was happy in the city where she had been assigned, thousands of miles from home. She replied, "Anywhere. Wherever Jesus wants me to be, that is where I'm happy." In the same way, learn to find your joy by trusting in God. After marriage you might never again have the time to serve God without restrictions.

The best husband and father will be a guy who is single-hearted for God. So be two of a kind. If you want a man of God, become a godly woman. After all, men of virtue look for women of virtue. Imagine all of the characteristics that you look for in a spouse —that he be faithful, holy, respectful, loving, pure, and so on— and ask yourself, "Judging by the way I live, do I deserve a guy like this?" If not, then become the woman who does. Everyone makes mistakes, but everyone is capable of turning things around and choosing to live a virtuous life.

As you grow in virtue, you will have a tremendous impact on men. Many women become discouraged because of the kind of guys they meet at school. But the character of the men that a woman attracts largely rests in her hands. One woman said, "He will be as much of a gentleman as she requires."[7] The fact is that the male desire to please females is a basic one, and a woman who sets high standards will be more likely to attract young men willing to meet them. If a young man wishes to enjoy a girl's presence, he will not be afraid to be a gentleman. When a woman says that this is unrealistic, she will continue to be frustrated and settle for less. If only young women realized their power to help boys become men!

Set the standard high. Look for a guy who takes the initiative to set pure guidelines for the relationship. Imagine if all the young women in a high school or college decided to do this. Sure, many of them might not have dates the next weekend, but it would send a clear message to the boys that girls are serious about being loved. Guys would soon be inspired to become worthy of a woman.

In the meantime, pray for your future spouse and for discernment in your vocation. I once read about a fifteen-year-old girl who felt she should pray for her future husband one random December night. When she met him sometime later, she found out that he was in a battle as she prayed, and nearly all of his fellow soldiers were killed, while his life was spared.[8] God hears our prayers.

So be at peace, and know that God cares about the desires of your heart. He who shaped the universe has not overlooked the smallest details.

One day in Calcutta a man who had a sick daughter came to Mother Teresa. She did not have the specific medicine that the child needed, since it had to be brought in from outside India. As they were speaking, a man came with a basket of medicine, and right on top was the exact one the child needed. Mother said, "If it had been inside, I would not have seen it. If he had come before, I would not have seen it. But just at that time, out of the millions and millions of children in the world, God in His tenderness was concerned with this little child of the slums of Calcutta enough to send, just at that time, that amount of medicine to save that child."[9] So know that your future is in good hands.

## 19

*Where, when, and how can I find the right girl for me?*

Here is how many singles see the world of relationships: "God created earth—that's 199 million square miles, for the record. Then God created my soul mate and put her out there somewhere. My job is to find her, and God's job seems to be to hide her from me for as long as physically possible. It is a delicate matter. If I sit at the wrong table during lunch, or do not keep my eyes constantly scanning, I might miss her. Destiny could slip between my fingers because I was careless. I'm prepared to exhaust myself until I find her."

If this rings a bell, then it is time to hand the matter over to God. Search Him out more zealously than you search for Miss Right. Do you think that if you remain single for a while to focus on God, He might let the woman He has planned for you slip by? Usually when we concentrate on serving the Lord, we give Him a freer hand with us precisely because we are not getting in the way anymore. I think that God waits on us sometimes and that our tinkering and impatience can keep His plans from unfolding in their fullness.

Think: "If I am called to marriage, then God wants my future wife to have the best possible husband. But I can't become that man of God by moping around until God brings me Miss Right. If I will be a father one day, then I'll need to give my kids the gift of faith. But how will I do that if God does not first give me the gift of faith? And how can He give me that gift unless He purifies my faith through trials?" This is the time when He can give you that gift. This is where God wants you right now.

Mother Teresa used to say of acceptance:

Every day we have to say yes. To be where He wants you to be. Total surrender: If He puts you in the street—if everything is taken from you and suddenly you find yourself in the street—to accept to be put in the street at that moment. . . . To accept whatever He gives and to give whatever He takes with a big smile. This is the surrender to God. To accept to be cut to pieces, and yet every piece to belong only to Him. This is the surrender. To accept the people that come, the work that you happen to do. Today maybe you have a good meal and tomorrow maybe you have nothing. There is no water in the pump? All right. To accept, and to give whatever He takes. He takes your good name, He takes your health, yes. That's the surrender. And you are free then. [10]

So right now embrace this season of singleness. Be there completely.

Have you ever had a conversation with someone while your eyes were darting all over and your mind was somewhere else? A few years ago I had a meeting with Father Michael Scanlan, my university's president. We spoke in his office for only twenty minutes, but I will never forget how present he was to me. He probably had a million other things to deal with, but he spoke to me as if I were the only person on earth. In the same way, we need to live entirely in the present moment, doing what we are doing, and being completely where we are. If God wanted us elsewhere right now, wouldn't we be there?

It is easy to waste our youth making a future event or person the cause of our joy. There is nothing wrong with looking forward to marriage, but if anticipation and daydreaming consume us, we become our own worst tormentors, and we do little to build up the kingdom of God. We can become so preoccupied with regrets about the past and anxieties for the future that we never sit still to enjoy the peace Christ offers us today. We can easily become so concerned with finding Miss Right that we miss out on the joy of the single life.

Do not give in to feelings of despair, but draw near to God if this is a time of loneliness for you. Avoid self-pity. When you feel lonely, minister to those who are far lonelier than you. Ask yourself: How many homeless people do I know by name? More importantly, look for those who are hungry for love within your own home. By being sensitive to the needs of those under your own roof, you are training yourself to be a better husband.

To find the right one, *become* the right one. It seems that most single people are more concerned about finding an ideal partner than they are about *becoming* the ideal partner. Perhaps this explains why they are having such a difficult time in their search. Therefore, become the man that God is calling you to be, especially by becoming a man of prayer. Do not wait for another person to complete you. Let God do that. Some guys think, "Since a wife is supposed to be your better half, I guess I'm only 50 percent complete until I find her. When I find her, she will fill my emptiness and take care of all of my emotional needs." If this guy finds a girl, it will not be a budding relationship; it will be a hostage situation.

We must be satisfied with being loved by God alone before we can truly love another. If you are in high school, realize that few guys meet their future bride during those years. You have plenty of time; there is no need to get into an intense relationship now. Most people find their spouses in college (or later) and do not get married until after graduation.

The second step is to go where the good young women are —at church youth groups, not at keg parties. Most importantly, seek God's kingdom first (Matt. 6:25–34). He is in charge, so be at peace because He knows well the plans He has in mind for you (Jer. 29:11–14).

## 20

*I am a freshman in high school and am dating a guy who's five years older than I am. My mom doesn't like him, so we've had to see each other secretly. What should I do?*

Ask yourself these questions: If you are having a secret relationship with a man who is willing to keep it hidden, what does this say of his character? It says that he is willing to be dishonest to get what he wants. If he is hiding a relationship *with* you, what makes you think he is not capable of hiding a relationship *from* you? Do you hope to marry a guy who is willing to hide a relationship? Beyond that, is there a reason he is not courting women his own age?

Also, examine how this relationship is forming you. To keep the relationship alive, you have probably lied to your family. But good relationships are founded on honesty with yourself, the other, your family, and God. To the extent that there is deception, there is an absence of love. The Lord has placed you within your family, under your parents' authority, for a reason. Do not let a guy come between you and them.

Whether we like it or not, parents have a lot of wisdom in this area—just as you will have a lot of wisdom when you become a mother. It takes maturity to realize that your parents may have valuable experience when it comes to relationships and that they want what is best for you. Older people realize that the younger you are, the more an age gap matters in relationships. While no one would see anything wrong with a thirty-seven-year-old man dating a thirty-two-year-old woman, it is more than a bit sketchy for someone your age to be dating a fourth-grader. In the high school to college range, age is still a factor.

In fact, while this can be hard for young people to accept, research shows that the place in the brain where reasoning and judgment take place is not fully developed until a person reaches his or her early twenties.[11] So there is a great deal of wisdom in deferring to the guidance of people who are a bit older.

Though this may be tough to see right now, the situation is dangerous. Why? Consider these statistics: 74 percent of girls who lose their virginity as teens lose it to an older guy.[12] In fact, the majority of teen pregnancies are caused by older guys.[13] Older guys are also more likely to transmit sexually transmitted diseases because they are more likely to have had multiple sexual part-ners.[14] Lastly, girls who date guys two or more years older are six times as likely to get drunk and smoke pot.[15] Even if the two of you are not sexually active, you can understand why your parents have some legitimate concerns.

You may say, "We're not into sex, drugs, or drinking. He's a good guy." But if you and he plan on making this relationship last, then the truth will be revealed. How many months and years of deception do you want to unveil eventually to your parents? If this guy hopes to be a son-in-law to your mom and dad, he's not going to make a good impression by lying to them for years. He will only create resentment. Have the courage and wisdom to step back and be honest with your family. If they want you two to stop seeing each other, honor their wishes.

In the meantime, do not worry that you will never find another guy who likes you. Think about whomever you had a crush on four years ago and look at how your tastes have changed since then. The same refining and clarifying of your interests will continue over the next several years.

Have confidence in love. If you sneak around, it shows a lack of confidence in your love for each other, as if the success of your love requires dishonesty. Have confidence in God as well. He can take care of things. All He asks in the meantime is that you honor your parents and wait to have the relationship until you are able to be honest with them about it. You will not regret it. Meanwhile, remember: "Love is patient and kind; love is not jealous or boastful; it is not arrogant or rude. Love does not insist on its own way; it is not irritable or resentful; it does not rejoice at wrong, but rejoices in the right. Love bears all things, believes all things, hopes all things, endures all things. Love never ends" (I Cor. 13:4–8).

## 21

*How come a guy will act interested in a girl, but after they sleep together he acts as if he doesn't know her?*

This kind of guy is not interested in guarding a girl's heart. His goal was sex, and her goal was intimacy. He got what he wanted. The thrill of the chase is over, and his respect for her is gone. She was only desirable as long as she was unattainable.

He might also feel uneasy around her because he used her.

When he did that, he missed the point of what it means to be a man. As a result, he probably feels shame when he sees her; her face might remind him of his emptiness. He might even feel sorry for her, so it is easier to ignore her. If a guy is exchanging sexual intimacies with a woman before he marries her, he has made the mistake of asking for her heart before he is willing to hold and guard it with his life.

Here is a glimpse inside the heart of an honest guy who did just this:

> I finally got a girl into bed—actually it was in a car—when I was seventeen. I thought it was the hottest thing there was, but then she started saying that she loved me and was getting clingy. I figured out that there had probably been a dozen other guys before me who thought that they had "conquered" her but who were really just objects of her need for security. That realization took all the wind out of my sails. I could not respect someone who gave in as easily as she did. I was amazed to find that after four weeks of having sex as often as I wanted, I was tired of her. I didn't see any point in continuing the relationship. I finally dumped her, which made me feel even worse, because I could see that she was hurting. I felt pretty low.[16]

During premarital sex two bodies are speaking a language of permanence that does not exist in reality. If either person's heart is invested in the union, that person will be disappointed, hurt, and angry when the breakup comes. One girl wrote, "I thought Mike really loved me, but last night we had sex for the first time, and this morning he told my girlfriend that he didn't want to see me anymore. I thought that giving Mike what he wanted would make him happy and he'd love me more."[17] To avoid this disappointment, a girl needs to realize that sexual intimacy is the culmination and reward of total commitment, not a way to keep a guy interested.

Unfortunately, many young women think that a physical relationship will draw a guy closer. I have seen plenty of relationships that started out fine, but as the couple became more physical, the emotional, social, and spiritual aspects of the relationship atrophied. (*Atrophy* is what happens to a body part when it is not used. For example, the muscles of a paralyzed arm will wither away.) That is what happens to the other dimensions of a relationship when physical intimacy dominates. The solution is restraint. A young woman will find the intimacy for which she yearns only by respecting herself.

## 22

*I am sort of seeing this guy, but he is still unsure of his feelings because he likes another girl too. I found out that he kissed this other girl, yet he wants to keep the door open in our relationship. What do I do?*

Shut the door. Here is why: This guy's actions are ruled by his emotions, not by principles. Therefore, even if he does commit to you, you can rest assured that the relationship will only be as stable as his feelings. Once they change, so will he.

Furthermore, if he kissed another girl while expressing an interest in you, what message would it send him if you stuck around? It would tell him that such behavior is tolerable. To a guy, it looks as if you're desperate for him to pick you. This will make him lose respect for you and will make you lose respect for yourself. So instead of waiting around, hoping that he will want you, shut the door and let him wish he deserved a girl like you.

When a woman does not demand the respect and commitment she deserves, she becomes her own worst enemy. Men treat her badly because she lets them. Therefore, don't be afraid to say to a guy, "I will not sit here while you flounder around in indecision. If you can't decide, I'll take that as a good-bye." When it comes to relationships, it is either 100 percent commitment or nothing. If he wanted to see other people, he should have had the guts to come to you and say so rather than sneak around.

On the other hand, if he had not committed to seeing you exclusively, then he was not being dishonest or breaking a commitment by seeing someone else. You may not like what he did, but that is one of the things that happens when you "sort of" see someone.

As you discovered, dragging on a vague relationship sets people up for problems. I'm sure you often hear of couples who say, "We're not boyfriend and girlfriend, but we are seeing each other," or, "We aren't dating, but he told my friend that we are a thing." Do not settle for a relationship that is just a "thing." A thing is something that grows out of the side of your foot. You deserve clarity when it comes to commitment. Girls who never learn to expect it often end up with a cohabiting boyfriend who, instead of proposing to her, gives her a "promise ring" because he is too scared to commit. She is flattered and pacified because any sign of commitment from him is exciting for her.

Now is the time to realize that great relationships do not "happen." They are the result of a conscious decision to respect yourself. You need to learn this respect for yourself so that you do not constantly end up with guys who refuse to respect you. In the situation you are in now, this guy only deserves to see you on a "more than friends basis" if he has clearly ended the relationship with this other girl and intends to be with you exclusively.

Even if he does, I would not jump back into a relationship with him. He needs to see that you are not waiting on him hand and foot, instantly available should he become tired of dating someone else. Take your time and do not exhaust yourself by clinging to him. Also, do not expect an overnight character change in him, no matter how eloquently he speaks about a change in his heart. Trust takes a long time to build, and if he expects you to trust him with your heart, there is a great deal of rebuilding that needs to happen. Since he has already broken some degree of a commitment to you once, there is no guarantee that this will not happen again.

Sometimes a girl will like a guy so much and will be so insecure that she accepts his deception and unfaithfulness as minor glitches in the relationship. He will say that he is sorry and he loves her, and she lets him right back to hurt her again. Do not make this mistake. Honesty is one of the most important elements in a good relationship. In the words of one marriage counselor, "To the extent that you are being deceived, there is no relationship."[18]

Also, if he has just ended a relationship, you do not want to get him on the rebound. Take a good look at why he is breaking up with this other girl. This says volumes about a person. As I said before, some people jump from one relationship to the other according to how strong the feelings are. When the feelings are weak, they jump ship; when the feelings are strong, they jump aboard. They think that once the feelings are gone, love is gone. It turns out that they love the feelings of being "in love" more than they love the actual person.

## 23

### Is it bad to date someone you met online?

Last week I was sitting in my truck at a stoplight when I noticed a bumper sticker on the car in front of me. It read: "You looked better on MySpace." After laughing, I thought of how well this sums up so many budding online relationships. When you meet a person online, both of you can be whoever you want. You choose what information you disclose and what pictures you share. As a result, personal faults are easily hidden. So no matter how much time you spend chatting with the other person online or over the phone, the relationship is not grounded in reality. In fact, I once received an e-mail from a young man who said that he had been dating a girl for over a year, "but we've never seen each other in person."

Because of Internet technology, people are learning to communicate more effectively through a computer than face-to-face. Instead of increasing their social skills, the Internet allows them to hide. For example, a seventh-grader recently asked me, "Is it wrong to use online dating services?" The guy was twelve!

While I know happily married couples who met through online Catholic dating services, I have met more teens than I can count who have ended up in unhealthy relationships that began through chat room discussions or Internet meeting sites. Aside from the obvious risks of meeting strangers online, such relationships have their own set of problems. For example, a couple who meet online may think their relationship looks promising because they spend four hours per night getting to "know" each other online. However, when the two finally meet in person, the relationship often becomes too physical too fast.

Other times one person discovers the hidden faults of the other, but feels too emotionally attached to get out of the relationship. Sometimes meeting a person online will create a long-distance relationship that never would have come into existence otherwise. More realistic local relationships are put on hold in favor of the budding romantic interest who lives eight hundred miles away.

Therefore I would not recommend starting a dating relationship with someone you randomly meet online.

## 24

*If you met a girl in her mid-twenties who was still a virgin, what would you think, really? Would you think that something was wrong with her? Wouldn't that scare you off?*

Speaking as someone who is in his mid-twenties, let me say this: nothing adorns a woman with as much beauty as purity! Nothing is more attractive than holiness. Anyone can recognize this. I once heard of a group of young men who called themselves the "Spur Posse." They competed to sleep with as many women as possible, but every one of them admitted that he wanted to marry a virgin. They all recognized that virginity was a priceless treasure. Unfortunately, they thought it was OK to sleep with the future brides of other men, even though they did not want anyone to touch the women they would marry.

In the book *When God Writes Your Love Story*, Leslie Ludy reported a conversation she overheard. Four men were speaking about what they looked for in a woman: " 'A woman who has mystery—who guards her heart and isn't easy to get.' 'A woman who has backbone. High standards.' 'A woman who is focused on God and isn't easily distracted by men.' 'A woman who doesn't throw herself at me, but allows me to win her heart over time.' " Leslie asked the men what their opinion was of girls who were easy. They all said, " 'A real turn off.' 'Totally unattractive.' " Leslie asked one more question, " 'How do you feel about a girl who is careful about guarding her emotions?' 'I have the utmost respect for a girl like that.' 'That's the kind of girl I want to marry.' 'If I'm interested in a girl, it may be frustrating if she doesn't fall for me right away, but deep down I am all the more intrigued by the challenge of winning her heart.' " [19]

If I were to meet a woman who was still a virgin (and there are plenty my age), I would not think that something was wrong with her. I would think that something was right with her. I would think, "Here is a woman who is willing to sacrifice for the sake of love. Here is a woman who knows the respect she deserves. Here is a woman who knows full well that her body is a temple of the Holy Spirit. Here is a woman."

Since virginity can be given only once, do not lose it. You lose keys and cell phones but your virginity is not meant to be lost, as if you had misplaced it somewhere. *Give* your virginity once and for all to the one true love of your life—your spouse—and to no other. This will be a tremendous blessing to your marriage. In fact, women who marry as virgins have a divorce rate 76 percent lower than those who don't wait for marriage. [20]

There is *nothing* wrong with you if you cherish the treasure of your virginity. Do you want to explain to your future spouse that you gave away your virginity in order to prove that you were normal or popular? Imagine the joy of being able to tell your groom that the gift of your body belongs entirely to him and to no other. Now imagine if you were not able to tell him that. You have saved it this long because you know its value, and you simply need a reminder that you are on track. You are.

The world talks so often about having "sexual experience" and being able to "perform" that it is no wonder no one seems satisfied. All the talk leaves people afraid to be inexperienced. But why? The marital act has nothing to do with performing. I do not know of anyone who had a panel of judges with numbered cards sitting in their honeymoon suite. Do not worry about not having enough experience. You and your spouse will have your entire married life to learn how to love one another.

Purity before marriage is beautiful and helps unite the couple for life. I have received several e-mails from husbands who are having difficulty in marriage because their wives had been with other men before them. The gift of a pure body, a pure mind, and a pure heart is the greatest gift you could ever give your spouse. Therefore, virginity does not scare me off. After all, the value of a gift increases immeasurably if it exists only for the one to whom it will be given. Anyone who thinks that having more sexual experience makes the gift of oneself better is like someone who thinks that if you chew your gum before you give it to someone, he will be more impressed by the gift. Prepare to give your future spouse the best gift you possibly can, and the Lord will bless you abundantly.

## 25

*I have decided to save sex for marriage, but I am unsure about being completely chaste with my boyfriend. Any advice?*

I am glad you recognize that chastity involves more than abstinence from intercourse, but there is a lot of wisdom in saving sexual arousal for marriage as well. The reason you hesitate to take this next step is that the connection between chastity and true love may still be hazy for you. Let's take a look at the link between the two.

We all desire love, but in the words of Pope John Paul II, "*Only the chaste man and the chaste woman are capable of true love.*"[21] He also said that "*purity is a requirement of love.*"[22] Why is this?

I think we can agree that it is easy to mistake physical intimacy for love. This is understandable, since physical intimacy has such a unifying power, which is an attribute of love. The problem is that lust also has a tendency to draw two people together. It is a counterfeit oneness that may be hard to distinguish from the real thing, especially if we have never known healthy intimacy before. The physical closeness seems to meet deep needs that may not have been filled elsewhere.

We all have a need to be loved, but some people stay in unhealthy relationships because it seems to bury the hurt and loneliness. This is where chastity comes in, because it alone has the power to differentiate between love and lust. For those who seek love, chastity is the answer.

Have you ever had a crush on someone and formed an idealized image of him, only to see a different person emerge when your emotions faded and reality set in? Was it the other person who changed, or was it you? He probably did not change at all. You just opened your eyes. Just as having a crush on a person clouds our objectivity, physical intimacy does the same. Personally, the more physical my relationships have been, the more difficult it was to judge their worth while I was in them. After a relationship ended, it was easier to evaluate how healthy the relationship was. But while I was in it—and to the extent that we were physically involved—it was tough to recognize that it was not worth keeping. Frequently we do not want to look at a relationship objectively because we do not want to admit that it is not love. We do not want to lose the other person.

Whenever love is present, there is a desire to please the other. This is especially common in young women who want to please guys in order to win their affection. However, love sometimes demands that we refuse to please the other, because what the other finds to be pleasing is not what is best for him. You would agree that when you refuse to have sex with a guy, it does not mean that you do not love him. It just means that you love him more than he may be able to understand.

Without a clear standard of purity in a relationship, couples begin to experiment with physical intimacy. Initial intimacies become familiar, and the couple gradually push back the boundaries in a desire to find new levels of excitement and closeness. Before long all that is left is sexual intercourse. When a couple depend on physical pleasure to feel close to one another, they may not realize that they hardly know how to express love in other ways. In the long run the couple's impatience for sexual oneness may contribute to their separation. They have deprived themselves of the opportunity to grow in love and thus to experience true joy.

Don't feel you will miss out if you live chastity to the fullest. Sure, you will experience an initial loss of the physical union that you desire, but you move beyond this when you see the value of the other person and the benefits of a chaste lifestyle. In the end the only thing you miss out on is the empty counterfeit of love. While chastity is not the easiest choice, it is the best one.

To see how this works on a practical level, consider your options. A guy who does not intend to save sexual arousal for marriage will often approach a date as a formality to get through before the real "fun" can start. When a couple is striving for purity, the dates can be enjoyed as time spent getting to know each other. You are free to fall in love for all the right reasons. If you do not embrace chastity but still wish to remain a virgin, where does this leave you? You will become all revved up, only to slam on the brakes repeatedly. Not only is this unloving because it arouses desires that you cannot satisfy morally, but it also leads to sexual frustration.

Often a couple will share the gift of sexual arousal to feel closer, but they end up feeling alienated from each other and regretful. They would be much closer if they entrusted the relationship to God and made sacrifices together to glorify Him. Love always involves struggle, so if they are both willing to be generous with God, this will create a union between their hearts that no illicit pleasure can match. Purity will become their superglue.

One man told me that the power of temptation rests on the deceptive promise that sin will bring more satisfaction than living for God. It is only God's way that can satisfy us. In the words of Psalm 16:11, "You show me the path of life; in your presence there is fullness of joy, in your right hand are pleasures for evermore." We all desire happiness, but sin and happiness cannot live together. Sin is a counterfeit of happiness that brings with it shame and regret. On the other hand, sacrificial love brings true joy, and a life of virtue brings happiness. Try it and see. You'll come to see why the Church teaches that chastity defends love from selfishness.[23] Where there is selfishness, there is no love. Where there is no love, there is no joy or peace. No wonder Pope John Paul II said, "Chastity is the sure way to happiness."[24]

## 26

*Sometimes my boyfriend respects my wishes, but sometimes he pressures me to do stuff that makes me uncomfortable. I don't want to lose him, so what should I do? I made some big mistakes in past relationships.*

I understand your fear of confronting your boyfriend, but the bottom line is that you must risk losing him. Every human being was created to be loved and never to be used. But if you are even slightly afraid that he will lose interest in you when you end physical intimacies, ask yourself: Is he interested in you or in pleasure? Deep in your heart I think you are afraid that he may be in this for the physical relationship. You have been used before, and your greatest fear is that you will be used again.

There are two options open to you. One is to give in to whatever he wants (which is no guarantee that he will stay). The other is to follow your intuition. Look into your heart to discover why you do not feel comfortable doing these things with him. It is probably because the acts degrade you. You deserve better.

Suppose that you were willing to give your boyfriend whatever he wanted, out of fear of losing him. Would his respect for you go up or down? Down. If you stand firm and show that you will not compromise your values, then he will respect you more—even if he leaves you because he is in search of a girl who does not know what she is worth. You must take this risk if you want love.

A young woman may abandon her morals because she likes

the fact that a boy desires her so much. She may be starving for love and willing to settle for lust. But what usually happens is that the guy loses respect for the girl, becomes bored, and leaves. Other times he sticks around as long as she is willing to satisfy his desires. I have heard of many young women who say they did certain things with their boyfriends because they thought that the guys would like them more. One girl wrote, "He had convinced me that what we were doing was OK, and so that is what we did. The whole time I felt I was doing something wrong, but I silenced myself for the good of him. Little did I know the effect this would have on me. It was as though someone had slowly scooped away at my soul and let it deteriorate."

You know in your heart that this kind of relationship is not what you are looking for. Another young woman shared:

> I had been told all my life that sex before marriage was wrong, but no one ever told me why. In the twelfth grade I found my-self dating one boy for a long period of time. We spent a lot of time alone, and as a result our relationship became more physical. I felt guilty, bitter, frustrated, and dirty. Because of those feelings I would say to him, "We need to stop having sex, or at least slow down." Well, we tried to slow down, but that didn't work. Instead of getting closer, we grew farther apart. After two years of dating, I finally said, "No more sex," and he said, "Good-bye." Since then, whenever I dated another person for a length of time, sex became a part of the relationship. Tears always came because I knew I had blown it again. [25]

If your boyfriend loves you, he will not pressure you to do things that make you uncomfortable. Suppose you say, "I don't feel comfortable doing that with you." If he responds, "Why not? You used to do it," or "What's your problem? Come on, I love you, this will make us so much closer," then he is not respecting you. Often a guy will insinuate that he really loves you but he may need to leave if his desires go unsatisfied. This is definitely not love. "Love waits to give, but lust can't wait to get." [26]

Ask yourself this question: When it comes to my body, will my boyfriend take everything I'm willing to give him? If this is the case, then he is not concerned about your soul. His goal is pleasure. While it may temporarily feel like love, you know in your heart it is not. For example, consider what a guy named Jordan said in an article in *Complete Woman* magazine: "Sex is extremely important to me. In fact, once I felt compelled to break up with a woman I really loved because we didn't have enough sex. . . . The lack of sex nearly killed me."[27] (Apparently he was rushed to the hospital for lack of sex.) If this is how Jordan treats the ladies he "really loves," it is hard to imagine how he treats other women.

Pray for courage and wisdom, and let your boyfriend know that you want to be pure from now on. Good relationships require good communication. You need to be open with your boyfriend about what is in your heart. You deserve a guy who will not only allow you to become pure but will take the initiative to keep the relationship pure.

Sometimes a guy will reply to his girlfriend's request to be pure by saying, "No more sexual stuff? That's OK—I just love being with you." The girl melts, but his behavior gradually returns to the way it was before. In these cases a girl needs to persevere in purity and see what happens. If he sticks with you as you grow in holiness, and he brings you closer to God by his actions, then the sacrifices you have made together will be good training for marriage.

As for now, the best thing you can do for your boyfriend is to grow in holiness yourself. It will inspire him to become worthy of you. When women are pure, they become "possessors of a deep and wondrous secret that is revealed only to the one who proves himself deserving of her."[28] This sense of independence in a girl appeals to guys. If women easily give themselves away, they should not be surprised to find themselves in a culture of men who feel no need to commit to them.

But is this guy the one for you? To be honest, I do not think so. I think you may know that and be afraid of starting over. Or perhaps you want to make this work out, so that you do not have to address the hurt. But it will be much better in the long run if you take a hard look at your situation now. One reason I doubt the strength of this relationship is because you said that "*sometimes* he will respect my wishes*.*" This is a big warning sign, suggesting that the rest of the time he is placing his hormones on a more important level than you as a person. That says a great deal about his character. Any guy can say yes to sex. But how many can say no? If he cannot say no to temptations now, how will he say no when temptations come in marriage?


## 27

*There is a guy I really like, but I am not sure if he is interested in me. I want to find out if he is, but I don't want to scare him off. Should I call and tell him, or should I play hard to get?*

Possibly neither. First of all, playing games is never a good idea. A girl who is real is much more attractive than a girl who wants to play mind games. After all, if you play games to make guys like you, then when do you stop playing? If you play hard to get to win a guy, then you may feel the need to maintain that teasing behavior to keep him interested. A mature relationship needs to develop without having to rely on games.

If you need to pretend to be someone you are not in order to win another's heart, then what will happen in the long run? The entire relationship will be built on deception. This is the opposite of love, which "rejoices with the truth" (1 Cor. 13:6, *NAB*). Love is patient, and it trusts that God knows what He is about. There is no need to take the situation into your own hands so that you can make things happen at your own pace. God's pace is much better.

But calling him up and telling him openly how you feel may not be a good idea either. To begin with, there should be a season of friendship before any romantic relationship. Failing to cultivate this could be harmful in the long run, since these things need time to build. Imagine a girl building a dollhouse. She is in such a rush to play with the finished product that she glues the house together in thirty minutes and moves all the furniture in. She ignores the directions to wait a day for the glue to dry before even touching the house. Naturally it collapses. Similarly, you must establish a foundation and give the friendship time to develop. If a relationship grows out of this, you will again be called to be patient. A lot of people become "more than friends" without spending much time *being* friends—which often ends up meaning they are really *less* than friends.

Without this foundation of friendship, revealing your feelings for him too soon could hinder mutual feelings from developing in his heart. If those feelings do take root in him, they will show in due time. But don't take the advice of the teen girl magazines that urge you to initiate things and make up for his supposed shyness. Resist the temptation to take matters into your own hands or to make excuses for why he hasn't asked you out yet.

There are two reasons for this. First, do you really want to date a guy who is scared to pursue you? Second, I can speak for all men when I say that we are drawn to women who have a sense of mystery about them. We need to wonder what you're thinking. We need to feel that asking you out is a risk. When you pour out all your feelings, it may temporarily flatter a guy, but he'll feel as if he's missing out on the thrill of winning you. Teen girl magazines may think that such advice is sexist, but the fact remains that men love the thrill of the chase, and women are worth the pursuit.

## 28

*My boyfriend has a lot of problems. I am scared of him sometimes, and my friends say that he is bad news. We have been pretty physical, but I want to stay in the relationship to help him. What should I do?*

No offense, but scientists recently discovered that feelings of romantic love tend to deactivate certain parts of the brain. For example, brain scans of people experiencing romantic emotions showed deactivations in the parts of the brain that make moral judgments (mesial prefrontal cortex, the parietotemporal junction, and the temporal poles). Other areas of the brain that were deactivated are responsible for judgment of negative emotions.

The scientists said that romantic love leads to "the suppression of activity in the neural machineries associated with the critical social assessment of other people and with negative emotions. . . . These findings therefore bring us closer to explaining in neurological terms why 'love makes [us] blind.' "[29] In other words, when you're in love with a guy, your brain is handicapped when it comes to judging the value (and morality) of a relationship. That's one reason why it's important to date only guys who have strong values.

The purpose of dating is to find a worthy spouse, not to rehabilitate a troubled guy. So it sounds as if you need to step back from this relationship. Many young women with good hearts want to play the role of therapist for a guy who has a rough life, but they end up wounded, and the guy is not much better off. A girl might stay in the relationship because she does not want to hurt the guy by leaving. But it will harm the guy (and her) more if she does not take a step back. Until he can deal with his problems in a way that is not destructive to him or to others, he is not ready to be in an intimate relationship. Friendship? Maybe. Dating relationship? Not now.

According to God's word, "The man of violent temper pays the penalty; even if you rescue him, you will have it to do again" (Prov. 19:19, NAB). It is not your job to save this guy from all of his problems. Let him know that you are praying for him but that you need space for yourself and stability in your life. This is not selfishness. It shows a healthy respect for yourself, and that is the foundation for any good future relationship.

If he tries to lay a guilt trip on you or intimidate you, it is all the more evidence that you need to back away. If he hurts you, then the sooner this ends the better. In the meantime do not use physical pleasure to cover up the pain of the relationship. Instead listen to your friends. They are there to look out for you, and I do not think you will regret following their advice.

A recent study showed that when it comes to predicting the success or failure of a relationship, few people know better than the friends of the girl. Not the couple themselves, not the guy's friends, but the girl's friends are often the most reliable judges of how strong a relationship is and how long it will last.[30] As Proverbs 27:6 says, "Faithful are the wounds of a friend." This means that although their advice may be painful to receive, it will be best in the long run to follow it.

As difficult as it may seem to walk away, it will only be more difficult later to patch up the hurt that has been caused by staying in the relationship too long. Two factors should influence this decision: You are worth more, and he needs this time to mature. If you do not understand your value in God's eyes, then it is easy to seek your worth in relationships, even unhealthy ones. Even an unhealthy relationship makes you feel desired, and so you settle for it.

Right now, while he is still single, the most loving thing you can do is to show him that he cannot deal with his hurt by hurting others. He needs to know that his behavior is unacceptable. Using a little child psychology may be helpful here. According to Drs. Cloud and Townsend, who offer parents advice on how to set boundaries with children, "Setting boundaries without setting consequences is a form of nagging. The disrespecter learns that his greatest problem is not the hurtfulness of his behavior, but only the annoyance of your complaining."[31] As long as you stay in the relationship and take the abuse, it sends him the message that his behavior is fine.

Therefore, don't spend your time trying to change your boyfriend. Instead, imagine what it would be like to be cherished by a man who would protect your purity and make you feel safe. Such men do exist.

### 29

*My friend is in high school, and she is always getting into bad relationships with college guys who don't respect her. Now a guy wants her to leave her mom and third stepfather and move in with him. What can I do?*

As you realize, your friend needs to take a break. Because she comes from a broken family, she may have a void in her life that should have been filled by the love of her father. It is common for a young woman who did not receive her father's love to jump into the arms of older guys to receive the missing affection, attention, and acceptance. One woman said, "I thought about the girl who this very night will lose her virginity because she is searching for her daddy's love. And I want to be able to stop her somehow and tell her that she will never find it in another man."[32]

Your friend might fear abandonment and may confuse the physical affection of boys with love. If she had a loving father who protected her and sacrificed for her good, then she would be more likely to wait for such a man to come into her life. Since she never received this gift, she does not know how a man should properly treat a woman.

There may also be a deep connection between the absence of her father in her life and her willingness to live with disrespect. Sometimes when a child had a distant or critical parent, the child may grow up wanting to please people who hurt her in order to receive their love. In trying to mend those original wounds, the girl may put up with just about any form of disrespect. These are deep problems, and living with a boyfriend will not solve them.

In fact, living with this guy is one of the worst things she could do. Go to the Q and A section of chastityproject.com to see research on cohabitation that shows the consequences of living together. Perhaps you can show your friend some of the facts in order to discourage her from moving in with him. If she wants a lasting relationship, then she needs to work toward it by making smart decisions for herself and her future.

She does not know what to expect from a man, so she will take what she is given. This is why she needs space to figure out who she is and what she really wants.

## 30

*How do you know if you should break up with a guy?*

Ask yourself the following questions (the more questions you answer with no, the more reason you have to break things off): Has my relationship with him brought me closer to God? Can I see myself marrying him? Would I like my children to grow up to be just like him? Am I dating to discern marriage? Do my parents approve of him? Is he 100 percent faithful? Do I feel safe, honored, and respected around him? Is he clean of any drug, alcohol, or pornography problems? Has this relationship helped me to become the woman I hope to be? Does he bring out the best in me? Does he respect my purity? Does he love God more than he loves pleasure? Can I honestly say that the relationship is emotionally, physically, spiritually, and psychologically healthy? Has the relationship brought me closer to my family and other friends? Ideally, you should be able to announce an emphatic "yes!" to all of the above questions. The more negative answers you have, the more reason you have to think twice about the relationship.

Saint Paul tells us that an unmarried woman is anxious about the things of the Lord, about how she can serve Him and be holy (1 Cor. 7). Are you free to be anxious about the things of the Lord, or are you consumed by emotional conflicts with your boyfriend or consumed by your relationship in general? Some young women are willing to stay in bad relationships so that they never have to be alone. They will put up with disrespectful behavior, compromise their values, and stay in dead-end relationships that should have ended long ago. Many couples become so close they feel as if the other person is their entire world. If they let the person go, they fear they will have nothing left and love will be lost forever. Do not give in to this fear.

If the guy has some major issues, do not move toward marriage expecting these issues to resolve themselves over time. This is denial. If he treats you disrespectfully, lovingly confront his behavior. If he listens, apologizes, accepts responsibility, and works to correct the behavior, then he is making progress. If not, then do not harbor false hope. If you want to know how the future will be with him, look at the past. The longer you wait to deal with his problems, the more burdensome they will become. Throughout all of this, he must have some personal motivation to change. All of the impetus should not come from you.

The presence of difficulties does not necessarily mean you need to break things off. It is common for couples to walk away from a relationship if things get tough. Your job is to discern if the issue is significant enough to merit a breakup or if it is a problem that can be solved. As you pray and ask the Lord for guidance, do not try to figure out the answers on your own. Turn to people you trust, such as family members, a priest, youth minister, or friends. Reflect on their input and have courage.

Whatever your decision, make it clear. The longer it flops back and forth, the worse it is. If you do break things off, do not worry. If he is the right one for you, then taking this time off will not hurt. Also, do not jump back into the relationship quickly if you see signs of improvement in his behavior. A person can manipulate another into letting him back even if he has not made a true change of heart. Resist the temptation, wait on God, and write a letter to yourself about why you broke up and what you are looking for in a spouse. When you feel the urge to jump back into the relationship for comfort, you will have a reminder of why you are holding out for God's best.

When you become close to a boyfriend, it can be easy to overlook his faults. One way to prevent this from happening is to make a calendar of his unhealthy behavior. For example, if he has a habit of being disrespectful or of flirting with other girls, mark this on a calendar every time it happens (without his knowledge). Ideally, you should leave him as soon as it happens. But if you don't feel strong enough to let go and you have the habit of justifying his behavior, it will be hard to deny the evidence when you see the pattern documented in your own handwriting.

If you break up, you might desire to "just be friends." But as long as one of you is still romantically interested in the other, this is not easy to do. If the two of you are to be friends again one day, you need space right now. When people try the "just friends" approach right after a breakup, it is usually because they are dragging their feet and do not want to let go. I have tried it before, and it can harm the friendship in the long run because the breakup is so drawn out.

And remember to take this to God in prayer. Ask Him what He thinks you should do. Sometimes we run around and grab what we want and rarely sit still long enough to hear Him. He will speak if we will listen. Until you do make a decision, live the virtue of purity in the relationship. This will help you to see more clearly. Also, chaste relationships tend to end on a happier note, since the couple did not do anything regrettable.

## 31

*My girlfriend of two years just broke up with me. I thought that she was the one, and I feel crushed. I'm not sleeping well, I've lost my appetite, and I can't understand why God would let this happen.*

I have been through a couple of tough breakups, and during those times Scripture was a great consolation. God wants us to remember that even when we know nothing about our future, "the Lord is trustworthy in every word, and faithful in every work" (Ps. 145:13, *NAB*). The Lord's timing is perfect, and His will is your refuge. His plan will be clear in time, so be still and know that He is God, that He is faithful, and that He knows exactly what He is doing. "The works of the Lord are all good, and He will supply every need in its hour. And no one can say, 'This is worse than that,' for all things will prove good in their season. So now sing praise with all your heart and voice, and bless the name of the Lord" (Sir. 39:33–35).

It is natural to feel a painful sense of loss during this time, but in the midst of this suffering, do not lose your peace. In the words of Saint Paul, "Rejoice always, pray constantly, give thanks in all circumstances; for this is the will of God in Christ Jesus for you" (1 Thess. 5:16–18). The prophet Nehemiah advises, "Do not be saddened this day, for rejoicing in the Lord must be your strength" (Neh. 8:10, *NAB*). Although rejoicing may be the last thing on your mind right now, God deserves our thanks just as much when times are bad as when everything goes our way. One of the most beautiful forms of praise to God is when we thank Him for His providence before we see it unfold. After all, is He less of a good God when we cannot fathom His ways?

Take this time to draw closer to God. As Psalm 62 says, "My soul rests in God alone" (Ps. 62:1, *NAB*). The more our peace depends on human beings, the more we will realize that another human being can never satisfy us. I sometimes imagine a little throne on top of the human heart, and we get to decide who sits there. We often place people there, and if things go well with them, life is beautiful. When things go wrong, and they do not reciprocate affection or say just the right thing, then we lose our peace. Only God deserves to sit on this throne, and only He can hold it in peace.

This is not to say that once we put Him there, nothing affects us. Trusting Him does not mean that we will never have feelings of hurt or confusion. It simply means that in the midst of the storm, we remain at peace even when it seems as if Jesus is asleep (see Mark 4:35–41). Now is a good time to make sure that all is in order in your life and that doing God's will is your number one priority. Sometimes we are so anxious about our relationships with others that we forget that the most important relationship in our lives must be our friendship with God. Pray that you may be single-hearted for the Lord.

Also, know that your suffering is not in vain. When you accept suffering, you can join it to the sufferings of Christ and offer it as a prayer. The apostle Paul said, "Now I rejoice in my sufferings for your sake, and in my flesh I complete what is lacking in Christ's afflictions for the sake of His body, that is, the Church" (Col. 1:24). If you need a suggestion regarding what to offer your sufferings for, I would ask that you offer some of them as a prayer for all of the teens I speak to about chastity. You can save many souls through your sufferings, although many people do not realize this. As Saint Thérèse of Lisieux said, "Sufferings gladly borne for others convert more people than sermons."[33] If we understand redemptive suffering, we will be able to find joy in our crosses. Blessed Mary Teresa of Saint Joseph wrote, "I have but one wish: to suffer as much as possible for this short while. It does not matter what kind of suffering, as long as it is suffering. From my heart I bless and thank all who have caused me to suffer. To suffer for God is the only joy which heaven does not have."[34]

So suffer well, be still, and trust the Lord. As the saying goes, there are years that ask questions, and there are years that answer.

# 3

# Preparing for Marriage

## 32

*How do you know if you should marry the person you are seeing?*

The most important decision you will make in life is to follow God. The second most important decision is your vocation. So make sure that God is guiding your choice. Talk to Him about your dreams, your joys, your problems, and your fears. It is common to meet people who select a spouse on their own, get engaged, and then only afterward ask God and their family to bless it. Try that the other way—start with God and your family—and things tend to run more smoothly.

Here are five practical points to consider when wondering if you should marry a specific person.

One: How is your friendship? It is easy to feel close to a person if you have been physically intimate, but how well can you honestly say you know this person? The more physically involved you have been, the more you will need to step back to evaluate the relationship. This is because physical intimacy clouds our judgment—which it should. One of the benefits of total physical intimacy for married couples is that it renders them less critical of each other. However, this clouding of your thinking belongs in marriage, not before.

Be honest in examining what truly unites the two of you. Is it a desire for pleasure or emotional gain? Is there an unhealthy dependency, where one or both of you has made an idol out of marriage, expecting that it will solve loneliness? How do the two of you deal with differences? Can you disagree lovingly, or are there some issues of manipulation, anger, or guilt that need to be sorted out first? Before marriage it is easy to maintain a good image, so make sure you have seen each other with your masks down, so to speak. Lastly, is there a real romantic interest? Some people say that romantic feelings are not that important, but there is grave reason for concern if these feelings are not present. This is not to say that you must feel constantly madly in love with each other. Most people do not struggle with the absence of feelings, but with infatuation. Just have the honesty to look at where you stand with this.

Two: Are the two of you on the same page when it comes to the size of your family? Does one of you expect one child, while the other envisions two minivans brimming with kids? Does one of you want kids right away while the other wants to wait ten years before having any children? If you have different dreams, then now is the time to be honest about your differences. More importantly, do you think that your prospective spouse would be a good parent? Or does he or she have habits that are destructive to a marriage and family, such as drug use, excessive drinking, pornography, sarcasm, anger, self-centeredness, or infidelity?

Three: Are you financially ready for a family? The book of Proverbs advises, "Prepare your work outside, get everything ready for you in the field; and after that build your house" (Prov. 24:27). We should not jump into marriage before we are able to care for a family financially. You do not need to have college money set aside for your kids before you get married, but you should be stable enough with your career that you will be able to carry the great responsibilities that come with the blessings of parenthood.[1]

Four: How is your prospective spouse's faith? Do you lead each other to God? Is your relationship centered on God? Do the two of you have different faiths? Does he or she have a faith at all? The Bible advises against marrying a nonbeliever (2 Cor. 6:14) because marriage is difficult enough without having differences on an issue that should be the foundation of your life together. If one goes to a Catholic and the other a non-Catholic church, then know that there will be trials as a result of this. The Church does allow mixed marriages, but advises against them because of the difficulties they present within marriage.

A husband and wife should be able to do more for God together than they can do apart. They should form a team, and to be effective they need to have the same goal in mind. So take this all to prayer, and trust that God will guide you. Some couples make the mistake of failing to ask for the Lord's guidance, while others overspiritualize the matter and will not move forward unless they receive numerous signs from heaven. God wants you to have confidence. Trust in Him. Use all the wisdom at your disposal, and then make a decision.

Five: What do your friends and families say? It is easy for a couple to become isolated and fail to consult the friends and families God has given them. They know your habits, your emotional health, your dreams, and plenty of things you probably wish nobody knew. But they love you nonetheless and can give some of the best guidance.

As I was finishing my master's studies, I was seeing a young woman, and we were looking toward marriage. We met with her parents to discuss our hopes. The parents approved of our relationship but saw marriage as something still several years ahead of us. At the time I was frustrated that they could not see how much we loved each other, but their wisdom prevailed and the Lord took us down different paths. Her family had a great deal of wisdom, and they knew that if we were to be together we would have to be patient and prayerful, waiting for the proper time.

Finally, know that if marriage is anything, it is a carefully planned leap of faith. You will need to weigh all the above considerations and more, pray about them, and move ahead. You can only know a person so well before you marry. This is because coming to know another person is not so much a destination as it is a lifelong process. Within marriage you will see strengths and weaknesses more clearly than ever before. Because of this there are inevitably going to be disappointments, but you should anticipate them with hope.

When difficulties arise—and they will come—they will test and affirm your love. Marriage is not an endless whirling romance, and your marriage will suffer to the extent that you expect it to fit that fairy tale. When the infatuation fades, some imagine that they must not have married Mr. or Miss Right. This is partly why so many divorces happen within the first few years of marriage. It is a shame that couples are not prepared to let their relationship breathe. We often have little faith when the time comes to exhale. There is a love waiting to grow, but it is a quieter love than a couple know at the start of their relationship. It is unfortunate that so few have the patience to wait and work in sacrifice to see it blossom.

*Successful marriages are not the result of finding the perfect person but of loving the imperfect person you have chosen to marry.* Therefore, do not allow yourself to be discouraged when you discover faults and annoyances that you never recognized before. It is said that after marriage, the man gets upset because the woman changes, and the woman gets upset because the man will not change. But when faults do come to the surface, we should not be set on "fixing" our spouse. We marry a person, not a project. We marry a human being, not an idealized image. Only when we let go of the idealized image and begin to accept and love our spouse will the deepest and most fulfilling kind of love appear. As a friend of mine once said, "I married her because I loved her. Now I love her because I married her."

When a couple understand these principles, they are mature enough to think about marriage. We are not eleven years old anymore, fluttering from one crush to another according to how fun the feelings are. When a relationship is based on an infatuation instead of a decision, it will last only as long as the infatuation does. We must be careful about what we base our relationships on, because finding the love that everyone longs for is a serious endeavor.

Pope John Paul II beautifully sums up all of these thoughts in his book *Love and Responsibility*:

The essential reason for choosing a person must be personal, not merely sexual. Life will determine the value of a choice and the value and true magnitude of love. It is put to the test most severely when the sensual and emotional reactions themselves grow weaker, and sexual values as such lose their effect. Nothing then remains except the value of the person, and the inner truth about the love of those connected comes to light. If their love is a true gift of self, so that they belong to the other, it will not only survive but grow stronger, and sink deeper roots. Whereas if it was never more than a synchronization of sensual and emotional experiences it will lose its *raison d'être* [reason for existence] and the persons involved in it will suddenly find themselves in a vacuum. We must never forget that only when love between human beings is put to the test can its true value be seen.[2]

### 33

*Divorce runs in my family, so I don't want to get married. Is that OK?*

I do not think that you are opposed to marriage; you are just afraid of getting a divorce. There is a big difference. I would imagine that the desire to give yourself completely to another and to receive the total gift of another is still in your heart. But because of the marriages you have seen, you have an understandable fear that a love like this is out of your reach. Do not be afraid.

While it is fine never to marry and to live the single or religious life instead, look at your intentions for avoiding marriage. Each vocation is a calling, and each requires courage, love, and sacrifice. God may call you to the married life and ask you to trust Him despite all the failed marriages you have seen. Just as there has been a rash of broken marriages in your family, perhaps God plans on using you to turn the tide for future generations. There is no reason why you need to follow in your parents' footsteps when you can make the decision to love so that your kids will want to follow in yours.

If we want a great marriage, we need to start building love's foundation now. Unfortunately, most people seem to spend more time preparing for their wedding than they do for their marriage. If we start disciplining ourselves now, we will have a firm foundation on which to build a lifelong love.

This is what I mean by preparation. While in high school I spent countless hours in batting cages. On one afternoon I hit thirty-eight consecutive rounds with the eighty-mile-per-hour pitching machine—which adds up to 684 swings. When I finished, my back was sore and I had blood blisters on my hands, but I did not mind because it was a time of serious training. You could have told me this was "repressive" training and that I should free myself from it, but it was not. I had a goal in mind. When I made my college baseball team as a freshman, I thought I had reached my goal, but the training had just begun. We would practice six or seven days a week for several hours at a time (not including games). This preparation was essential if we ever hoped to have a successful season.

Unfortunately, some couples spend less time getting ready for a lifetime of marriage than we spent preparing for a few months of baseball. If I wanted a good batting average, I would train myself to read a pitcher and hit his curve. If we want successful marriages, we need to train ourselves in the virtues that hold marriage together: humility, servanthood, purity, honesty, faithfulness, and so on. Begin fostering these virtues in your life now, and you will have more confidence in the hope of a lasting love. Then, if God chooses to call you to a vocation other than marriage, you will have the peace of knowing that you did not avoid marriage because of fear but embraced another vocation because you heard His voice and followed it.

## 34

*What role does physical attraction play in a decision to date someone?*
*Should a person value personality more than attraction?*

Many people make the mistake of thinking that they should pursue a relationship with someone because they feel such strong feelings of attraction. We are all attracted to what is beautiful, but that does not mean that we should pursue each beautiful person we see. For example, even in marriage there may be times when you experience feelings of attraction toward people other than your spouse. Needless to say, such attractions are not a sign that you should leave your husband or wife.

Being attracted to another person is wonderful, and I would not recommend that a couple get married if they are not attracted to each other. This is the natural way that God has made us. However, if a woman marries a man only because of an intense physical attraction, or a man refuses to get married because he cannot find a Christian Barbie doll, then there is a problem. We are not to expect flawless perfection in the other. If we do, then the flaw is not in the others but in us. We may need to readjust our priorities so that love does not pass us by. As one man said, "God help the man who will not marry until he finds a perfect woman, and God help him still more if he finds her."[3]

The book of Proverbs says: "Like a golden ring in a swine's snout is a beautiful woman with a rebellious disposition. . . . Charm is deceptive and beauty fleeting; the woman who fears the Lord is to be praised" (Prov. 11:22, 31:30, *NAB*). These verses do not mean that physical attraction is bad but that other factors, such as the person's personality and spirituality, are more important. When the beauty fades—and the external beauty will fade —then who are you left with? Ask yourself this question now instead of later. Look at a same-sex grandparent of the person you would like to marry. Now add all the internal qualities that your potential spouse has. Can you say that you would still want to spend your life with him or her? You should. An easier way to test your attraction is to pretend you are blind. Now ask yourself how attractive the other becomes.

A relationship stands on whatever foundation you choose. If a couple build their relationship on the foundation of pleasure, the relationship will last as long as the pleasure is sufficient. If it is based only upon looks, then when the looks fade, so will the relationship. Since judgment is easily clouded by physical beauty and the infatuation it inspires, make sure you have role models who can provide you with guidance.

## 35

*I really like the dating scene and the freedom to see different women without having to settle down and get married. Is that OK?*

I think that you need to take an honest look at your motives. When you enter into these temporary relationships, what is your goal? The natural response may be to say that you date around simply to have a good time. But ask yourself if perhaps these short relationships are a shield for you. Do they cover up a deeper fear that you might not be able to have a lasting relationship? Is this a way to guard yourself from becoming too involved with the demands of love? We men must have the courage to meet those demands if we intend to hold the heart of a woman. This may be risky and uncomfortable for us, but as C. S. Lewis wrote, "The only place outside Heaven where you can be perfectly safe from all the dangers and perturbations of love is Hell." [4]

I once read that "young love is a flame; very pretty, very hot and fierce, but still only light and flickering. The love of the older and disciplined heart is as coals, deep-burning and unquenchable." [5] If you want to find unquenchable love, you must come to grips with the fact that love is not free. It costs everything, but this total gift of ourselves is precisely what makes us most free. It liberates us from the prison of doing everything for our own sake. Otherwise we will die having learned to love no one but ourselves. In the words of Pope John Paul II, love "draws one out of the shell of individualism and egocentrism."[6] It sounds weird, but we do not know freedom until we give it away for the sake of love. That is why it exists: so that it can be surrendered. If we live for ourselves, we miss the point of our existence, because we have been created to love as God loves.

I would challenge you not to invite the interests of a woman unless you are interested in considering her as a possible future spouse. In a speech to college men, Pope John Paul II noted that we men have a lack of willingness to give: "We are quite ready to take, or conquer, in terms of enjoyment, profit, gain, and success . . . . Then comes the question of giving, and at this point we hang back, because we are not prepared to give."[7] But as he said elsewhere, "The person who does not decide to love forever will find it very difficult to really love for even one day."[8]

## 36

*I have met this great girl, and she is exactly what I have been hoping for. I really want to marry her someday. Do you have any tips for how to keep from messing this up?*

Entrust this relationship to God. He is the Master Builder, not you. David wrote, "Unless the Lord builds the house, those who build it labor in vain. Unless the Lord watches over the city, the watchman stays awake in vain. It is in vain that you rise up early and go late to rest, eating the bread of anxious toil; for he gives to his beloved sleep" (Ps. 127:1–2). Also, let the peace of Christ reign in your heart. Your task is to take this to prayer so that you can determine the will of God and follow it.

Where do you start? Build the foundation of a graced friendship before jumping into romance. If and when a relationship starts, you will want to have a clear sense of direction in it, looking toward marriage. After all, this is the reason to date. As for now, there is a lot of wisdom in taking it easy. If it is love, then this time of anticipation will not hurt.

In a relationship that is new and exciting, people often stay up to the wee hours of the morning pouring out their life history and emotional secrets. They feel incredibly close because they know so much about each other's past. Other couples dive headlong into a deep spiritual relationship as well. People in both situations, if they value chastity, also will be working to hold back on the physical side of things. But the intimacy of hearts has moved so fast that the physical side yearns to catch up. Picture a slingshot primed to launch. A similar tension results when you move too fast on emotional matters and then cannot, morally, match that emotional depth with a corresponding physical intimacy. So take it easy. I do not intend to put a damper on love but to help you pace yourself so that love reaches its fullest potential. Take your time and allow trust to develop and strengthen.

Also, take the initiative to make the relationship godly. At the same time do not attempt to be her spiritual guru or father in the faith. She is not to be under your tutelage as if she is your student, disciple, or child. It is easy for a good-hearted young man to want to assume these roles for a young woman, especially if she has not been involved in her faith for long. Progress toward God side by side.

Involve your families, and tap into their years of wisdom. One man with a great deal of insight on the topic of relationships is Dr. James Dobson, who offers this advice in his book *Love Must Be Tough*:

> Don't let the relationship move too fast in its intimacy. The phrase "too hot not to cool down" has validity. Take it one step at a time. . . . Don't call too often on the phone or give the other person an opportunity to get tired of you. . . . Don't be too quick to reveal your desire to get married—or that you think you have found Mr. Wonderful or Miss Marvelous. If your partner has not arrived at the same conclusion, you will throw him or her into panic. . . . Do not expect anyone to meet *all* of your emotional needs. Maintain interests and activities outside that romantic relationship, even after marriage. . . . In addition to the many moral, spiritual, and

physical reasons for remaining virgins until marriage, there are numerous psychological and interpersonal advantages to the exercise of self-control and discipline. Though it's an old-fashioned notion, perhaps, it is still true that men do not respect "easy" women and often become bored with those who have held nothing in reserve. Likewise, women often disrespect men who have only one thing on their minds. Both sexes need to remember how to use a very ancient word. It's pronounced "NO!" [9]

Dobson also notes that the relationship must be able to breathe. Do not be afraid to give each other some space, because relationships thrive best when there is freedom, respect, and confidence. The less one exhibits these characteristics, the more likely he is to have difficulty in romantic endeavors.

Lastly, realize that too many people see marriage as a finish line. They often arrive there exhausted, only to discover that the real work has only begun. Making a lifelong love is a demanding task that yields its priceless fruits only to those who love with patience and fortitude.

In the meantime work to better yourself. Becoming a saint is the best gift you could ever give to your wife and children. Work vigorously against your defects, and do your best to improve as a man of God each day.

## 37

*Should I move in with my boyfriend before we get married? It seems like a smart move, because you want to really know a person before you commit to life together.*

Most cohabiting couples who hope to marry see their arrangement as a good test run, a way to make sure that they are compatible before tying the knot. After all, who wants to go through a divorce?

Aside from all the spiritual factors regarding premarital sex, we should take a look at what researchers have found about living together before marriage. Two researchers summarized the findings of numerous studies by stating that "expectation of a positive relationship between cohabitation and marital stability . . . has been shattered in recent years by studies conducted in several Western countries." [10]

What the studies discovered is this: If you do not want to get divorced, do not move in until after the wedding. Why is that? Consider the following facts about cohabitation: Most couples who live together never end up getting married, but those who do tie the knot have a divorce rate nearly 80 percent higher than those who waited until after the wedding to move in together. [11] Couples who cohabited prior to marriage also have greater marital conflict and poorer communication, and they made more frequent visits to marriage counselors. [12] Women who cohabited before marriage are more than three times as likely to cheat on their husbands within marriage. [13] The U.S. Justice Department found that women who cohabit are sixty-two times more likely to be assaulted by a live-in boyfriend than by a husband. [14] They were also more than three times as likely to be depressed as married women, [15] and the couples were less sexually satisfied than those who waited for marriage. [16]

From a standpoint of marital duration, marital peace, marital fidelity, physical safety, emotional well-being, and sexual satisfaction, cohabitation is not exactly a recipe for happiness. Even *USA Today* reported, "Could this be true love? Test it with courtship, not cohabitation." [17] Even if you do not think that your boyfriend would be abusive or that you would get depressed, the divorce rate speaks for itself.

Like all of us, you dream of a lasting love. If you are serious about making this relationship work, save your marriage before it starts and do not move in until after the wedding.

## 38

*Why are the divorce rates so high for couples who lived together before marriage?*

There are a number of reasons why cohabiting couples have higher rates of separation. For one, cohabiting couples are usually sexually active, and according to the journal *Adolescent & Family Health*, "those who have premarital sex are more likely to have extramarital sex (affairs)—and extramarital sex contributes to many divorces." [18] However, since I would imagine that most cohabiting couples remain faithful in marriage, the infidelity link can account for only some of the increased divorce rate.

Even when the couple remain faithful, cohabiting undermines commitment, since it is assumed that if one person finds enough faults in the other, he is free to leave. However, successful marriages are not the result of a lack of annoying qualities in the other; they are the result of choosing to love and forgive the other daily, with all his or her imperfections. It is the ability to sacrifice that holds marriages together, not the absence of nuisances. Couples who refuse to cohabit before marriage and refuse to engage in premarital sex seem to have a better understanding of the notion of sacrifice than couples who give in.

The desire to "test drive" a marriage demonstrates a lack of understanding regarding what makes a marriage work. It also shows a real lack of faith in one's love for the other. In one sense the couple is saying that they desire intimacy, but on the other hand they want to leave a way out if the partner does not measure up. This sows seeds of doubt and distrust from the start. Some couples seem to be under the impression that a good relationship will not have disappointments. When they marry and the disappointments come, they often bail out.

G. K. Chesterton said, "If Americans can be divorced for 'incompatibility of temper,' I cannot conceive why they are not all divorced. I have known many happy marriages, but never a compatible one. The whole aim of marriage is to fight through and survive the instant when incompatibility becomes unquestionable. For a man and a woman, as such, are incompatible." [19]

If you want a marriage to last, take an honest look at what makes love work. According to Pope John Paul II,

> We love the person complete with all his or her virtues and faults, and up to a point, independently of those virtues and in spite of those faults. The strength of such a love emerges most clearly when the beloved person stumbles, when his or her weaknesses or even sins come into the open. One who truly loves does not then withdraw his love, but loves all the more, loves in full consciousness of the other's shortcomings and faults, and without in the least approving of them. [20]

This is why the slogan "Love is blind" is off the mark. Infatuation is blind, but love has both eyes wide open. That way we can see and know the other person fully, so that we can love him or her completely. Married couples often say that they really did not know their spouse fully until years into marriage, but dating couples who are infatuated feel they know everything about each other. It takes a lifetime to truly know the other, and cohabiting couples seem afraid of that task.

If things are running smoothly for a cohabiting couple, they may head toward marriage thinking, "Well, we haven't been fighting much lately, and after living together for this long, I sure don't want to start over with someone else. Why don't we just make it official?" These couples often find it difficult to explain exactly what marriage is. You go through a big ceremony, get a piece of paper and new Tupperware, and go back to what you were doing before. This undermines the meaning of marriage as a covenant that two people make with God. Since they think less of marriage, they are less likely to work tirelessly to preserve it. Even when cohabiting couples do not end up marrying, their breakup can be as wrenching as an actual divorce.

Some people assume that living together is not a problem as long as the couple is not sleeping together. But there is a problem: they are putting themselves in an occasion of sin. They are also causing scandal (giving bad example) to neighbors, who will reasonably assume they are sleeping together. By living together they are also saying that they lack confidence in their relationship.

Waking up in the same house on a daily basis with a person you love is a gift that should be reserved for marriage. Stealing all the privileges of marriage in advance reminds me of my childhood, when I would beg my parents for early Christmas gifts every day the week prior to Christmas. If they had allowed me to open all but one (which they did not), Christmas would not have seemed that big a deal. The same goes for marriage.

Lastly, consider the fact that Joseph and Mary did not need to cohabit to have an exemplary marriage. So why do we?

## 39

*Is it OK to have sex while you're engaged? After all, you're going to get married anyway.*

Engagement is a special time, and during this period couples may feel that they are "almost married," but in reality being married is like being pregnant—you either are or you are not. No matter how committed a couple may feel, until they actually pledge themselves to one another on their wedding day, they cannot pledge themselves to one another with their bodies in bed.

Some might feel that this idea is old-fashioned. It is definitely old, but it still works. Waiting to receive each other from the Lord allows the couple to establish authentic intimacy. By waiting on God and focusing on what he is calling them to, the couple receive the freedom to see that intimacy is not simply about how close your body is to someone else's. A healthy relationship does not require sex in order to be intimate. Love is patient, and a man and woman who are confident in their love know that they will have the rest of their lives to enjoy sex. But now is their *only* time to prepare for marriage—to lay the foundation for the rest of their lives together.

Waiting to share the gift of sex should be seen not as a passive delay of passion but as an active training in faithfulness. In the words of the *Catechism of the Catholic Church*,

> Those who are engaged to marry are called to live chastity in conti-
> nence [abstinence]. They should see in this time of testing a discov-
> ery of mutual respect, an apprenticeship in fidelity, and the hope of
> receiving one another from God. They should reserve for marriage
> the expressions of affection that belong to married love. They will
> help each other grow in chastity.[21]

Don't you want to know *before* the wedding if your spouse will be able to resist temptations *after* the wedding?

Since engagement is a time to prepare to become a sacrament, the months preceding a marriage are a time of serious discernment. By having sex during this time, couples hinder their ability to look at the relationship clearly. They feel so close as a result of sex that they are often unable to look at the past, present, or future critically. The sexual intimacy may even blind them from seeing that their relationship lacks real intimacy, and it may prevent them from bringing to the surface worries or hesitations they may have. In fact, sex may cover up defects of love.

When a woman says yes to her boyfriend's proposal, this is not the end of their discernment process for marriage. Until they pronounce their vows, no permanent commitment has been made. Imagine if you were engaged, but you knew in your heart that you needed to call off the wedding. Consider how much more difficult it would be to break an engagement if you were already sleeping with your fiancé.

Some people ask, "Well, how do you know if you want to marry a person if you don't sleep with her?" I would reply, "How do you know you should marry her once you have slept together?" If anything you are less clear-minded, because *sex is not designed to be a test to find a good spouse.*

Just because a person is capable of physical intimacy does not mean that he or she is capable of the other kinds of intimacy that hold a marriage together. Because sex has the power to bond, the experience may seem wonderful in the initial stages of a relationship, and both partners will feel quite "compatible." But think about a couple you know who have been married for fifty years. They sit on their front porch swing, smiling with all their wrinkles at each other. They are still together because they have been refined by the fires of love, not burnt by the counterfeits of lust.

So why *not* wait for the honeymoon? I know of couples who were sexually active long before their wedding, and when they arrived at their honeymoon suite, they immediately fell asleep. They had been there and done that, so why not rest up for something new and exciting—like jet skiing? They only robbed themselves. On the other hand, one woman who saved that gift for the honeymoon said that it was *"unspeakably worth the wait."* [22] How often do you hear of promiscuous couples experiencing such joy?

If a man and woman refuse to wait, what are their motives? Does impatience, lust, or pride motivate the couple to disobey God? These vices only harm a marriage. It is through humility, obedience, chastity, patience, and a willingness to sacrifice that a couple build a lifelong love. So why not practice these virtues now?

In the meantime, know that each time you resist sin you bless one another. In addition, God has issued a special challenge to men. When a man perseveres in the virtue of chastity, he helps fulfill that challenge: to love his bride as Christ loves the Church, to give himself up for her, that he might sanctify her, that he might present his bride to God "without spot or wrinkle or any such thing, that she might be holy and without blemish" (Eph. 5:25–27). A man should consider his acceptance of this challenge to be the measure of his love for his bride. Imagine Christ hanging on the cross, saying to you, "This is how I got my bride to heaven. How else do you think you will get yours there?" When an engaged man embraces such a challenge and grows in purity with his fiancée, you will notice on his wedding day that his bride's soul matches her dress. She glows.

If we do not understand these principles, perhaps we do not

understand marriage. Is it merely a public declaration of the love that a bride and groom feel? Is the wedding a decorative formality, or is God present there, establishing a supernatural bond—a covenant with the couple that can only be severed by death?

At every sacramental marriage a spiritual reality *will* take place on that altar when a man and woman become a husband and wife. The couple enter into a union that is a sacrament. That night, the marital embrace will become the visible expression of this union blessed by God. Until the marriage vows have been said, a woman is not a wife and should not be treated as one.

When a husband gives his body to his bride and a bride gives herself to him, their bodies speak the truth: "I am entirely yours." On the other hand, sex anywhere but in marriage is dishonest. No matter what, it cannot say, "I am entirely yours." Therefore, having sex during the engagement is not a matter of "peeking under the wrapping paper." It is a matter of completely missing the point of sex and marriage.

If you are engaged, ponder for a moment the gift of your partner. Look how generous God has been with you. When you come to the altar, do you not want to give God a gift in return? Do not come empty-handed. Make the sacrifice to keep your engagement pure, so that you come to the altar with this gift for him.

### 40

*If an unmarried couple get pregnant, should they get married?*

There is no simple answer to this, since each situation and relationship is different. What I would recommend in most cases is that the couple wait at least until the child is born to make a decision. There is so much to consider in those nine months that the couple will not be in the best frame of mind to discern marriage.

There are at least four options open to the couple: to place the child for adoption and have the couple go their separate ways; to place the baby for adoption but stay open to marriage; to get married and raise the child together; or to keep the baby and not get married. All four options will be difficult, so it is important that the couple seek the best advice they can find. By talking to parents, priests, and counselors at crisis pregnancy centers, the couple will be able to make the best decision for the child and for themselves. If you know someone who is pregnant and needs help, call (800) 866-4666 to find a local crisis pregnancy center for them.

## 41

*I am in college and met a great young woman, but she has already been married and divorced. Is it wrong to date her?*

There are a couple of things to consider here. If she was married and her spouse is still alive and their marriage has not been annulled, then for practical purposes she is not available for you to date. You must consider her a married woman, regardless of whether the state recognizes her as legally married or whether she no longer lives with her husband. When a person is married, he or she is married until death. Only if the Church determines that the presumed marriage was never valid can the person be considered available while the former partner still lives.

This is why Jesus said, "Whoever divorces his wife and marries another, commits adultery against her" (Mark 10:11). This includes doing anything with a divorced person that you would not do with a married person. This is a difficult saying, but it came from the mouth of the Lord.

## 42

*Isn't an annulment the same as a divorce?*

No. A divorce is a legal decree that a valid, legal marriage has been *done away with*. In the eyes of the state, a marriage can be real and still be dissolved. The Church, however, recognizes that before God a valid marriage between two baptized people can *never* be dissolved, that spouses are bound to one another as long as they live. An annulment, therefore, is not a decree that this bond has been dissolved but that, on investigation, no marriage bond ever existed.

When two people seek to be united in Christian marriage, certain realities must be present in order for that union to take effect. For example, if one partner is being forced into the marriage, or if one does not intend to be faithful or to be open to children, he or she is not entering what God considers a marriage. Therefore the marriage is not valid, no matter what the state may think about it. (There are other conditions, but I mention these for starters.)

Imagine that a couple went through a wedding ceremony, but the bride was being forced to marry the groom. Even though it looked like a wedding, there was no valid marriage. Since there was never a marriage to begin with, they are not bound to each other. Their "marriage" could be declared null—found by the Church to have no existence in the eyes of God. Since God has not joined them together, they are free to marry other people. Even Jesus spoke of this in the Gospel of Matthew, when He forbade divorce and remarriage, "unless the [first] marriage is unlawful"—that is, null (Matt. 19:9, *NAB*).

So an annulment does not end a real marriage but declares that there never was a sacramental marriage to begin with. The Church goes through a long investigation to determine if the marriage was validly contracted. If it was, then even if the marriage turned sour years later, the Church cannot dissolve that. (The couple may separate if necessary, such as in the case of abuse, and even may obtain a civil divorce, but neither is free to remarry.) When a valid marriage has taken place between two baptized persons, only death can sever that bond.

## 43

*Did Jesus say that everyone's marriage would be ended in heaven? I thought that what God has joined no one could separate.*

In Matthew 22:30 Jesus said that in heaven, people are neither married, nor are they given in marriage. In order to see God's ultimate plan for the sacrament of marriage, we need to understand what marriage is.

A sacrament is a sign Jesus established in order to give us grace. By spousal love the married couple make visible to the world the love that God has for all of us. God's plan for humanity is that mankind be united to Him in a way that is similar to the way husbands and wives are united to each other. Throughout the scriptures, it is clear that God wants to espouse us to Himself. In the Old Testament, Israel is even accused of adultery when the people turned away from God. In the New Testament, the Church is called the bride of Christ, and heaven is described as a wedding banquet. In marriage, couples are living images of this deeper spiritual reality. This is God's vision and purpose for every marriage.

But as great as weddings are, they are just shadows of the reality of the one eternal marriage. Earthly marriages were created for Earth, but as Saint Paul says, "When the perfect comes, the imperfect will pass away" (1 Cor. 13:10). When a married couple go to heaven, the sacramental marriage (like all other sacraments) will pass away and be fulfilled by the reality that it now points to or veils. So we *will* have marriage in heaven: the union of us all as the bride of Christ with the heavenly Bridegroom at the eternal wedding banquet. God makes His proposal to us in this life, and if we accept it, heaven is the consummation.

Marriage is intended both for the raising of children and to promote the good of the spouses, including their growth in holiness. Since everyone is perfected in holiness in heaven and everyone will already have been born, the purposes of marriage will have been completed. So where does this leave married couples when they get to heaven? Because sin will be gone and everyone will be filled with God's love, those who were husband and wife in this life will be able to love one another with an intensity never known to them while on earth. They will live like the angels, in continual worship of God. They are the bride of Christ, and even if their earthly marriage was not made in heaven, it will be fulfilled there.

# 4

# How Far Is Too Far?

## 44

### *Is it wrong to flirt with guys?*

Flirting means different things for different age groups. When I was in second grade, if I liked a girl, I would throw a rock at her. (Fortunately for women, I have made some progress in this area.) When we matured to the fourth grade, things got more sophisticated: a girl would ask her friend to pass a note to a boy, inviting him to check the appropriate box if he was interested in her. By sixth grade the tactics were more refined, and a girl might have her friend "accidentally" shove her into a cute boy as they walked out of class. This is all amusing, but by junior high the girls leave the notes behind as they start to realize what interests guys. This is when flirting can become a problem.

The basic definition of *flirt* is to tease or toy with another; to pay romantic attention to someone without serious intentions. To the degree that one is being impure or dishonest, flirting is wrong. There is nothing intrinsically wrong with letting another person know you are attracted to him. The problem comes when you lead him on for the sake of amusement or to boost your self-esteem, usually while causing him to have impure thoughts or desires.

If you are attracted to another, be pure and honest in your dealings with him, and the Lord will bless your friendship. There is nothing wrong with being playful with the person and going out of your way to meet him. Just make sure integrity motivates your tactics. If you are an affectionate girl, be careful about how you express this. A guy might perceive your affection as a hint that you want him to do more with you. This is because affection usually does not come naturally for guys. It is out of the ordinary, and so the guy may associate it with something sexual.

The best approach is to make your intentions for purity clear, and make sure that your words, your actions, and your outfits convey the same message. Also consider this: Lots of guys will date a flirt, but who wants to marry one? If a girl is flirty toward me, what reason do I have to think that she is not flirting with other guys? A girl is much more attractive if she does not flutter around trying to get attention.

One reason a girl may be a flirt is because she wants to be loved. The attention might soothe a wounded self-esteem, but in the end it is like trying to survive on a diet of cotton candy: it tastes sweet but leaves her malnourished. Before a woman can love a man fully, she must realize that only God can completely satisfy her deepest desires for love. Until then she'll be looking to guys to fulfill her, instead of looking to God to help her to love them. When a young woman sits still long enough to hear God and when she sees with her heart how he looks at her with love, she recognizes the lewd comments and looks from various guys as nothing more than counterfeit love.

As Mother Teresa often said, "Stay close to Jesus. He loves you." By the side of Christ a woman finds her independence. When she stands beside Christ, and He reveals her worth to her, she no longer depends on the approval of random guys to build her self-worth.

## 45

*Is French kissing wrong? Everyone I talk to gives me a different answer.*

When it comes to sins of impurity, many people think, "If it's a mortal sin, then I don't want to do it. But if it's a venial sin, then I don't want to miss it!" We need to drop this minimalist idea that focuses on how much we can get away with before we offend God. Even the smallest sin divides, while purity ignites true love. Elisabeth Elliot wrote in her book *Passion and Purity*, "How shall I speak of a few careless kisses to a generation nurtured on the assumption that nearly everybody goes to bed with everybody? Of those who flounder in the sea of permissiveness and self-indulgence, are there any who still search the sky for the beacon of purity? If I did not believe there were, I would not bother to write." [1]

I used to take for granted that everyone knew that French kissing is sexually arousing, especially for a guy. But I have met women who act surprised when they find out that a man is sexually aroused by passionate kissing (or before then). French kissing is deeply unitive, since the penetration of one person into another is part of becoming one with him or her physically. This passionate kissing tells a man's body that it should prepare for intercourse, and when a man is aroused, generally he is not satisfied until he is relieved.

Therefore, French kissing teases the body with desires that cannot be morally satisfied outside of marriage. For the couple that is saving sex for marriage, French kissing is like a fifteen-year-old sitting in a car in his driveway, revving up the engine while keeping the car in park because he knows he does not have the license to drive.

I believe that the moral problem with French kissing is harder for girls to accept, because they tend to be aroused sexually in a more gradual way than guys. If a woman's arousal could be compared to an iron heating up, a guy's could be compared to a light bulb. Sensual reactions in guys tend to be more immediate, and when the flame of sexual arousal is ignited, a man often wants to go further. He might be content for some time with just kissing. But when a couple have passionate make-out sessions and try to draw the line there, one of two things will eventually happen: either the original boundaries will disappear, or frustration will set in. In the one case sexual arousal does not seem so scandalous, and the couple begin to justify new forms of physical intimacy. Perhaps they will stop the first, second, or third time, but gradually the old boundaries will be pushed back because they begin to experience the intoxicating bonding power that God has in store for couples in marriage.

Otherwise, one of them may end up hearing the same thing this girl did: "My boyfriend and I don't go any further than making out, but recently he said to me after we were kissing, 'Don't you ever just get . . . bored?'"

I often receive e-mails from abstinent couples who say that they really love each other and want to stay pure, but they keep falling over and over into the same sexual sins. They have stirred up that desire, and they are finding that such desires are not easily tamed once they are awakened. These couples want to sit on the fence and keep some sexual intimacy while avoiding going "too far." But they're realizing that men and women are not made to work that way. Angelic purity is easier to live out than 50 percent purity, because you're not constantly teasing yourself.

Nevertheless, some say that French kissing is really no big deal and does not mean anything. But isn't there something in you that wants it to be a big deal? The more of ourselves we give away, the less we value the gift of our body and our entire self (and people will respond by treating us with less respect as well). Ask yourself what your kisses are worth. Are they a way to repay a guy for a nice evening? Are they a solution to boredom on a date? Are they a way to cover up hurts or loneliness? Even worse, are they merely for "harmless" fun? If the answer to any of these questions is yes, then we have forgotten the purpose of a kiss and the meaning of intimacy. So do not segregate parts of your sexuality as "no big deal." Your entire body is an infinitely big deal, and this includes your kisses. If we realize this, the simplest of kisses becomes priceless and brings more closeness and joy than 100 one-night stands.

What happens to the unsuspecting teen is that the initial intimacy and excitement of a kiss is worn thin when he or she begins to give it away as if it's a handshake. The profound meaning and depth of simple acts of affection are slowly lost. The world would like to tell us that we're acquiring better dating skills, but we're really just numbing ourselves.

So before you go there again, consider saving the passion for your bride or groom. Not only will your purity be a gift to your spouse, but it will make his or her affection seem more unique to you as well. In the long run this will bond the two of you much closer than all the "experience" the world recommends you have before marriage.

In high school, I didn't think twice about this kind of kissing. I figured that other people were doing worse things, so it wasn't that big a deal. Now I wish more than anything that I had reserved such kisses for my bride, instead of dispensing them to girls I never saw again after graduation. But at the time I didn't think about the future. I just looked at the classmates around me and figured that this was the way life was supposed to be.

When my relationships matured and deepened and I began taking them to prayer, I gave up this kind of kissing because it would always ignite the desire to go further. It was also pushing other aspects of the relationship to the side. I knew in my heart that I could not say with confidence that this kind of intimacy was pleasing to God.

So I had a talk with a girlfriend at the outset of a relationship, and we agreed to sacrifice that. This was a huge blessing, and I was immediately able to see that the relationship was more holy and joyful. We were not perfect, but I saw for the first time that the more passionate kissing there was in my relationships, the less there was of everything else. This was not something I could understand until I gave it up.

I encourage you to give it a shot. Give up French kissing until you are married. Keep the affection simple. If you have a difficult time accepting this, then have the honesty to ask yourself why. If you could not French kiss your boyfriend, would that hinder your ability to love him? Would not being able to French kiss your girlfriend hinder your ability to glorify God or to lead her to heaven? How much are our intentions directed toward our gratification, and how much to God's glorification?

Simply put, sexual morality is about glorifying God with your body. The way you use your sexuality should reflect your love for God and should express the love of God to others. If an area seems gray, then do not go there. Do only those things that you confidently know glorify God.

If you struggle with this issue, take it to prayer. If you truly wish to know the will of God as it relates to purity, I know He will show you. You just have to sit still long enough to listen. Sure, this is difficult, but love is willing to sacrifice big things as well as small ones for the good of the beloved.

More and more often I hear of couples who save their first kiss for the wedding day. At first this sounded crazy to me, but then I noticed that they were not giving up kissing on the lips because it was evil or because they could not control themselves but because they cherished a simple kiss so much that they wanted God and the world to witness their first one. Their first kiss could be offered as a prayer.

With all this having been said, we should not be stuck on how close we can get to sin. When our hearts are right with God, we are concerned with what is truly pure and how we can glorify God with our bodies. We want every act of affection to be a reflection of the fact that He is first in our lives. Until that is the case, then we'll have a terribly hard time discerning love from lust.

## 46

*Is oral sex OK, so that you do not go all the way?*

If you are being called to marriage, then right now your future spouse is somewhere out there. Do you ever wonder what she or he is doing right now? Maybe he is running drills during basketball practice, or maybe she is laughing with friends at a coffee shop as they cram for a test. Suppose that he or she is elsewhere, namely at the house of a person who finds him or her attractive. The parents are not home, and as you read this, that person is trying to talk your future spouse into having oral sex.

If you could speak to the heart of your future spouse right now, would you say, "Oh, go ahead—just make sure you don't go all the way, honey!" Probably not. You would also have some words for the other person, such as, "That's my bride!" or "That's the man who will one day kiss my children good night." You would feel offended by what that person is trying to get from your future husband or wife.

One reason why oral sex is gaining popularity is because people think that it is a safe alternative to sex. Although you will not get pregnant from it, it is anything but safe. I once asked a microbiologist which STDs you could *not* get by means of oral sex. She stood there thinking for a while and said, "I can't think of *any* that you can't get from oral sex (including HIV)." Sure enough, doctors today are seeing dramatic increases in cases of oral gonorrhea and herpes.[2] According to the *International Journal of Cancer*, cases of oral HPV (human papilloma virus) are reaching "epidemic" levels,[3] and now HPV is the leading cause of throat cancer.[4] Other forms of head and neck cancer can also be caused by orally transmitted HPV.[5] Oral sex is anything but safe.

Some people resort to oral sex so that they do not lose their virginity. Although you do not *technically* lose your virginity by having oral sex, it still robs you of innocence and puts you in situations where you could easily lose your virginity. It does not relieve sexual tension in a man but creates it and reinforces in him the myth that he has sexual "needs" that must be met, even at the expense of a woman's dignity and innocence. The bottom line is that you don't need oral sex to keep from going all the way. You need grace, courage, and self-respect.

We need to take an honest look at our motives. Why would we do this anyway? Why would a person become upset if he or she were not allowed to have oral sex? Recently I was invited to speak to a high school morality class. When I arrived the teacher said to me in front of the class, "We've been having a big debate about oral sex. They do not see anything wrong with it. What would you say?" Everyone in the class looked at me and awaited my response. I said what came to mind: "If a guy needs to place his genitals into the mouth of his girlfriend in order to show her what she means to him, then it shows exactly what she means to him."

## 47

*Is foreplay with your boyfriend wrong, even if you really love him and just want to get as close as possible? I see myself marrying him someday.*

Although I was not alive in the 1960s, I understand that at the time there was a big "free love" movement. Apparently it had one fatal flaw: the promoters of this sexual revolution had no idea what constituted freedom or love. The people assumed that if there were mutual feelings between two people, they should be free to have sex. I agree that we should be free to do whatever love calls us to do, but we need to make sure that it is love that is calling us. It is easy to be moved by infatuation, loneliness, or lust and to mistake any of these for love because the feelings are so strong. Many people assume that if a couple has a strong desire to be sexually intimate, then that is a sign of love indicating they should do whatever they wish, provided they both feel comfortable with it.

So if you deeply love a person, are committed to him, and see yourself marrying him, why can't you express that in whatever way you want? After all, when you love someone, you desire union with him. I would say that as long as a couple only *see* themselves being together for life and can only *talk* about marriage, then they should only *see* themselves having marital relations in the future, within marriage. Until the reality of marriage is there, the expression of marital oneness is dishonest. Even if I reserve sexual arousal for a person I hope to marry, this does not make my actions moral.

You mentioned that you wanted to get as close as possible to your boyfriend. Many young women suspect that physical intimacy will draw a guy closer to them, but this tactic often backfires. One girl said that, in her quest for pleasure, she was "painfully disappointed when I found only guilt instead of freedom, pain instead of love, and suffering instead of pleasure. Instead of drawing my boyfriend and me closer together, a sexual relationship only drove us further and further apart." [6]

Perhaps the easiest way to find out if our actions conform to authentic love is to imagine God sitting on a nearby sofa watching us. If His presence would cause immediate shame or the desire to stop dead in our tracks, we need to ask ourselves why. If God is love, and we "really love" the other person, shouldn't we be thrilled to have Love Himself witness everything we do together?

That awkwardness in our hearts is there because deep inside we know that our actions are not loving. There are two essential elements of love. The first is the desire for union. (I would say you have got that.) The second and more important element of love is to desire what is best for the other, to desire God and heaven for him. It elevates the desire for union so that the two want to be together not for just a night but for eternity. Both elements must be present for love to exist. If I crave unity with a woman, but I do not desire her salvation, call it whatever you want, it is not love. After all, the purpose of foreplay is to prepare for sex. Since you're not married and therefore not ready for sex, foreplay will only bring about greater temptations, not greater love.

If you are unsure whether a particular action could be sinful, then love demands that you refuse to go there. Suppose I put a teaspoon of powder into a cup of tea for my wife. I look at the bowl where I got the powder. It reads "sugar" on one side and "rat poison" on the other. Do I say, "Oh, it's probably not poison. I'll give it to her anyway"? If I loved her, then I would never do something that was possibly lethal for her. Similarly, even if I were not convinced that a particular action with her would be sinful, I would still avoid it if there were good reason to believe that it might be harmful to her soul. Since her soul is more important than her body, I should have all the more concern to protect her salvation.

Also, consider the heart of this guy's future wife, in case you do not end up marrying him. I think that most sincere people who become physically intimate before marriage can see themselves marrying their partner. But most do not end up marrying each other. I have been in a few long relationships, and in each one marriage was a real possibility. In one case we were even trying on rings. The Lord had different plans for us. Not long ago I went to her wedding, and she married a friend of mine! Watching them exchange vows and kiss at the altar made me take a deep look at the relationships I have had in my life. Take the same look, and honestly ask yourself if your actions are in any way defrauding the future bride of the guy you are dating.

## 48

*Is it OK to hook up with a girl even if we aren't dating?*

The term "hooking up" can mean a lot of things, but it always means some kind of casual sexual contact, up to and including intercourse itself. Regardless of what you mean by it, you should not be having sexual contact with anyone who is not your wife. Even if you both like it, it shows mutual disrespect because you are exchanging a sign of commitment, love, and unity that does not exist.

Speaking of such relationships, Pope John Paul II said, "Deep within yourself, listen to your conscience which calls you to be pure. . . . A home is not warmed by the fire of pleasure which burns quickly like a pile of withered grass. Passing encounters are only a caricature of love; they injure hearts and mock God's plan."[7]

In the long run, no one benefits from these kinds of relationships. I read of one young husband who said, "I would do anything, *anything*, to forget the sexual experiences I had before I met my wife. . . . The pictures of the past and the other women go through my head, and it's killing any intimacy. The truth is, I have been married to this wonderful woman for eight years and I have never been 'alone' in the bedroom with her."[8]

When you "hook up" for fun, physical intimacy begins to lose its depth, greatness, sacredness, and power to bond two people.

Sex is shared as easily as a handshake, and the couple lose all reverence for the sacredness of each other's body. You begin thinking that physical pleasure is basically for fun and can solve the problem of boredom or loneliness. This leads to the idea that as long as two people agree to do something, then it is OK to do it. Often this is nothing more than two people agreeing to use each other for mutual gratification. They receive the physical pleasure of being held and the emotional pleasure of being desired, and they remain together so long as they are a source of pleasure for each other. This is not far from prostitution.

You both desire and deserve love. But as long as you are treating one another as objects, you will never be satisfied because neither of you is giving or receiving real love. Have the courage to admit your mistakes with women, and do not fall back into the habit of using them or allowing yourself to be used. If you cannot lead a woman to holiness when you are not that interested in her, how will you lead a woman to God when you are head over heels in love with her? If you can be trusted with the smaller things, you will be responsible with the larger ones.

When you do meet someone you are seriously interested in, take it slow. Intense physical intimacy at the beginning of a relationship is a cover-up for the absence of love that failed to develop. The real love that you long for takes patience and purity. In fact, purity is the guardian of love.

## 49

*How come everyone blames the guys? Girls today are just as sexually aggressive.*

Men often receive the blame because we bear a particular responsibility for the wounds inflicted on women. Like it or not, there is no way around this. The world has a double standard. A guy is considered a "player" when he is sexually active, but a woman who lives the same lifestyle is called a "slut."

Nevertheless, the pressure goes both ways. There is no doubt that there are many young women who are more sexually aggressive than their dates. But take a look at the reasons why. When a guy is sexually aggressive, it is usually because he wants to satisfy his sexual desires. With young women there is often a different motive. Look into the heart of a young girl who is forward and physical. Odds are that she has been used before, and now she shuts off her emotions from her physical actions. In the words of *Complete Woman* magazine, one of the positive aspects of first date sex is that it "makes you briefly forget your huge self-esteem problems." [9] What they failed to mention was that first-date sex *causes* huge self-esteem problems.

Many men have no qualms about having a one-night stand because they are more able to perform the sexual act as if it were merely a physical event. Women's hearts and bodies tend to be more integrated. One girl said:

> Most of all, at the gut level, there was a desire for intimacy, a desire for marriage, a desire for commitment, a desire for fulfillment and a desire to hear the words "I accept you." . . . As an attempt to find fulfillment and acceptance, "rolling in and out of bed" became a common pattern for me, a balm to cover my fears. Fulfillment took the scope of a few hours instead of what I had imagined— a lifetime. The fears produced the truth: I had become bored *and* boring; I didn't find any lasting acceptance of me; I didn't find my ideal mate. [10]

When you find a woman who is having one-night stands, you will notice that it is often a kind of protection for her heart. She has been hurt before. She may have no boundaries when it comes to her body, but there is a mile-high wall around her heart. She stoops to the level of a temporary physical relationship to prove that she can be as carefree about sex as some men are. It keeps her from having to be vulnerable, and it gives her a false sense of being in control of her life. She is losing the ability to bond, but it is all an effort to numb the interior wounds and find something that feels like love in order to smother the emptiness.

This is known to some people as "liberation." One man noted, "Most young women strike me as sad, lonely, and confused; hoping for something more, they are not enjoying their hard-won sexual liberation as much as liberation theory says they should." [11]

When a young woman encounters the inevitable hurt that accompanies the misuse of sex, she may shut men out of her life or immerse herself in physical relationships in order to forget the wounds of her heart. Imagine that a woman spilled ink on a white carpet. The stain runs deep, so instead of taking the time and effort to scrub it out, she dyes the whole carpet the same color as the ink. This makes the original stain much less noticeable.

That is what is going on in many hearts. A woman who has been broken from sexual encounters tends to minimize the hurt. One way to do this is to jump into numerous affairs as if they were no big deal. By doing this she hopes to convince herself that there is no need for healing. One high school girl told me why she had done all sorts of things with guys: "I was only doing it because I had this total and complete lack of love in my life."

Some young women may lower their standards so that they will feel desirable and worth something. Women know that guys like sex. So sex becomes bait to win the attention of a man. Other young women may have been reserved about sexual matters, but because of a mistake or a wound from the past, they figure they no longer deserve a good guy. A girl like this may even assume that a man does not like her unless he makes sexual advances toward her. As you see in all these cases, the physical tends to be an avenue for the fulfillment, burial, or protection of the emotional.

I go into all of this psychology because the solution to the double standard you mentioned is not to place more blame on women. Rather, if a man understands the source of a woman's sexual aggressiveness, he'll be more concerned with reminding her of her dignity than with exposing her shame.

## 50

*Exactly how far is too far to go with a girl? Be specific.*

I will give some specifics, but before I do, we should lay down a foundation. If we are asking how close to sin we can get girls, we are asking the wrong question. We need a change of heart. We need to start asking, "How close to God can I get her? How far

can I go to lead this girl to holiness and guard her innocence?"
Until we have this transformation of our heart and will, it will
be difficult to determine where to set the physical boundaries in
a relationship. Also, whenever we operate with the "how far is
too far" mentality, where do we usually end up? More often than
not, we end up going right up to that boundary and inching it
forward each time we visit it.

We need to remind ourselves that purity is not simply a matter
of staying on one side of a line we have drawn. It is a battle for
our hearts and minds as well as our bodies. Just because a guy has
not crossed a line does not mean that he is pure. It may mean that
he has never had the opportunity to cross it.

Anyway, here are a few guidelines for how you can know how
far is too far. Whenever you are considering doing something
with a girl, ask yourself if you would do that if her parents were
in the room. Or imagine the expression on her dad's face if he
were to walk in on you. In our hearts we all know what is pure
and pleasing to God. Let this sink in. Often we get so involved
in intense relationships that it is hard to sit back and look into
our hearts. One young man said, "I heard somebody say that you
can judge your own character by the things you do in private. I'd
take that a step further and say you can judge your own character
by the things you do with your girlfriend." [12]

Some people assume, "As long as I'm being a virgin, I'm being
good." They compare themselves with others who are sleeping
around, and as long as they see the world from that perspective,
they feel that they are right on track. Meanwhile, they give away
bits of themselves in passing relationships, all under the pretense
that their classmates are worse.

Do yourself a favor: do not get technical about drawing a line
at virginity and saying that all else goes. If you cannot decide if a
particular action is "too far," imagine your future bride or groom
sharing that act with another person. If the thought of this makes
you hesitate, listen to your conscience. Make decisions now that
would bless the heart of your future spouse, not wound it. (And
do not be quick to discuss the specifics of your prior experience

with potential spouses; a lot of that information could do far more harm than good.)

So where does the line go? For starters, know that the line begins in your mind. As soon as you begin to lust after a girl, stop. In regard to physical lines, an easy guideline to remember is, "Don't touch what you don't got." Also, I recommend no passionate kissing, kissing below the chin, or lying down together. That may seem extreme to some, but the more you become sensual and physical in a relationship, the more the relationship begins to revolve around that.

I will admit that this sounds a lot like no, no, no, and no, but think of it like this. There is a highway in California that runs up the coast. It is a gorgeous ride that takes you along the side of a sheer cliff that drops hundreds of feet to the ocean. Imagine that you were cruising along in your priceless sports car, and the passenger with you remarked, "Man, there is another one of those stupid guardrails. And look, another sign saying there is a sharp turn ahead. I hate how the California highway system inhibits your freedom and tells you what to do." Odds are, you would not let the guy drive your car.

When we hear different moral laws about our sexuality, they are there for the same reason that guardrails and signposts mark a person's drive along the Pacific Coast Highway. If you want to express your freedom as you drive off the cliff, you are free to do so. But the purity of your soul is worth much more than a car. The Church's moral laws are there for our sake, so that we do not fall for counterfeit versions of love.

If you have tried everything else for years, try purity. You will not regret it. Each year I speak to over one hundred thousand teens about dating, sex, and relationships, and I have never met one who regretted what he or she did *not* do with a date. I have never had a high school girl come up to me in tears after a chastity talk because she did *not* sleep with her boyfriend. I have never had a guy confide in me that he was scared to death that his girlfriend was *not* pregnant. They regret what they have done, not what they have saved.

Imagine you were dating a beautiful young woman you hoped to marry, and she had never kissed anyone because she wanted only her husband to know the touch of her lips. What man would not be flattered by her integrity and purity? What man would send her away to go a little further with the other guys? If we would be so honored by her, why would we not want to make a woman feel honored in the same way?

## 51

*If a song has a few sexual lyrics about women, does that make it wrong to listen to?*

Imagine settling down with a beautiful wife one day and having a baby daughter. She looks just like your wife, and you are in love all over again. Now imagine the lyrics of the song you mentioned being sung about your little princess. Would you sing along? Would you download a copy of the song or blare it from the speakers in your car stereo? Odds are, you would shatter the CD. If that is the case, why do we celebrate music that degrades the daughters of our heavenly Father?

Our answer? "Well, it sounds cool."

I will grant that it is difficult to let go of music we like. Getting rid of CDs you enjoy may feel like an amputation. It is painful. At the beginning of my conversion, I had tons of music that I would not sing in church. But I did not want to let go of it. It was "my" music, and I liked it. I figured, "I'm not a bad person because of it. I'm not going to go have a one-night stand after listening to it. I just like the music." So I clung to it. But God has a funny way of asking for things that we do not want to give up.

I did not want to be fanatical about it, so I started by getting rid of my worst CD. There comes a feeling of peace when you know you are giving something up for the love of God. I eventually let go of one CD after another until my entire collection was purged. So give it a shot. Give Him your worst, and He will give you His best.

A friend of mine once said, "If it's not of God, then I don't want anything to do with it." Life for her was black and white, and all she cared about was glorifying God with the short amount of time He gave her on Earth. Saint John Vianney had the same outlook on life. In his words, "Here is a rule for everyday life: *Do not do anything which you cannot offer to God.*"[13] So if you know a song has parts that are displeasing to God and are likely to drag you down spiritually, listen to another song.

Better yet, take some time to listen to nothing. Because we live in such a technological age, it is difficult to discover the value of silence. For this reason Pope John Paul II recommended to young people that if they want to encounter Christ, "above all, create silence in your interior. Let that ardent desire to see God arise from the depth of your hearts, a desire that at times is suffocated by the noise of the world and the seduction of pleasures."[14] By creating more room for silence in your life, you'll find it easier to listen to God. And what He has to tell you is more valuable than anything.

## 52

*My girlfriend and I have decided not to have sex. Is it wrong to sleep in the same bed occasionally?*

It is understandable that a couple would want to lie down together. After all, who would not want to wake up next to their loved one? However, this kind of intimacy belongs only in marriage. To lie down with a woman in bed is marital. When we use the expression, "They slept together," we usually are not thinking about sleep at all. But this phrase is used because the marriage bed is reserved for the marital act.

In Hebrews 13:4 we are told to keep the marriage bed undefiled. It is to be sacred, and this means it is to be set apart for holy use. The holy use that God has in mind is marital union. In your heart you know that this belongs in marriage, because if you knew that sleeping in the same bed with her was pleasing to God, you would not have asked this question.

If you want to save sex for marriage, sleeping in the same bed is not the best way to guard that commitment. Granted, you may not be having sex, but as Proverbs 16:18 says, pride goes before a fall. There is wisdom in avoiding occasions of sin and not trusting ourselves too much.

Promise each other that the next time the two of you share a bed, it will be as husband and wife. There is a time and a season for everything under the sun, and as difficult as it may be, purity calls you to make this sacrifice. After all, if the Lord calls you to marry her, you will have the rest of your life to fall asleep looking at her.

# 5

# Pornography and Masturbation

## 53

*What is wrong with looking at pornography? It's not like you're getting a girl pregnant or spreading STDs.*

When Jesus warned that anyone who looks lustfully at a woman commits sin with her in his heart (Matt. 5:28), He spelled it out in no uncertain terms that it is not enough to avoid pregnancy or STDs. It is not even enough to avoid impure sexual contact; we must also resist impure sexual thoughts and looks.

The problem with using pornography is that it emasculates men, degrades women, destroys marriages, and offends the Lord. You may be thinking: "That's going a little overboard, don't you think? I mean, what's wrong with checking out a few Internet sites?" Take a look at the effects of pornography, and you will see why real men do not use it.

What does pornography do to a man? For starters, because it cripples his ability to love, it robs him of the capacity to be a man. The essence of manhood consists in readiness to deny oneself for the good of a beloved. This is why Saint Paul reminds husbands in his Letter to the Ephesians that their love must be like that of Christ, who allowed Himself to be crucified for the sake of His beloved, the Church (Eph. 5:21–33).

Pornography defeats this calling. Instead of denying himself for the good of the woman, a man, through the use of porn, denies the woman her dignity in order to satisfy his lust. In essence, pornography is a rejection of our calling to love as God loves. It is no wonder that those who use it are never satisfied. Only love satisfies. One marriage therapist noted, "People who use pornography feel dead inside, and they are trying to avoid being aware of that pain. There is a sense of liberation, which is temporary: that's why pornography is so repetitive—you have to go back again and again."[1] Her insights are well understood by those who have felt entrapped by the allure of lust. One recovering porn addict admitted that viewing pornography "brings intense disappointment, precisely because it is not what I'm really searching for. It's rather like a hungry person standing outside the window of a restaurant, thinking that they're going to get fed."[2]

In a way, the fact that pornography allows men to indulge their lust without having to worry about pregnancy or STDs is part of the problem. It encourages him to live in a world in which sexuality offers only pleasure without meaning or consequences, in which "no one gets pregnant, no one catches a disease, no one shows signs of guilt, fear, remorse, embarrassment, or distrust. No one suffers from the sexual activities of others and the men, at least, are always carefree, unrestrained. . . . The priority of lovingly protecting one's partner is of little concern in pornography because no harm seems possible."[3] Living in a world of fantasy allows a guy to escape from reality and evade the demands of authentic love. Therefore, it does not liberate him. It enslaves him.

Put simply, pornography is the renunciation of love. As the writer Christopher West said, "[Pornography] seeks to foster precisely those distortions of our sexual desires that we must struggle *against* in order to discover true love."[4] For the person who indulges in porn, the purpose of sex becomes the satisfaction of the erotic "needs," not the communication of life and love. Pornography trains a man to value a woman only for what she gives him rather than for the person she is. Because he is so focused on what he is getting, he doesn't learn to give.

Some guys will slough this all off, saying, "Boys will be boys," or "I'm just appreciating the beauty of womanhood," or, "I like the articles in the magazine." Sometimes they will realize how unconvincing these arguments are, and they will become resentful, saying, "You want to repress sexuality and rob women of their freedom. It's unhealthy for you to have such little appreciation for women!" This defensive attitude is apparent in the way strip clubs advertise themselves as "gentlemen's clubs" for "adult entertainment." Why would a man feel the need to justify his behavior as "gentlemanly" or "adult"? A man does not need to announce that he is a gentleman, nor do adults need to remind others that they are mature. Actions speak for themselves.

Yet even when a man's lack of self-control makes him immature and his behavior cannot be reconciled with the title "gentleman," he still feels a need to identify with authentic manhood. No matter how far we fall, Christ has still stamped into our being the call to love as he loves. If we untwist the lies and humbly come before the Lord in our woundedness, he will raise us up and make us true men.

What does pornography do to women? Since it trains men to think of women as objects to be used instead of persons to be loved, guys speak of them as objects and treat them as objects. One long-time producer in the porn industry admitted "My whole reason for being in this industry is to satisfy the desire of the men in the world who basically don't care much for women and want to see the men in my industry getting even with the women they couldn't have when they were growing up. I *strongly* believe this, and the Industry hates me for saying it."[5] He added that the porn industry is simply "a playpen for the damned."[6]

When men learn their concept of intimacy from videos and magazines, they may accept the idea that a woman's no is actually a yes and that she enjoys being used. This can lead to a rapist mentality. Consider, for example, a study done in the Oklahoma City area. When 150 sexually oriented businesses were closed, the rate of rape decreased 27 percent in five years, while the rate in the rest of the country increased 19 percent. In Phoenix, Arizona, neighborhoods with porn outlets had 500 percent more sex offenses than neighborhoods without them.[7]

Ted Bundy raped and killed dozens of women. Sentenced to die in the electric chair, he requested that his last interview be with Dr. James Dobson, the founder of Focus on the Family. In that meeting Bundy talked openly about pornography and told Dr. Dobson that his struggles all began there. He explained that all his fellow inmates had an obsession with pornography before going to prison. Porn magazines and videos lay at the root of innumerable rapes and murders. Countless victims of child molestation also report that their abusers exposed them to pornography in attempts to seduce them. No one can tell the husbands, siblings, children, and parents of those violated and deceased women that pornography is harmless. Besides, wouldn't it infuriate you if a guy simply looked at a woman you loved in the same way he looked at pornography?

What does pornography do to marriages? To be blunt, pornography is the perfect way to shoot your future marriage in the head. Imagine that a young man has a habit of using pornography, and he does not reveal this to his fiancée. He hopes that once he is married, the desires for illicit sexual arousal will subside. But what becomes of his lust once he marries? It does not disappear; it is foisted upon his wife. The pornography has trained him to react to the sexual value of a woman and nothing else. He has trained himself to believe that women should be physically flawless and constantly sexually accessible. Even if he rejects this intellectually, the fact remains that pornography has warped the way he looks at women. One psychologist who specializes in sexuality problems noticed, "the more time you spend in this fantasy world, the more difficult it becomes to make the transition to reality."[8]

Provided a man's wife is a life-size Barbie doll with a squad of makeup artists and hairdressers who follow her around the house, things might run smoothly for a time. But when reality confronts fantasy, the man will be left disillusioned, and the woman's self image will suffer. No real-life woman can ever fulfill his disordered desires and fantasies. They focus solely upon self-centered gratification rather than mutual self-giving and joy in pleasing one's spouse.

One woman explained that if a man's real-life partner is not always as available sexually and willing to do whatever he wishes as the women he has fantasized about, he may accuse her of being a prude. If she looks normal, and unlike the models he has come to adore, he may accuse her of being fat. If she has needs, unlike the passive images in the magazines, then she may seem too demanding for him.[9]

In other words, he will be quick to blame his disorder on her; his fantasies will have robbed him of the ability to be truly intimate with his wife. One reason he is unable to have healthy intimacy with his wife is because intimacy is not an escape from reality but the capacity to see the beauty of the other. The presence of lust in the heart of the man blocks his ability to view the woman as a person. He has reduced her to an object and ignored her value as a person. When this happens he forfeits love. True intimacy is impossible.

It has been said that the problem with pornography is not simply that it shows too much but that it shows too little. It reduces a woman to nothing more than her body. Thus a man will assume that the greater the body, the greater the value of the woman. With this mindset men not only expect their future wives to look no less perfect than Miss September; they also don't appreciate a woman's most beautiful and precious qualities, since a centerfold display can never reveal these. This drives men to look elsewhere in an impossible quest to satisfy their lust. After all, pornography fosters the false mentality that casual, uncommitted sex is the most fulfilling and enjoyable. Who does not want to be fulfilled?

One response to the marital dissatisfaction often caused by pornography habits is to bring pornography into the bedroom. This is a vain effort on the part of the man to have the illicit excitement he has formed an attachment to. The poor wife may allow this, but the joy of loving has escaped the man, who no longer sees the value of the person and the need to deny himself for her. Married couples who use pornography find that their marital problems only worsen. If a husband needs to pretend that his wife is someone else in order for him to be excited, then he will become less and less drawn to her. Instead of making love to her, he is destroying love between them. At the very moment he is supposed to be renewing his wedding vows with his body, he's committing adultery in his mind.

Because the effects of pornography are so severe, Christian men have an obligation to rid their lives of it. According to Pope John Paul II, God "assigns the dignity of every woman as a task to every man." [10] When we act in a way that is contrary to the dignity of women, we act contrary to our own dignity and vocation as men. For this reason, the Holy Father says, "each man must look within himself to see whether she who was entrusted to him as a sister in humanity, as a spouse, has not become in his heart an object of adultery." [11]

Even if pornography had no adverse effects on people, we must never forget that sin is not simply a social matter. We owe it to our neighbors to love them, but we also owe it to God to honor Him in all our actions and thoughts. To lust after His daughters is a grave sin, even if no one becomes pregnant as a result of another's imagination. "So shun youthful passions and aim at righteousness, faith, love, and peace, along with those who call upon the Lord from a pure heart" (2 Tim. 2:22).

## 54

*I have been looking at porn on the Internet for years, and I am finding it practically impossible to overcome the habit. How do I finally rid myself of the stuff?*

Be assured that where sin abounds, grace abounds all the more (Rom. 5:20). I recommend four steps that will help you resist the temptation in the future.

First, you must become a man of prayer. Prayer is essential for those who want to persevere in purity (this applies to women as well). In particular, go to Mass often, receive the sacrament of reconciliation whenever you fall, and develop a strong devotion to the rosary and to Saint Joseph. This is pretty much a one-two-three punch for fighting temptation.

Second, do whatever you can to rid yourself of occasions of sin. If you have pornographic magazines or videos, throw them all away immediately. Since the Internet has been a problem, at the very least you should install filtering software on your computer.

You might even want to consider whether there is any way you can take a break from using the Web entirely, or go a while with minimal Web access (perhaps with the images turned off in your browser or with a text-only browser, like Lynx, that does not use images). Another useful strategy is to put holy objects and pictures wherever you had the images. If it is on the Internet, put a crucifix or picture of Our Lady on top of the computer, and have a sacred image for your screen saver or computer wallpaper. You could also make the sign of the cross, or bless yourself with holy water when you feel tempted. Saint Teresa of Avila said, "I know by frequent experience that there is nothing which puts the devils to flight like holy water." [12]

Third, find a person with whom you can be honest about your habit, and be accountable to him. A priest, family member, youth minister, or good friend should be able to help you win the battle. With their help, take advantage of the accountability software at covenanteyes.com. As the Bible says, "Two are better than one. . . . If they fall, one will lift up his fellow; but woe to him who is alone when he falls and has not another to lift him up. . . . And though a man might prevail against one who is alone, two will withstand him. A threefold cord is not quickly broken" (Eccles. 4:9–12). It is also helpful to have this person in your life as an example of how to treat women. Pope John Paul II said, "Men must be taught to love, and to love in a noble way; they must be educated in depth in this truth, that is, in the fact that a woman is a person and not simply an object." [13]

Fourth, take a look at your motivation to overcome the habit. Are you simply trying to conquer the temptations because the habit is embarrassing or because you are afraid you will be caught? Elevate your motivation so that you are working to overcome the problem for the sake of love. Do it for the love of God and to make yourself worthy of your future bride.

When a person looks at pornography, on some level he is looking for love. It is a warped attempt to give of yourself and receive another. The fantasy woman may seem as if she is entirely yours, although a million other men feel the same way toward her. If a young man longs for love, then he must strive to acquire the self-lessness that will enable him to properly love a woman. Getting rid of porn should not be seen as a loss but as an opportunity to grow in that selflessness.

Imagine that you found the woman of your dreams and got married. As you carry her across the threshold of your honeymoon suite, she wraps her arms around your neck, looks into your eyes, and whispers how excited she is. She tells you that she has waited all her life for this day, and to make it extra special, she has been looking at thousands of pornographic images of men on the Internet. You would probably drop her on the floor. You see, not only should we wait for our spouses with our bodies; we must wait for them with our minds. So for the sake of love, trash the pornographic magazines, Web sites, and videos. If you are called to the sacrament of marriage, isn't your bride worth waiting to see, instead of filling your mind with images of other women's bodies?

If you persevere in the battle for purity, you can and will lose the desire to look at pornography. You will not lose sexual desire, but when you see women degraded, you will be filled with pity for them instead of lust. In the words of C. S. Lewis, "Lust is a weak, poor, whimpering whispering thing when compared with that richness and energy of desire which will arise when lust has been killed." [14] When you empty yourself for the good of a beloved, you will see that the passing satisfaction of porn is an illusion.

### 55

*I threw away all my pornography a long time ago, but how do I clear my head of all the images stamped into it? I go to confession and Mass, and I pray regularly, but I feel like the images are branded in there.*

As you've discovered, the "just don't think about it" approach doesn't work. When you look at pornography, your brain releases epinephrine, which burns the pictures into your memory. As a result, there's no easy way to make the memories instantly disappear. But they can be healed.

As strange as it sounds, *the antidote to pornography is to love the women in pornography.* When a man understands the dignity of womanhood and the truth about his call to love, he is able to transform temptations into opportunities for grace and virtue. So every time one of those impure images pops into your mind, take that as an occasion to pray for that woman's conversion. Pray specifically for her, and lift her to Jesus. This makes up for the times you have lusted after her but will accomplish even more. If you persevere in this practice, I would imagine that the thoughts subside considerably. Stay strong, because resisting these temptations will foster in you the virtues that make for great dads and husbands.

Other than this, continue with your prayer life and remain pure in your day-to-day relationships. And finally, deepen your devotion to Mary. We need to have our image of womanhood redeemed, and praying a daily rosary is an ideal way to begin this reconstruction.

## 56

*What is wrong with masturbation? I think of it as getting rid of your temptations without leading anyone into sin.*

Masturbation does not "get rid of" temptations any more than prostitution does. Both may temporarily relieve sexual desires, but our goal as Christians is not simply to get rid of temptations but to glorify God with our bodies. The idea that masturbation can be used to decrease sexual desires is like saying that lighter fluid can be used to extinguish a fire. If anything, masturbation incites lustful thoughts and teaches a person that he or she deserves—and needs—sexual gratification whenever the desire arises.

To understand why masturbation is wrong, we need to step back from the world's constant clamoring for the fulfillment of sexual "needs" and go back to God's plan for sex. Sexuality is meant to be a gift between a husband and wife for the purpose of babies and bonding. When it is taken out of that context, the gift is degraded and, in the case of masturbation, altogether ceases being a gift. The purpose of sexuality is abandoned, because the center of the sexual act becomes "me" instead of "we," and the person is trained to look to himself for sexual fulfillment. The gift of sexuality is misused for the sake of lifeless pleasure.

When people misuse their sexuality in this way, they may begin to use pleasure to change their mood, release tension, or forget their loneliness. Masturbation becomes an escape. It may pacify them, but it will never satisfy them, because they will always want more. They use the fantasies of their mind and the pleasures of their body to flee from reality and the call to love. Their goal in sexual activity has been reduced to merely receiving pleasure instead of showing love. If men and women have trained themselves to use their sexuality in this way, why would this suddenly change once they are married? The husband or wife will simply use the spouse as a substitute for the fantasies. The problem is that the lust will be transferred to the other, not healed within.

Furthermore, if the person has formed a habit of using lust as a means of dealing with stress, he or she may continue to turn to various forms of lust (porn, masturbation, infidelity, and so on) as a remedy to the stresses within marriage. Instead of seeking consolation in a healthy manner, the person learns to find solace in pleasure.

Getting married will not cure one's problem with masturbation. Because masturbation has trained disordered impulses in the person, the true pleasures of marriage—though far superior—may not appease his or her warped attachments. Where will one turn to find those pleasures within marriage? Often he or she will continue to struggle with masturbation, to the sorrow and distress of the spouse and to the detriment of the marriage.

A person who does not preserve his own purity when alone will have a difficult time remaining pure with another. If he lacks self-control when alone, he will be unable to properly give himself to his spouse when the time comes. You cannot give what you do not possess. So if you do not have self-control, you cannot truly give yourself to another. To the extent that there is no gift of self, there is no love. Therefore, if you want to be able genuinely to love your spouse, you must build self-mastery.

57

*Someone at school said that it was unhealthy not to masturbate, and in the long run it could be harmful to your body if you don't. Is that true?*

This is a myth. When a man's body needs to release seminal fluid, this will come in a natural manner during nocturnal emissions (wet dreams). There is not a constant buildup of pressure that will harm an individual unless he masturbates. The next time you hear a claim like this, ask the person to show you the scientific evidence to support what he or she is saying.

If anything, the scientific evidence seems to show that masturbation is harmful for both men and women. If you have ever taken a class in psychology, you probably learned about Pavlov's dog. Pavlov was a guy who rang a bell every time he was about to feed his dog. The dog came to associate the bell with food, and it would begin salivating at the sound of the bell. This is known as a trained response.

The human mind can be trained in the same way. In fact, the pleasure center of the brain is the most easily trained part of the human mind. This center is called the Medial Pre-optic Nucleus (MPN), and when the body experiences great pleasure, as in a sexual release, this part of the brain is rewarded. According to the research of Dr. Douglas Weiss, when a person experiences sexual arousal, the brain releases endorphins that help train the MPN to associate pleasure with whatever the person is doing, looking at, smelling, and so on. Unconsciously, a person forms a bond between a particular image, scent, or person and the feeling of sexual pleasure.[15] This is why porn magazines often contain perfume advertisements. When a man associates a smell with an erotic image, he'll be more likely to buy the fragrance for the unlucky woman in his life.

This scientific discovery sheds new light on Saint Paul's words: "Do you not know that he who joins himself to a prostitute becomes one body with her? For, as it is written, 'The two shall become one flesh. . . .' Shun immorality. Every other sin which a man commits is outside the body; but the immoral man *sins against his own body*" (1 Cor. 6:16–18).

When a person experiences sexual pleasure while lusting after another online or in his imagination, he is training his brain to be stimulated by fantasy images. If this is what a man's or woman's brain identifies as the cause of sexual joy, then where does this leave his or her spouse one day? The person is not a fantasy image, but a real human being. Yet instead of being able to take joy in the actual person in the marriage bed, the individual trained by masturbation may be driven to find stimulation in inner fantasies even while trying to make love to a spouse. Men and women may look to adultery, strip clubs, pornography, or a disordered lust for one another to satiate their desires. Often, especially for men, the habit of masturbation continues in order to take care of sexual "needs." This obviously doesn't make for more intimate marriages.

Now, this does not mean that you are doomed to a dysfunctional marriage if you have ever experienced sexual pleasure on your own or with anyone other than your husband or wife. However, it does mean that you will have obstacles to overcome that those without such a history will not struggle with. The brain can be retrained, but it will take time according to how well-entrenched the habit of lust has become.

This should show us that God's plan for our sexuality is stamped into our anatomy. When people live according to God's truths, their bodies will associate sexual joy with their spouse. God has designed our bodies to ensure that a married couple will be physiologically drawn to each other. Their minds have been trained that way. As the Bible says, "Let your fountain be yours alone, not shared with strangers. And have joy of the wife of your youth. . . .

Her love will invigorate you always, through her love you will flourish constantly" (Prov. 5:17–19, *NAB*).

## 58

*I have formed a real habit of masturbation and do not know how to stop. What would you say is the best way to overcome this?*

Prayer and patient perseverance. As you begin the battle, know that God is pleased with your desire for holiness and that his grace is working in your life. He will complete the good work he has begun in you (Phil. 1:6). Come to Him in prayer and ask Him often for the grace to be pure and specifically to overcome this habit.

The number one prayer you can offer is the holy sacrifice of the Mass. There is enough grace in one Communion to make you a saint. Tap into that fountain of purity!

Spend an increased amount of time in personal prayer as well, and speak openly to Jesus about your struggles. Also pray the Hail Mary three times each day for purity of mind, body, and heart; frequent the sacrament of reconciliation; read Scripture; pray the rosary; make the stations of the cross; and develop a devotion to Saint Joseph. These form an arsenal of weapons against any sin.

If you need to confess the same sin repeatedly, do so. The devil will try to discourage you, saying, "Hey, you've been back in the confessional so many times with this sin. Why don't you give up? You can't win." Recognize these thoughts as a temptation and turn immediately to prayer. Know that the patient is healed who shows his wound to the physician. The confessional is the medicine box, Christ in the priest is the doctor, and that is the last place the devil wants you to be. You are on the winning team, and the Lord will not let you be snatched from his hand. You cannot do it alone, but you can do all things through Christ who gives you strength (Phil. 4:13).

Certainly, if you own any pornography, swimsuit posters, or vulgar music, get rid of them immediately. For the sake of love, guard yourself against such contamination. Replace these things with Christian music and put holy images in your room, especially where you usually fall into the sin. If you have a habit of watching a lot of television, find something else to do, such as exercise. This helps release tension and makes the body easier to master. Television is idleness filled with temptation, and that is kindling for the fires of lust. Saint Robert Bellarmine warned, "Flee idleness, for no one is more exposed to such temptations than he who has nothing to do." [16]

To help you grow in discipline, set reachable goals. For example, make a commitment not to masturbate for three days, a week, a month, or whatever you feel is a reasonable time. When you have made it to that point, you will have an increased sense of confidence that you do have control over your body. Then, without falling back, bump up the time and abstain for a longer period. Keep this up until the vice is overcome.

During this time of discipline, give up tiny things. For example, skip salt on your fries, or skip seconds at a meal. These small sacrifices will help you grow in self-mastery, so that you gain self-control. After all, we are slaves to whatever rules us. The difference is like that between a jockey who has no control over his horse, which gallops wildly through gardens and living rooms, and a jockey who has control and can win races and stop on command. That is a person fully alive.

This kind of self-control is challenging, but with the grace of God, all things are possible. If you ask for purity, not one grace will be lacking. Be patient with yourself, and do not give in to discouragement. According to the Gospel of Luke, "By your endurance you will gain your lives" (Luke 21:19). The prize of true love awaits those who are truly free, because they are the only ones capable of giving and receiving.

# 6

# Homosexuality

## 59

*I go to an all-guys school, and my friends and I sometimes make fun of effeminate guys. Is that wrong?*

It is wrong. To help you understand why, imagine what it would be like to be in their place:

Imagine being in middle school, and as your buddies began to talk about their feelings of attraction and love for girls in your class, you noticed that you didn't feel the same desires. You listened to their stories and played along with their conversations and jokes, but you always felt that you were on the outside, looking in. As the months and years drew on, you felt all the emotions and excitement of romantic attraction that they did—but not for girls. Because you feared their rejection, you kept silent about your attractions, and told absolutely no one. For months and even years you were afraid to tell anyone what was stirring within you. Feelings of isolation, confusion, shame, loneliness, and despair seemed to suffocate you at times. Finally, once you were in high school, you found others who felt the same way you did. At last, you felt understood and accepted. But the more you associated with them, the more you felt rejected by others. You suffered repeated humiliations from bullies, and wondered what your parents would think if you ever told them. Would they reject you as well? Because you sometimes struggled to accept yourself, you even wondered if God Himself would accept you.

Now that you've taken a moment to enter into the life of one of these individuals, imagine the impact your jokes would make on him. At an all-boys high school, it's common for guys to be concerned about whether they're athletic enough, smart enough, popular enough, and so on. But the way to find acceptance is not to tear others down. That doesn't make you any more of a man. In fact, it is a sign of male insecurity for a guy to belittle other men in order to establish his own masculinity. A real man is secure enough in his manhood to treat all guys with dignity, including those he considers to be effeminate. Keep in mind, though, that not all effeminate guys are attracted to other guys, and sometimes the most masculine-looking men experience same-sex attractions.

I went to an all-guys high school, and I sadly confess that I took part in mocking such guys as well. Our jokes, mannerisms, and impersonations were a constant announcement to the world that none of us understood manhood yet. Lurking under the mockery, though, was the knowledge that we would feel equally afraid and alone if we were the ones experiencing same-sex attractions.

If you want to prove your manhood to the world, be virtuous. In fact, the word virtue means "manly strength." As a display of such character, I would challenge you to go and ask forgiveness from those you have mocked. Such an act of humility might go a long way to healing some of the abuse that these individuals might have suffered in their lives.

In the future, stop such conversations and refuse to take part in the behavior. Whatever we have done to another, we have done to Christ Himself (Matt. 25:31–46).

## 60

*What causes homosexuality? Is it OK to be gay if you are born that way?*

The origins of same-sex attractions are not fully understood, and many people who experience such feelings do not choose or want them. There has been much debate over the question of nature versus nurture, but scientists have been unable to find a genetic cause for homosexuality. Dr. Dean Hamer (who coined the phrase "gay gene") said, "We have not found the gene—which we don't think exists—for sexual orientation."[1] Another study concluded,

"Critical review shows the evidence favoring a biologic (genetic) theory to be lacking."[2] Although genetic factors might play a role in sexual attractions, we know that it is an overstatement to say that their genes cause people to be "born gay." After all, identical twins share the same genes, but do not always share the same sexual attractions. Furthermore, if some men and women are "born homosexual," why do their reproductive systems compliment the opposite sex? The mystery that science seeks to explain is why their bodies are oriented one way, while their desires point them in the opposite direction.

There may be genetic factors that have yet to be discovered, but this is beside the point, according to one columnist on a homosexual advocacy Web site. In his article "Nature? Nurture? It Doesn't Matter," he explained the origin of homosexual attractions:

> We discover them; we do not invent them. So we must be born this way, right? Wrong. For several reasons. No one is born with romantic feelings, much less engaging in sexual conduct. That comes later. . . . The fact is that there are plenty of genetically influenced traits that are nevertheless undesirable. Alcoholism may have a genetic basis, but it doesn't follow that alcoholics ought to drink excessively. Some people may have a genetic predisposition to violence, but they have no more right to attack their neighbors than anyone else. Persons with such tendencies cannot say "God made me this way" as an excuse for acting on their dispositions. . . . We do not determine whether a trait is good by looking at where it came from (genetics, environment, or something else). . . . Remember: bad arguments in favor of a good cause are still bad arguments—and in the long run not very good for the cause.[3]

Even this gentleman, who sees nothing wrong with embracing the homosexual lifestyle, recognizes that we can't merely look to genetic or even environmental factors in order to approve or condemn human behaviors.

He's right. If homosexual attractions have their origin in biological or environmental factors, then those things should be studied for their own sake, not for the sake of making ethical judgments based upon them. Some people who identify themselves as gay or lesbian are offended by the idea that their attractions might have been influenced by their upbringing or life-experiences. But these things influence all of us, and even if people's unchosen attractions were not shaped by their past in any way, their past may have shaped the sexual behavior they did choose.

Many psychologists believe that the development of homosexual desires is sometimes rooted in an individual's upbringing.[4] Here are some ways in which this could be the case:

One: Sometimes the person experienced sexual abuse. Certainly not everyone who suffers sexual abuse develops homosexual attractions, and not everyone who has homosexual attractions was abused. But if a man abuses a girl, she may subconsciously think, "Men must all be like you, and no man will do that to me! I don't want to be hurt that way again." At times, homosexual relationships become a shield for the heart and a sort of haven to escape the hurt of abusive relationships. It is understandable that a person hurt in the past would want to avoid future relationships that cause pain—and pain may be all a person knows of the opposite sex. Also, children who are sexually abused by a member of the same sex can become confused about their sexual orientation.

Those who experience same-sex attractions should not dismiss this connection simply because they have not experienced it themselves. I recall having a long and friendly conversation with a teenage girl and her girlfriend. Over the course of our discussion, she mentioned that she used to date guys. I asked her if anything particular made her lose interest in them. She replied, "No, I was born lesbian." Sensing some hesitation on her part, I asked, "Are you sure? Nothing turned you off from guys?" She quietly answered, "I was raped four times, if that's what you mean." Who could blame this young woman for being repulsed by men and finding greater security in the companionship of another female? The purpose of recognizing a connection between sexual abuse and homosexual attractions or behavior is not to condemn the person but to assist him or her in healing the original wound instead of running from it.

Sometimes the abuse a young person witnesses is not sexual. One individual who experiences same sex attractions shared with me the following scenario: "A female witnessing an abusive father with her mother often times views the mother as weak and splits from identifying with her mother. She tells herself that she doesn't want to be like that (weak). She feels anger toward her father and even anger toward the mother for not defending herself. Often times, the girl will identify with the father's emotions seeing that he gets his way and is in control. Thus, the young girl takes on male traits (i.e. tomboy)." While these childhood experiences might have played a role this person's future relationships, it should be noted that each person processes suffering in a different way. Some young girls who witness domestic abuse might respond by avoiding marriage, while others might focus on marrying a kind husband. The point is that human experiences often shape human behavior, and those who experience same-sex attractions are not immune from such influences.

Two: Sometimes the opposite-sex parent is too enmeshed in the life of the child. For example, a mother and son can rely too exclusively on one another for needs that should be met elsewhere. Through this behavior a mother might inadvertently impede a boy's masculine development, which might lead him to feel that he "doesn't belong" among his peer group. This can contribute to gender identity confusion in the child.

Three: The same-sex parent may be emotionally or physically absent, which could lead a child to think that he or she is unloved. This perception has power—even if it is untrue. For example, imagine a father who works tirelessly in order to provide for his family. He was raised in a home that wasn't particularly affectionate, and he isn't the best communicator. His children might assume he doesn't like them, although they probably mean everything to him.

In the case of a young man, the real (or perceived) absence of a father may lead to feelings of inferiority or rejection by peers when it comes to things such as athletic endeavors with other guys. This can cause a young man to feel an inability to relate to men, and yet a yearning to be accepted by them. If his own father failed to affirm him as a man, he'll naturally look for that masculine affirmation elsewhere. If he begins to explore homosexuality in response to this yearning, he may gradually come to believe that his orientation is homosexual. But the attraction may have existed simply because others possessed a degree of masculinity that the young man admired and feared he lacked.

These three considerations do not apply to everyone. Each person's experience is as unique as the individual himself or herself, and there's no such thing as a "one-size-fits-all" explanation to such a complex topic. Those who experience same-sex attractions will rightly explain that not everyone with such attractions has had traumatic life experiences or dysfunctional families. But the fact remains that both positive and negative experiences can shape our attractions. There are external factors in all our lives that go back beyond what we remember and that influence us in some way. The brain is an organ that can be shaped throughout our lives, and this is true of all people, regardless of to whom they are sexually attracted.

People have spent decades searching for genetic clues in order to better understand sexual orientation. In their quest for microscopic evidence, they miss what is plainly revealed in the body. God made us male and female, and our bodies reveal that we are called to make a gift of ourselves. However, this gift of self doesn't need to be expressed in a sexual way. We are made in the image and likeness of God, and only by loving as God loves will we find true fulfillment and meaning in our lives.

Some people mistakenly think that the Church condemns people for experiencing same-sex attractions. The Church would be unfair if it did this. Sin is something you choose, but attractions are not chosen. Therefore, it is not a sin to experience homosexual attractions or temptations. For good reason, the Church distinguishes between the person, the inclination, and the actions.

Although our attractions in themselves are not sinful, they can lead us to sin. For example, Scripture and Church teaching condemn homosexual actions (Rom. 1:24–27; Gen. 19:1–29; 1 Tim. 1:8–10; CCC 2357–2359). However, a person does not need to give in to his or her temptations. As the Bible says, "No temptation has overtaken you that is not common to man. God is faithful, and He will not let you be tempted beyond your strength, but with the temptation will also provide the way of escape, that you may be able to endure it" (1 Cor. 10:13). Although temptations and attractions are not chosen, we do have a choice regarding them: Do we reinforce and intensify them or do we seek God's help when the desires arise? By looking to the examples of unmarried people such as Pope John Paul II, Mother Teresa, and Jesus, a person who experiences same-sex attractions can see that it is possible to give up certain pleasures in this life in order to experience a deeper union with God, now and in the life to come.

It might seem far-fetched to compare yourself to these individuals, but it's important to realize that there are other people living this out in the world. You may not see them, but they are there, striving to live a holy life through the joy of pursuing fulfillment in Christ above all else. I know some of them, and they radiate a peace that is rooted in self-honesty about their attractions and about their ultimate identity in Jesus Christ. They are seeking to grow in holiness and are amazing examples of how Christ's love can *and does* transform lives and bring joy!

The Church has canonized saints who have struggled with all kinds of difficulties, and I look forward to the day when the Church will canonize people who experienced same-sex attractions and chose to glorify God with their bodies through a life of purity. This isn't a naïve wish on my part. The friends I know who are living such a life serve as a powerful reminder to me that God is calling each one of us to holiness, regardless of our attractions.

## 61

*Recently I've been feeling attraction for some other guys at my high school. I have not told anyone yet because I don't even understand what's going on in me. I love God, but I'm scared and I don't know what to do. Any advice?*

Do not be afraid. God loves you, too, and your attractions will never cause Him to love you any less. During the teenage years, the body develops rapidly, spurred on by profound hormonal changes. Because of this, teens are sometimes puzzled by all the feelings they experience. As a young man matures, he will often seek to identify with what is masculine. Sometimes this desire to identify with a guy who is particularly masculine may be misinterpreted as the beginning of homosexual attractions.

This admiration for a member of the same sex is not uncommon during adolescence, for girls or for boys. During this time, young people are trying to discover who they are. They often go through a process that moves them from a strong interest in same-sex friendships to a primary interest in opposite-sex relationships. It is not unusual for adolescents to feel confusion in the midst of their rapid sexual development, identity search, and maturing of interests. Sometimes feelings of same-sex attraction will come and go, and other times they will last quite a while. Some guys experience same-sex attractions, then the feelings dissipate and they eventually fall in love with a woman and get married.

Let us assume, though, that the attractions and even temptations do not subside. The world will tell you that you shouldn't be ashamed of those desires, but should "come out" and embrace the homosexual lifestyle, because that's your identity. To do otherwise, in the eyes of the world, would be disingenuous, unhealthy, and repressive. What does the Church say about this? Indeed, there's no need to be ashamed of something you never chose. You didn't ask for these feelings, so there's no need to live in shame because of them. But it's a mistake to think that this *is* your identity. We are much more than our sexual attractions, and the Church invites us to recognize that truth.

I have friends who experience same-sex attractions, but some of them do not prefer to be called "gay" or even "homosexual." They feel that such labels would define them by their sexual desires, and that would minimize them. After all, we should not define ourselves by our struggles or sexual attractions. A "homosexual" is not who you are. You are a guy with many talents, desires, gifts, and other characteristics, but most important of all, you are a beloved son of God, and *that* is your identity. As one friend explained to me, "The Church calls us to be honest with ourselves about the existence of our sexual attractions (whatever they may be), but also to be honest with ourselves about what identity we choose to embrace. We can choose to place God above our sexuality, or sexuality above God. Our sexuality (though a very important gift) does not belong at the center of our embraced identities."

During an interview, someone once asked Mother Teresa for her views on homosexuality. She announced that she did not like the word "homosexual." She paused the interview and told the reporters that if they had any more questions about "homosexuals," they would refer to them from now on as "friends of Jesus." This is how the Church invites us to view all people; especially those who might feel misunderstood, unloved, or unwanted.

You are not alone in what you are experiencing. Within the Church, there is an organization known as "Courage" that exists to provide support for those who experience same-sex attractions and want to glorify God with their lives. (See couragerc.org.) Some people who experience same-sex attractions also pursue counseling to find encouragement and to help them make sense of their attractions. If you feel that would be helpful, you can find a good list of counselors at catholictherapists.com.

If desired, counseling can be a great blessing because it helps you to understand yourself, and self-knowledge is always a good thing. I remember listening to one man who had lived a homosexual lifestyle say that after years of being immersed in that culture, it finally dawned on him that he wasn't "homosexual." In his words, he was "homo-emotional." Because he never had a loving father, he longed for the approval, attention, and affection of a man, and the world taught him to sexualize his problems. After looking for fulfillment in a sexual way, he discovered that none of those relationships brought him what he desired.

What many people who experience same-sex attractions have discovered is that the Church does not condemn or hate them, but calls them to a life of heroic virtue. As one man said on his blog:

> Where are all these bigoted Catholics I keep hearing about? When I told my family [of my same-sex attractions] a year ago, not one of them responded with anything but love and understanding. Nobody acted like I had a disease. Nobody started treating me differently or looking at me funny. The same is true of every one of the Catholic friends that I've told. They love me for who I am. Actually, the only time I get shock or disgust or disbelief, the only time I've noticed people treating me differently after I tell them, is when I tell someone who supports the gay lifestyle. [Chastity]?! You must be some kind of freak. . . . Would I trade in my Catholicism for a worldview where I get to marry a man? Would I trade in the Eucharist and the Mass and the rest of it? Being a Catholic means believing in a God who literally waits in the chapel for me, hoping I'll stop by just for ten minutes so He can pour out love and healing on my heart.[5]

Despite the positive experiences of the gentleman above, your fears might still make you feel alone. You are not. A large fellowship of men and women is growing closer to God while carrying this same cross and persevering with joy in the virtue of chastity. Even those who do not experience same-sex attractions are walking alongside you in the struggle to place God's will before our own desires. Because of original sin, all of us experience the effects of the Fall. Theologians explain that we all have weakened wills, darkened intellects, and disordered desires—all of us. Same-sex attraction is only one manifestation of the universal human condition. Therefore, if we accept the fact that our sexual desires are part of our fallen nature, we can also accept the fact that Christ has promised to redeem them. This does not always mean that our attractions will change, but that He'll give us the grace to put

Him first in our lives and then follow Him. The Church does not expect or require people to change their attractions, as if such feelings can be controlled by a simple act of the will. Therefore, don't assume that your holiness is measured by how much you "reverse" your desires. Although you might fear that your temptations will pull you away from God, if you invite Him into your life, this trial might be the means by which you most intimately encounter His healing presence. The key, though, is listening to His voice instead of the voices of the world. Do not be afraid or lose hope. Come to God in prayer to be loved by Him as you are. He will do the rest.

## 62

*If two people of the same sex really love each other and are willing to stay faithful for life, why can't they get married?*

If you're like me and you have friends who experience same-sex attractions, you know that this is a deeply personal and sensitive issue. Although some people who experience these attractions are opposed to re-defining marriage,[6] others who wish to marry often feel that the Church is discriminating against them and is unfairly opposed to their desire to simply love one another. However, the issue of same-sex marriage isn't ultimately about equal rights, bigotry, hatred, or even about homosexuality.

The issue is about the definition of marriage and who has the authority to define it. For example, if a woman wanted to marry two men, the Church does not believe it has the authority to redefine marriage in order to accommodate her wish. Similarly, if a husband decided he no longer wished to be married to his wife, but instead wanted to marry another woman, the Church does not have the authority to pretend he could be validly married to anyone other than his wife. As Jesus said, "Every one who divorces his wife and marries another commits adultery" (Luke 16:18).

The Church recognizes that Jesus' teaching on marriage can be a cause of suffering for those who desire to live otherwise. But by upholding God's original plan for marriage, the Church is not expressing hatred toward any group of people. Rather, the Church believes that although some things in the Gospel are difficult to accept, we will only find fulfillment by trusting in God's plan for our lives.

The reason why people of the same sex who love each other and are willing to be faithful for life cannot get married is because there is more to marriage than love and faithfulness. These are necessary elements, like two legs of a four-legged chair, but they are not the only ones.

One reason why our modern culture doesn't understand why two people of the same gender cannot marry is because contraception has divorced procreation from sex. If heterosexual couples engage in sexual activity that is ordered against the transmission of life, why can't members of the same sex do likewise?

To understand why marriage requires the union of a man and a woman, we need to define the essential characteristics of marriage and sex. When a man and woman make love, they are renewing their wedding vows and promises with their bodies. Such a concept is easy to understand when you consider the essence of marriage.

For a valid marriage to take place, the union must be free, total, faithful, and ordered toward procreation. All these characteristics are necessary. For example, who would consider a marriage to be valid if the husband forced the woman to marry him? What about a couple who agreed to marry and have children, but refused to be faithful? According to the Church, these would not be real marriages, even if the couples had legal marriage certificates. Similarly, if two people cannot have the kind of sexual relations that are designed to give life, they are incapable of marriage.

Because of this, some argue that the Church is "discriminating against gays." This is an understandable reaction, but realize that the Church is not singling out same-sex couples. In fact, the Church also believes that heterosexual couples are incapable of marriage if they are impotent. Not to be confused with sterility (a condition in which a couple is able to have intercourse but unable to have children), impotency means that a person is incapable of having intercourse.

Ever since the beginning, the marital embrace has been an essential and integral part of marriage. In Genesis we read, "A man leaves his father and his mother and clings to his wife, and they become one flesh" (Gen. 2:24). In marriage, the total gift of one's self becomes indissoluble through the total gift of one's body. This is how a marriage is consummated.

Just because two people are engaging in some kind of sexual embrace, it does not make them one flesh. For example, if a husband and a wife only engaged in the kind of sexual activity that a same-sex couple engaged in, the husband and wife would not have consummated their marriage.

The reason why only male and female bodies are capable of becoming one is because they are made for each other. Of all the biological systems in a person's body (circulatory, nervous, digestive, and so on), only the reproductive system cannot fulfill its purpose without uniting to a member of the opposite sex. Consider what happens when the cord of a lamp is united to a power outlet. Because the two were made for each other, light is created. The same is true with sexual complementarity and the creation of human life.

Because members of the same sex have bodies that are not created to receive one another, they physically cannot express the vows of marriage. This inability of the bodies to become one expresses the deeper reality that they were not meant to give themselves to each other in marriage. Therefore, the Church has no authority to marry a couple who cannot speak their wedding vows through their bodies. A nonmarital relationship cannot be declared a marriage. This is not easily understood by a culture that separates sex from marriage. Not surprisingly, the culture that first demanded sex without marriage now demands marriage without sex.

Some advocates of same-sex marriage point out that the Church allows opposite-sex couples to marry even if they can't have children. However, if a husband and wife are unable to have children because of sterility, they would still be truly married because they are still capable of becoming one flesh. The validity of their marriage does not depend on what happens in the woman's womb several hours or days after they become one flesh. Although children are the possible fruit of their union, their union is still real even if conception does not occur.

The comparison of homosexual couples to sterile heterosexual couples falls short because sterility is a dysfunction for heterosexual couples, but is natural and necessary for the homosexual couple. If you're looking for similarities between heterosexual and homosexual couples, look at the couple using birth control. Their sexual acts, just like homosexual acts, are ordered against the transmission of life. Many people don't know this, but if a couple gets married and intends to use contraception and never have children, the Church does not recognize their marriage as valid. If they set their wills against life, then the Church says that no marriage ever existed between them. They walked into the church as two singles, and they left as two singles. In the eyes of the Church the same would be true of a homosexual "marriage," even if it was recognized by the state.

Marriage is not something that was invented by the Catholic Church—or by the government. In fact, the traditional view of marriage (as the life-long, faithful union of one man and one woman) pre-dates Christianity, and can be found in civilizations throughout history. The reason for this is simple: Couples have intercourse, intercourse makes babies, and babies need parents who stay together. Whereas a mother has no choice but to be present at the birth of her children, one of the historical purposes of marriage was to bind a father to his offspring publicly. Although that might not sound romantic, cultures have always known that the stability of every civilization depends upon the stability of its families. Thus, the institution of marriage has always been intrinsically ordered toward procreation and family life. In fact, the word "matrimony" literally means "the duty of the mother."

Let us assume, though, that marriage doesn't need to be ordered toward bodily union and family life. If marriage were redefined to be about emotional union and cohabitation, why would it need to be permanent? Why would it need to be sexually exclusive or restricted to two people? Many same-sex couples agree that faithfulness and permanence are essential to marriage. But the fact remains: If the traditional view of marriage discriminates against same-sex couples, then won't the mere recognition of same-sex marriage discriminate against others who wish to have "marriages" that aren't monogamous or permanent? How could those who favor same-sex marriage legally refuse marriage to them?

*The Advocate*, a popular gay-advocacy magazine, explained this well when it stated:

> Anti-equality right-wingers have long insisted that allowing gays to marry will destroy the sanctity of "traditional marriage," and, of course, the logical, liberal party-line response has long been "No, it won't." But what if—for once—the sanctimonious crazies are right? Could the gay male tradition of open relationships actually alter marriage as we know it? And would that be such a bad thing? . . . perhaps now is the perfect time for the gays to conduct a little marriage makeover.[7]

In God's eyes, marriage is supposed to be a sign of Christ's love for His bride, the Church (cf. Eph. 5). As young people today know, marriage is already broken enough. A redefinition of marriage would further obscure and contradict this sign of God's free, total, faithful, and life-giving love. As one professor and proponent of same-sex marriage wrote, "conferring the legitimacy of marriage on homosexual relations will introduce an implicit revolt against the institution into its very heart."[8]

Another consideration that needs to be made is the issue of children and their well-being. If a person is in favor of same-sex marriage, then he or she will necessarily need to approve of genetically engineering motherless and fatherless children. After all, same-sex married couples want to have children of their own biological makeup. To do this, they use techniques such as in vitro fertilization, artificial insemination, and surrogate motherhood.

Deliberately creating motherless or fatherless babies is a social experiment that shows a lack of concern for children. Approving of this is equivalent to saying, "Being raised by your biological mother really isn't any better than being raised by your dad's male partner." Granted, it's not always possible for both biological parents to raise a child. Some children need to be adopted. But a mom cannot be replaced by two dads, or even by two hundred of them! Just ask anyone who has lost his or her mother to divorce or death. Likewise, dads don't make good moms. Both are unique and unrepeatable.

One man who was raised by two moms said of the experience, "I was aware of it at a very early age. I lived that absence of a father, experienced it, as an amputation."[9] He is not alone. One famous lesbian celebrity adopted a son, and was asked what she'd do if he wanted a dad. She replied that when he was six, he said, "I want to have a daddy." Her answer to that was, "If you were to have a daddy, you wouldn't have me as a mommy because I'm the kind of mommy who wants another mommy. This is the way mommy got born." He said, "OK, I'll just keep you."[10] The son was made to feel that if he wanted a dad, he'd be rejecting her. She also shared that her son now knows that "There are different types of people; that he grew up in another lady's tummy, and that God looked inside and saw there was a mix-up and that God brought him to me." In other words, because God didn't want him to have a dad, he intervened to prevent such a mistake. Another case of a boy adopted by a gay couple was published in *The American Journal of Orthopsychiatry*. In the article "Recreating Mother," it explained that one of the dads hired nannies to care for him, but fired them when he became too attached. This happened three times, and the boy was seeing a therapist for his psychological problems by the age of four because he wanted to "buy" a mom.[11]

Same-sex parents undoubtedly care for their children. They cheer for them at their kindergarten plays, comfort them in times of sorrow, and make many sacrifices for them. The same could be said of single parents, stepparents, or adoptive parents. None of this changes the fact that kids do better when they live with their own mom and dad. It seems that the only people who refuse to admit this are those who lobby for same-sex marriage. If it's biologically necessary for men and women to cooperate in order to create children, shouldn't we believe that both parents are equally necessary for the developmental well-being of those children?

Although the world has taken this for granted for thousands of years, some modern sociologists have attempted to show that same-sex parents are just as capable as biological parents of raising happy children. But consider the following facts: If a girl does not grow up with her dad, she's more likely to suffer sexual abuse and experience out-of-wedlock teen pregnancy, while fatherless boys are more likely to become involved in crime and end up in prison. [12] Extensive research has shown that children raised by same-sex parents don't do as well as those raised by their married biological parents. [13]

Some homosexual activists object to these findings, arguing that other studies have shown the opposite. What they don't realize is that their conclusion is inexplicable: Long before the same-sex marriage debate ever surfaced, decades of extensive research showed that children do better when raised by their biological parents than in any other arrangement (stepparents, single parents, and cohabiting heterosexual parents). [14] Why should one expect same-sex unions to offer a parental benefit that heterosexual adoptive parents can't even offer their children? Furthermore, if two dads can raise a child just as well as one mother and one father, then why couldn't one father and two wives raise a child better than anyone?

Many people who have same-sex attractions yearn to become fathers and mothers, and these desires are healthy, good, and understandable. But in the end, a child's right to live with his father and mother should take precedence over anyone's desire to have a child. Simply put: The rights *of* children should come before the right *to* children.

All the issues mentioned above are emotionally volatile and often ignite heated debates. Those who argue in favor of same-sex marriage claim that others need to learn to celebrate diversity and become more tolerant. But at the same time, such advocates will not tolerate those who believe in traditional marriage. Laws are enforced against those who do not agree with the alternative lifestyle, and same-sex marriage is portrayed in the media as a human-rights issue, equivalent to interracial marriage. But if belief in traditional marriage is on par with racism, then those who support it will be viewed like racists. They will be scorned and looked down upon as close-minded, hateful bigots.

Because young people are especially aware of the harm caused by social isolation and bullying, many of them dismiss the Church's teaching on homosexuality. They mistakenly assume that the Church's message contributes to hatred and unjust discrimination. Largely because of the media, teenagers today experience overwhelming social pressures not to "hate gays"—as if the invitation to chastity involved anything other than profound love and respect. Young people, perhaps more than others, realize that everyone experiences an ache to satisfy the deepest desires of his or her heart. We not only have *right* to that fulfillment, God has *destined* us for it. No one should prevent another person from finding it! However, our ultimate fulfillment cannot be found in any human relationship. If God created us to experience perfect fulfillment, perhaps we ought to trust Him when He says that it can only be found by following Him.

What is often overlooked amidst the heated rhetoric is that the Church is calling all people—regardless of their sexual attractions —to love. As surprising as it may sound, the Church today does not forbid people who experience same-sex attractions to love one another. In fact, the Church seems to be the only institution that is inviting them to love. We are created for love, and our lives make no sense if we don't experience it. However, we often need to grow in our understanding of what love really means. If two members of the same sex love one another, they will do what is best for each other. They will encourage one other to identify themselves as beloved children of God who happen to experience same-sex attractions, rather than people who are defined by their sexual urges and happen to believe in God. They desire union because of their love, but true love desires more than physical and emotion union; it desires the good of the other. It desires heaven for the other person and will encourage him or her to embrace the virtue of chastity. This is not a renunciation of love, but a profound and courageous expression of it.

# 7

# Contraception

## 63

*Why doesn't the Catholic Church allow married couples to use contraception?*

Contraception is nothing new; history records people using various methods of birth control four thousand years ago. Ancient people swallowed potions to cause temporary sterility; they used linens, wool, or animal skins as barrier methods; they fumigated the uterus with poison to keep it from bearing life. The Romans practiced contraception, but the early Christians stood out from the pagan culture because they refused to use it.[1] Scripture condemned the act (Gen. 38:8–10), as did all Christian denominations before 1930.

At that time the Anglican Church decided to allow contraception in some circumstances. They soon gave in on the issue altogether, and before long virtually all Protestant denominations followed suit. Yet the Catholic Church stands fast on the teaching of historic Christianity. But why? Why doesn't the Church "get with the times"?

The modern world has trouble understanding the Church's stance on contraception because the world does not know the purpose of sex. The writer Frank Sheed said that "modern man practically never thinks about sex." He dreams of it, craves it, pictures it, drools over it, but never pauses to actually *think* about it. Sheed continued: "Our typical modern man, when he gives his mind to it at all, thinks of sex as something we are lucky enough to have; and he sees all its problems rolled into the one problem of how to get the most pleasure out of it."[2]

But we should put more thought into the matter. Who invented sex? What is sex? What is its purpose? What is it worth? For starters, God invented sex. Since He is its author, He knows its meaning and purpose better than we do. God has revealed that the purposes of sex are procreation and union (babies and bonding), and that the sexual act can be thought of as the wedding vows and promises made flesh. On a couple's wedding day, they promise that their love will be *free, faithful, total,* and *open to life.* Each act of marital intercourse should be a renewal of these vows.

Some couples say that they will be *open to life* but will contracept between kids. In other words, they will be completely open to life—except when they sterilize their acts of love. Imagine if they had the same mentality with other parts of the wedding vows. Can a wife say she is *faithful* except when she has affairs? Can she say that she will give herself *totally* to her husband as long as he's rich? Can a husband say the marital act is *free* except when he forces himself upon his wife? All this is absurd, but contracepting couples contradict their own vows in a similar way when they refuse to be open to God's gift of life. When it comes down to it, they are afraid of what sex means.

But sex is more than the wedding vows made flesh. It is also a reflection of the life-giving love of the Trinity. In the words of Carlo Cardinal Martini, "In the Bible, the man-woman couple is not meant to be simply a preservation of the species, as is the case for the other animals. Insofar as it was called to become the image and likeness of God, it expresses in a bodily, tangible way the face of God, which is Love."[3] God's plan for us to love as He loves is stamped into our very being, and so there is really only one question to ask when it comes to sexual morality: "Am I expressing God's love through my body?" When a married couple does this, they become what they are—an image of Trinitarian love—and through this they unveil the love of God to the world.

The act of life-giving love between a husband and wife is also meant to be a mirror of the love Christ has for His Church. We should ask ourselves: "If we consider the relationship between Christ and His Church, where does contraception fit into the picture? What is contraceptive about Christ's love?"

Beyond the theological implications, consider the consequences of contraception in society. When contraception spread among Christians, the Catholic Church warned about the harm it would inflict on relationships. Rates of marital infidelity would increase because spouses could be unfaithful without fear of pregnancy. Since contraception offers an easy way to elude the moral law, there would be a general lowering of morality. The Church "feared that the man, growing used to the employment of anti-conceptive practices, may finally lose respect for the woman, and no longer caring for her physical and psychological equilibrium, may come to the point of considering her a mere instrument of selfish enjoyment, and no longer as his respected and beloved companion." [4] Furthermore, if people could separate making love from making life, then why would those acts that are unable to make life (homosexual sex or masturbation) be forbidden? With the increase in contraceptive use, it would become increasingly difficult to view sexuality as a sign of God's love.

Some argue that the Church restricts women's freedom by opposing contraception. However, the sour fruit of contraceptive "liberation" is manifested most clearly not by arguments but by the lives of those who accept such false ideas of freedom. Consider the following question that one young woman sent to Dear Abby: "I am a twenty-three-year-old liberated woman who has been on the Pill for two years. It's getting pretty expensive and I think my boyfriend should share half the cost, but I don't know him well enough to discuss money with him." [5]

In the words of Christopher West, "If the real problem behind women's oppression is men's failure to treat them properly as persons, contraception is a sure way to keep women in chains." [6] The earliest feminists opposed contraception for this reason, and some modern feminists still realize that contraception is the enemy of women's liberation. [7]

Anthropologists who study the origin and destruction of civilizations have noted that societies that do not direct their sexual energies toward the good of marriage and family begin to crumble. [8] Therefore the Church does not hesitate to point out the vast implications of contraception. The love between a husband and wife holds a marriage together. A strong marriage holds the family together. Strong families hold society together, and a civilization will stand or fall upon this. "The future of humanity," according to the Church, "passes by way of the family." [9] If it can be shown that contraception compromises intimacy between a husband and wife, invites selfishness into the marital act, and opens a door for greater infidelity, then contraception is a cancer to civilization itself.

## 64

*If the Church forbids contraception, does it expect married women to have fifteen kids?*

Although the Church is opposed to contraception, it is not opposed to the responsible regulation of births. Couples may use Natural Family Planning (NFP) to avoid pregnancy if they have a just reason to do so.

Since a woman can conceive on only a limited number of days of each cycle, a couple who are practicing NFP will refrain from intercourse when the woman has a chance of conceiving. This method is often confused with the outdated calendar "rhythm method," but in reality it is very different. With an effectiveness rate above 99 percent, NFP is far more reliable. [10] NFP is also an effective means to achieve pregnancy, since the couple have a deep understanding of the woman's fertility. And by monitoring the woman's fertility, they are more aware of reproductive problems that may need treatment.

One husband noted that a couple may have good reasons to delay pregnancy, "but God has taken care of that already. So deeply has He wrought His purposes into us that a woman's body not only bears fruit but has seasons . . . providing not only for bringing babies forth but for spacing them. There is no need to thwart the design, to artificially block fertility during a naturally fertile time. One only has to wait for a few days. If that is too difficult for us, something is wrong." [11]

Many people think that the Church's opposition to contraception is an attack on the freedom of women to have control over their bodies. Nothing could be further from the truth. The Church insists that we have control over our bodies (*CCC* 2339). By having control over one's body, a person is able to make a gift of one's self.

The contraception industry would like its customers to believe that contraception grants them control over their bodies, relationships, and sex lives. While contraception offers a person the ability to live without true responsibility, that is not freedom. Freedom can be attained only through self-control. Some people use birth control to make up for their lack of self-control. Thus they never experience genuine freedom.

Contraception can never make woman free. To treat pregnancy as if it were a disease implies that there is something defective in the way she was created—that her fertility is a curse. That is not a very liberating experience for any woman. For years those within the contraception industry have been trying to convince women that they should ingest chemicals or insert devices in order to become sexually liberated. NFP beautifully contradicts such a mentality, because it does not treat a woman's body as if it needs to be subdued by drugs or shielded behind barriers in order to function properly; it just needs to be understood. This invites the man to treat the woman's fertility with reverence instead of disdain. He learns that his wife's body has been perfectly made. *This* is true sexual liberation.

## 65

*If couples are using NFP to space births, what is the difference between that and contraception?*

There are at least four enormous differences between NFP and contraception. The first is the morality of the act; the second deals with the fact that some contraceptives work by causing abortions; the third issue pertains to adverse side effects caused by contraceptives; and the last issue deals with the fruits of NFP.

Suppose that a married couple is using contraceptives for the same reason another couple is practicing NFP. Both couples already have children and hope to have more. But for good reasons they need to space the next birth by a couple of years. Both have the intent to regulate births, and responsible parenthood allows couples not to have more children than they can care for. However, the good intent of a couple is not sufficient to determine the morality of their act. For example, if two women wanted to avoid becoming overweight, one might go on a diet, and the other might binge and purge (bulimia). Both may stay slim, but one exercises the virtue of temperance, while the other succumbs to gluttony and unnatural, unhealthy behavior.

Similarly, the Church's condemnation of contraception does not imply that the couple has bad intentions but that they are using a means that is immoral. Married couples are free to have intercourse (or to agree to abstain from it) on any given day, regardless of the wife's fertility. But when they do join as one flesh, they must not frustrate the purpose God designed that act to have. It is God alone who has the power to create an immortal soul as a result of the marital act, and to contracept is to say that God's presence is not desired. Clearly then, a couple abstaining from sex for a just reason cannot be compared to a couple who sterilize their acts of lovemaking in order to enjoy the pleasure of the marital act apart from God's design.

The reason the Church denounces contraception is not because it is artificial. After all, the Church allows the use of countless artificial drugs and other technological advances that medicine can offer man. However, these are to be used to heal dysfunction and promote the proper functioning of the body as God designed it. Contraception does the opposite: it *prevents* the natural functioning of the body.

Therefore, the moral difference between NFP and contraception is that contraception deliberately interrupts, sterilizes, and works against (*contra*) conception, while NFP respects the way God ordained conception to occur. In no way does NFP interrupt or sterilize an act of intercourse. NFP couples are not acting against the way God has designed fertility but are working with it.

Another major difference between NFP and contraceptives is that some birth control methods work by causing abortions. For example, the birth control pill, the morning-after pill, the patch, the intrauterine device (IUD), and Depo-Provera (the shot) sometimes work by preventing a newly conceived child from attaching to the uterus. This causes a first trimester abortion to occur—without the mother even knowing it.

All contraceptives have potential adverse side effects, most of which affect the woman. In question 69 I go into detail regarding the side effects of contraceptives. Here I will simply point out that depending on the method used, these may include a heightened risk of breast cancer, a greater risk of contracting a sexually transmitted disease, migraine headaches, high blood pressure, fatal blood clots, increased fetal abnormalities, and toxic shock syndrome.

Finally, consider the implications of the fact that *couples who use NFP have a divorce rate of 1 to 3 percent.*[12] In one study there were zero divorces out of fourteen hundred NFP couples.[13] Keep in mind that more than half of all marriages end in divorce. The striking correlation between NFP and strong marriages is an important indication of the close relationship between NFP and the way God designed marriage and sex to work.

Also, NFP offers something else that contraceptives cannot: an understanding of how to time intercourse to achieve pregnancy. Further, NFP couples are in a much better position to teach their teens about sexual self-control. A couple should not expect their children to follow the Church's teachings on sexuality outside of marriage if they as parents are not willing to follow the Church's teachings on sexuality within marriage. It would be like a parent saying to their teen, "You need to obey God and abstain from sex for about a decade, but I won't obey God and abstain for a week."

Despite all these differences between contraception and NFP, it can be abused. Because NFP is so effective in regulating births, a couple could take on a contraceptive mentality and close themselves off from the gift of life. Therefore, it must be practiced responsibly and only when there is just reason to do so.

When we consider the positive impact of NFP on a marriage and the potential dangers of contraception, the most loving option becomes obvious.

## 66

*Why do NFP couples have such low divorce rates?*

The low divorce rate among couples practicing NFP reflects a combination of factors. First, couples with strong relationships may be more likely than other couples to choose to practice NFP. After all, NFP depends on some of the same virtues as marriage itself —commitment, communication, consideration, and self-control. Couples who reject NFP as "too much trouble" or "too restrictive" all too often turn out to be the same couples who ultimately find the demands of marriage itself to be too much to handle.

Second, NFP helps strengthen marital relationships. On the most basic level, since the spouses are not constantly sexually available to the other, it keeps them from taking the other for granted. Often women rightly complain that the use of contraception has lowered their sense of worth.

I recently received a letter from a woman who said that while she and her first husband were using contraception, she felt like a "toy or a recreational vehicle." The contraception made her husband assume that she was always sexually available, and she felt used and taken for granted. She has since been married in the Church and has used NFP for years. In her words, "a chaste marriage is the ultimate!" After abandoning contraception and switching to NFP, another woman said, "I now know the true meaning of the word 'intimate.' "[14]

When was the last time you heard a woman say that using a spermicide is "the ultimate!" and that after using a condom she finally knew the meaning of intimacy? The enthusiasm has never been there because no woman wants to be at war with her body. Sure, she may want to delay pregnancy, but she has never been ecstatic about the methods commonly offered to do that. She may seem content, but she silently wishes there was a better arrangement.

NFP is this better way, and couples who make the switch are more than pleased with the results. One way to measure a couple's satisfaction with a method of spacing births is to look at how many continue to use it over time. For example, spermicides have a 42 percent annual continuation rate; the condom, 53 percent; the shot, 56 percent; the diaphragm, a 57 percent rate; and the Pill, 68 percent.[15] What about NFP? Research of 1,876 couples using the Creighton Model of NFP showed that it has an annual continuation rate of 89 percent—which is higher than any form of reversible contraception.[16]

The Church explains that the practice of NFP "favors attention for one's partner, helps both parties to drive out selfishness, the enemy of true love, and deepens their sense of responsibility."[17] Many men do not realize that there is a time for a wife to be sexually intimate and a time for her to have some space. Men who sacrifice to give a woman that freedom improve the unity and intimacy of the marriage. The relationship has space to breathe. In the words of one husband, "It's wonderful because it almost creates the honeymoon over and over again."[18]

All-Pro NFL quarterback Philip Rivers pointed out that self-control "doesn't end when you get married. Chastity is still part of your marriage." He and his wife practice NFP, and he admitted that "it can be hard as ever sometimes. But it makes us stronger and love each other more. It allows you to love in many different ways. . . . That part of our relationship has strengthened us."[19]

During the times of abstinence, the spouses learn to express love in nonsexual ways. As a result, the intimacy between them deepens. In the meantime their anticipation of the marital act will intensify its joy. Furthermore, even the act of abstaining from intercourse can be a loving gesture, since not having more children at that time may be best for the family.

At times couples resort to sex as a way to solve problems, when in reality they are only burying the issues under a false sense of closeness. Since complete physical intimacy is not always possible for the couple practicing NFP, they cannot as easily use the feeling of physical intimacy to cover up conflicts. This opens a door for them to deepen their ability to communicate and solve problems. As a result, their exchange of the marital act is not as likely to be a means to bury problems but an opportunity to celebrate their love.

The use of contraception also fosters a level of rejection between spouses. By sterilizing the act of intercourse, the woman is saying that she wants to make love, but will kill any sperm that come her way.[20] The man is saying that he accepts everything about the woman except for fertility. He gives everything to her except his potential fatherhood. The language of sex should be that of complete self-donation, but that is impossible with contraception. Since the body reveals the person, a rejection of the body is a rejection of the spouse.

Also, couples who reject contraception are less likely to see children as a burden. Because of their generous spirit, they tend to have larger families, and divorce rates are highest where children are fewest. NFP couples also tend to take their faith, and therefore the sacrament of marriage, more seriously than the average contracepting couple. Lastly, since the couple never sterilize acts of intercourse, they are truly renewing their wedding promises each time they exchange the marital act. Knowing that they are not blocking God's plan for life and love, their times of unity as one flesh take on the joy, peace, and freedom that come from obeying the Lord and His bride, the Church.

## 67

*Isn't using birth control better than having unwanted teen pregnancies and abortions?*

Look at both these issues and judge for yourself if contraception is part of the solution or part of the problem.

Because of the widespread use of birth control, more people than ever have sex without intending to have children. Sex out of wedlock has become far more common, and more sex means more babies. Some argue that teaching people how to use contraceptives will alleviate the problem. But research shows that "programs in safer sex education and condom distribution have not reduced the out-of-wedlock birth rates among sexually experienced teens. . . . The fact is, increased condom use by teens is associated with *increased* out-of-wedlock birth rates."[21]

A few years ago in Colorado, one school began passing out condoms to the students. Within three years the birth rate rose 31 percent above the national average, and in one school year one hundred births were expected among the twelve hundred students. The administrators were described as "searching for explanations."[22]

When unwanted pregnancies occur, many turn to abortion as a solution. In fact, studies show that about half of all unintended pregnancies end in abortion.[23] Some argue that increased use of contraception could have lowered these abortion rates. However, the research institute of the nation's largest abortion provider admits that *most women who receive abortions had been using birth control during the month they became pregnant!*[24] Such couples feel that the "fault" of the pregnancy can be blamed on the failed contraception, but by contracepting they have already set their wills against new life. Since contraception treats pregnancy as if it were a disease, many people conclude that abortion must be the cure.

I once saw a condom advertisement that called pregnancy "the mother of all nightmares." With this mentality it is no surprise that the sex researcher Alfred Kinsey said, "At the risk of being repetitious, I would remind the group that we have found the highest frequency of induced abortion in the group which, in general, most frequently used contraceptives."[25] Even a former medical director of Planned Parenthood admitted in 1973, "As people turn to contraception, there will be a rise, not a fall, in the abortion rate."[26] Fifty million abortions later, no one can dispute his prediction.

Lastly, it should be noted that anyone who believes that contraception decreases abortions ignores the fact that hormonal birth control can cause abortions.[27]

Mother Teresa did not need to see the statistics. She was well aware of the connection between contraception and abortion when she said in a speech in the presence of Bill and Hillary Clinton:

> The way to plan the family is Natural Family Planning, not contraception. In destroying the power of giving life, through contraception, a husband or wife is doing something to self. This turns the attention to self and so destroys the gift of love in him or her. In loving, the husband and wife must turn the attention to each other. Once that living love is destroyed by contraception, abortion follows very easily.[28]

## 68

### If couples do not use contraception, won't the world become overpopulated?

Contraceptives are not needed to plan family size. In Calcutta, NFP has proven to be a practical alternative that works effectively. The *British Medical Journal* reported, "Indeed, a study of 19,843 poor women in India [practicing NFP to delay pregnancy] had a pregnancy rate approaching zero."[29]

But is there an overpopulation problem? Especially in the 1960s and 1970s, people feared that the world's population would soon outstrip its resources. Books predicted that the earth would run out of natural resources, such as gas, lead, and petroleum. Widespread catastrophes were feared, and some predicted that hundreds of millions of Americans would starve to death. Indeed, the world saw an exponential growth in population in the 1900s. However, much of this was a result of advances in medicine. Because the average life expectancy was lengthened, there were more people alive than ever before.

Now life expectancies have begun to level out, and although

the population continues to increase, the 1970s doomsday predictions have faded away. In fact, many countries are now facing economic difficulties as a result of underpopulation.[30] Global fertility and birth rates have been rapidly decreasing for more than twenty-five years.[31] Almost every developed country in the world has a below-replacement fertility rate.[32] The fertility rate of developing nations tends to be higher, but according to the United Nations Population Division, between 2005 and 2050 the worldwide number of children (persons under fifteen) will decline.[33]

While some people predicted that there would be too many children, others feared that humans would run out of space. However, humans occupy only 1 to 3 percent of the Earth's surface. If you gathered every human being on Earth, we would all fit in Jacksonville, Florida. If everyone moved to Texas, each person would have more than a thousand square feet in which to live.[34] This provides more living space than people have in San Francisco and only slightly less than they have in the Bronx.[35]

The problem is not a lack of space but an unjust distribution of resources. One researcher noted that "according to the Food and Agriculture Organization, world food supplies exceed requirements in all world areas."[36] Besides, farmers use less than half of the land that can be used for agriculture. Human poverty is the result of bad economic policy, war, and corrupt governments, not overpopulation. (For more on this, see pop.org.)

## 69

*How reliable are the different kinds of contraception, and what are their side effects?*

There are many methods of contraception. Each carries with it some risk of harmful side effects, many of which are downplayed in our modern culture. Although some side effects are common and others are rare, men and women should be aware of all of the possible consequences. Furthermore, people are often led to believe that most birth control methods are 99 percent effective in preventing pregnancy. In order to clarify these matters, here's a sobering look at the facts for some forms of birth control.

## Anti-Fertility Vaccines

For decades research has been underway to create vaccinations against pregnancy. These drugs are different from other methods of birth control because they use the woman's immune system against her own baby. Thus they are called "immunological contraceptives."

One such vaccination being tested is the anti-hCG vaccine. HCG stands for human chorionic gonadotrophin. This is a hormone that is produced by a newly conceived baby when he or she is only a few days old (a blastocyst). Once hCG is produced, it signals the mother's body to release other hormones that will sustain a healthy pregnancy. When a woman takes a pregnancy test, she is looking for elevated levels of hCG in her system.

The hCG vaccine will create antibodies in a woman that will attack hCG, resulting in the death of the baby. In order to make this work, scientists put a molecule in the vaccine that links hCG with diphtheria or tetanus. These are diseases that a healthy immune system will attack. The version of the toxin is not sufficient to infect the woman with the disease, but it is enough to stimulate her immune system to respond to hCG as if it were a disease. After receiving the vaccination, the woman's body will be tricked into killing off any future unborn children. Her progesterone levels will drop, and the lining of her uterus will shed, preventing a pregnancy from being sustained.

Another form of the anti-fertility vaccine is known as TBA (Trophoblastic Antigen). It trains the woman's immune system to attack the trophoblast, which is a layer that surrounds and protects the embryo. As is the case with the anti-hCG vaccine, when a woman uses TBA, the baby dies before the mother is aware of the pregnancy. Because her menstrual cycle is uninterrupted, there is no way for her to know when these early abortions occur.

The side effects and effectiveness of these methods have yet to be established. However, the editor of the *International Journal of Risk & Safety in Medicine* wrote, "[The development of immuno-contraceptives is] asking unnecessarily for trouble . . . Whatever risks there are can hardly be predicted in any test. But what we know of physiology suggests that they could be very serious."[37]

Controversy has surrounded the development of these vaccinations, especially because they are being tested on women in developing nations without informed consent. Such women (and their unborn children) are being used as living laboratories. Also, it would seem to be a dangerous idea to tamper with the immune systems of women who live in countries ravaged by HIV. Thankfully, many health movements and human rights groups across the globe continue to protest the development and testing of anti-fertility vaccines.

## Birth Control for Men

Several new birth control methods for men have been in the works, but the Food and Drug Administration (FDA) has approved none of them—yet. Some scientists are working on a pill that will deform a man's sperm. Others are testing an Intra Vas Device (IVD) that consists of silicone plugs that can be surgically inserted into a man's vasa differentia (the tubes that transport a man's sperm). Still others have created a shot that can be injected into the vasa differentia, which will permanently block the transport of sperm. Another injection will partially block the passage of sperm, and damage the ones that pass through. Other drugs aim to prevent a man's sperm from being able to attach or enter a woman's egg.

One of the most talked-about forms of male contraception is hormonal birth control. One way this would work is through injecting the man with a synthetic female sex hormone (progestin) in order to halt sperm production. By acting on the pituitary gland in the male brain, the two hormones that signal the testes to produce sperm can be reduced. When this was tested in men, it was decided that the men should also rub testosterone gel on their shoulders, because progestin decreases testosterone.

Other scientists are developing a 1.6-inch progestin implant that can be inserted under the skin of a man's arm. This would be supplemented with testosterone shots every three months. Since men might not go for birth control that requires routine injections, other researchers have proposed an implant that would contain both testosterone and progestin. But most guys probably won't be too thrilled about any kind of birth control surgically inserted under their skin.

A male birth control pill is also in the works. It could work by increasing the level of testosterone in the man. Through a chain of biological reactions, this would cause the man's body to halt sperm production. With the added testosterone come side effects, however, such as acne, weight gain, prostate gland growth, and abnormal liver function.

With all these new drugs, one can only imagine the side effects that will inevitably be discovered. For example, what will happen when a chemically deformed sperm successfully impregnates a woman?

Gels, shots, pills, implants, herbs, patches, and everything imaginable have been proposed, but nothing has been licensed in the United States yet. One reason for this is because the drug companies behind these products are afraid of how many men will sue them for the inevitable side effects.[38]

It is astounding how far mankind will go in order to avoid the demands of self-control.


## Birth Control Pills

Although most people assume that oral contraception was invented in the 1960s, the practice dates back thousands of years. Some ancient civilizations created drinkable potions of plants and tree bark. According to some reports, extract from the silphium plant was so effective in preventing pregnancy that the plant was used to extinction over fifteen hundred years ago![39]

In the Middle Ages new concoctions were invented, some of which proved to be fatal for the women, who didn't realize the drawbacks of drinking mercury, lead, arsenic, and strychnine. Even when women did not ingest the medicine, they were often subjected to bizarre practices. Some civilizations urged women to wear amulets that contained the liver of a cat or the earwax of a mule![40] Over time, advances in medical technology replaced such superstitious and ineffective methods.

In the early 1900s, scientists began to experiment with the fertility of animals by using orally administered hormones. Some methods proved to be effective, but mass-producing enough hormones for human use seemed impractical. Scientists required gallons of urine or thousands of pounds of organs in order to extract a few milligrams of sex steroids.[41] When a chemist in the 1940s was able to produce hormones from certain plants, researchers no longer needed the ovaries from more than two thousand pregnant pigs to create one milligram of progesterone. With only five gallons of liquefied roots of Mexican yams, he could create three kilograms of hormone. With continued progress in the development of synthetic hormones, oral contraception became a reality.

In 1950 Planned Parenthood invited an American biologist named Gregory Pincus to create an "ideal" and "harmless" form of birth control. As it usually does, research began on animals, such as rabbits and mice. Within a few short years, social workers in Puerto Rico were handing out oral tablets to women throughout the barrio. One witness recalls, "Women were told this was medicine that would keep them from having children they couldn't support."[42] What these women did not know was that they were being used as test subjects. During these clinical trials, three women died of complications that arose from taking the drug. As a result, the researchers changed the dosage and continued testing.[43]

Further studies were conducted in the United States and abroad, and the FDA approved the birth control pill for contraceptive use in 1960. It didn't take long before safety concerns began to crop up, including the Pill's tendency to increase a woman's risk of suffering heart attacks and strokes. By 1970, the FDA initiated efforts to give information about the drug to the women who used it. As scientists learned more about the harmful chemicals in the Pill, they sought to experiment with different levels and types of hormones.

Over time the chemicals in the Pill have changed considerably. For example, when the Pill was first approved, it contained five times as much estrogen as some of today's birth control pills.[44] Estrogen enhances clotting of the blood, and so the higher dosage of the hormone led to many injuries related to blood clots, such as strokes and heart attacks. Because such levels of hormones were dangerous and unnecessary for women, the FDA told doctors in 1970 to prescribe the lowest possible dose of estrogen available at the time. Sales of the higher-dose pills began to drop. In 1973 those in the population control business saw the opportunity to obtain the high-dose pills at a low cost and spent millions of dollars buying up the leftover stock for shipment overseas for use by women in developing nations, despite the safety concerns.[45]

In order to prevent pregnancy, birth control pills employ several mechanisms. First, the synthetic hormones may convince a woman's body that she is pregnant. This can stop the ovaries from releasing an egg. The Pill also makes it difficult for the sperm to reach the egg, because the hormones thicken the cervical mucus. Normally, on the days of each month when a woman is fertile, her cervical mucus has microscopic channels in it that make it easier for the sperm to travel to the egg. The mucus also nourishes the sperm, allowing them to live longer. However, when a woman is infertile (which is true for the greater part of each month) her cervical mucus changes. It looks more like a mesh or net at the microscopic level. The Pill causes the woman's body to produce this type of cervical mucus on a continual basis, thus making it difficult for the sperm to live and move. The Pill also creates changes in the uterus and fallopian tubes that can interfere with the transport of sperm.[46]

Despite the hormones' ability to prevent the release of eggs, sometimes a "breakthrough ovulation" takes place. How often this happens depends upon several factors, such as which kind of pill the woman is taking, how consistently she takes her pills, and even how much she weighs. Even with correct and consistent use of the Pill, some formulas allow ovulation in less than 2 percent of cycles, while others allow a woman to ovulate during 65 percent of her cycles.[47]

When a woman ovulates, she can become pregnant. However, the Pill has mechanisms that can cause an abortion before a woman knows that she has conceived. If a sperm does fertilize the egg, the newly conceived baby (zygote) may be transported more slowly through the fallopian tubes because of how they have been altered by the Pill. Thus, the child may not reach the uterus, where he or she needs to implant and receive nourishment for the next nine months. Because the fallopian tubes are changed, the baby may accidentally implant there, causing an ectopic or "tubal" pregnancy, which is fatal to the baby, and can also be life-threatening for the mother.

If the baby is able to travel safely to the uterus, he or she may not be well received. One reason for this is that the chemicals in the Pill thin out the lining of the woman's uterus (the endometrium).[48] As a result, the baby may not be able to implant. At other times the child will attach to the wall, but he or she will be unable to survive because the normally thick and healthy uterine wall has shriveled and is therefore unable to nourish the baby. The Pill also impacts the woman's progesterone level. This causes the lining of the uterus to break down and eventually shed as it would in a menstrual cycle, further denying the baby's attempt to implant.

Many doctors are concerned about the fact that women often are not informed that the birth control pill can cause an abortion as well as prevent pregnancy. One medical journal declared,

> If any mechanism of any OC [Oral Contraceptive] violates the morals of any particular woman, the failure of the physician or care provider to disclose this information would effectively eliminate the likelihood that the woman's consent was truly informed and

would seriously jeopardize her autonomy. Furthermore, there is a potential for negative psychological impact on women who believe human life begins at fertilization, who have not been given informed consent about OCs, and who later learn of the potential for postfertilization effects of OCs. The responses to this could include disappointment, anger, guilt, sadness, rage, depression, or a sense of having been violated by the provider.[49]

Unfortunately, not all doctors are aware that the Pill can act as an abortifacient. Dr. Walter Larimore admitted that he prescribed the Pill for nearly twenty years—and used it in his own marriage —before anyone informed him that it could have such an effect. When another doctor clued him in, he said that he had never heard of such a thing, and that the claims seemed to be "outlandish, excessive, and inaccurate."[50] He began a search of the medical literature, "to disprove these claims to my partner, myself, and any patients who might ask about it." However, what he discovered compelled him to stop using the Pill in his medical and personal life. Reviewing the information, he realized how many doctors (and patients) were ignorant of the abortifacient potential of the Pill. It was a humbling realization, considering that ever since the 1970s, the patient package insert for birth control pills explained how the drug reduces the likelihood of implantation.[51] After informing his colleagues, Dr. Larimore noted, "several said that they thought it would change the way family physicians informed their patients about the Pill and its potential effects."[52]

Because many physicians felt that it was unfair to leave women in the dark, some of them submitted a proposal to the American Medical Association (AMA) calling for a vote on whether doctors should tell patients that birth control pills can act as abortifacients. However, in 2001 the AMA voted overwhelmingly against the proposal.

One reason why certain doctors may not tell women about the abortifacient nature of the Pill is that some physicians do not believe that pregnancy begins with fertilization. Until the 1960s, when the Pill was invented, it had been taken for granted that the union of the sperm and egg signaled the beginning of pregnancy.

In 1963 even the United States government published health information declaring that anything that impairs life between the moment of fertilization and the completion of labor is to be considered an abortion.[53]

Because many women would never have agreed to use a drug or device that could cause an early abortion, those in favor of such contraceptives knew that the issue had to be resolved. In 1964 a Planned Parenthood doctor speaking of another type of abortifacient birth control recommended that scientists not "disturb those people for whom this is a question of major importance." He added that judges and theologians trust the medical community, and "if a medical consensus develops and is maintained that pregnancy, and therefore life, begins at implantation, eventually our brethren from the other faculties will listen."[54]

One year later the American College of Obstetricians and Gynecologists (ACOG) decided to redefine pregnancy. In its words, "conception is the implantation of a fertilized ovum."[55] Instead of defining conception as fertilization, ACOG decided that life begins nearly a week later, at implantation. At the time they said that this was because pregnancy could not be detected before then. Today science is able to detect pregnancy before implantation,[56] but the ACOG still won't correct its definition. The original change had nothing to do with a scientific discovery in women's health, reproduction, or biology. Unfortunately, doctors today are split on the issue.[57]

Regardless of a doctor's personal opinions, few women are ever informed about this issue. Feminist author Germaine Greer wrote, "Whether you feel that the creation and wastage of so many embryos is an important issue or not, you must see that the cynical deception of millions of women by selling abortifacients as if they were contraceptives is incompatible with the respect due to women as human beings."[58]

Sometimes, all of the Pill's mechanisms fail to prevent pregnancy and successful implantation. It is often said that with optimum use of the Pill, it should have an effectiveness rate of 99 percent. Therefore, it is said to have a "method" failure rate of about

1 percent. However, in typical use the rates change significantly. This can be caused by many things, such as a woman's forgetting to take her pill or taking it at the wrong time of the day. Thus the actual rate, called the "typical" or "user" failure rate.

For the first year of use for women under the age of twenty, the Pill has an annual failure rate of 8 to 13 percent.[59] One study that followed sexually active teenage girls on the Pill found that 20 percent of them became pregnant within six months![60] The typical failure rate of the Pill has been shown to vary according to such factors as a woman's age, race, marital status, education, and economic status. For example, one large study showed that poor teenage girls who lived with their boyfriends had a 48 percent chance of getting pregnant during their first year on the Pill, whereas a wealthy married woman over the age of thirty had a 3 percent chance of pregnancy.[61]

There are numerous health risks in taking the Pill, since it contains potent synthetic hormones. According to the drug information that is included in birth control pills, the user may experience the following side effects: heart attack, blood clot, stroke, liver cancer, breast cancer, gallbladder disease, headache, bleeding irregularities, ectopic pregnancy, weight gain, mental depression, yeast infection, changes to the curvature of the eye, excessive hair growth in unusual places, loss of scalp hair, acne, partial or complete loss of vision, and more.[62] Some of these adverse reactions are rare, and others are more common, depending upon the type of pill and the particular woman who takes it.

The risk of breast cancer is especially worrisome for young women, since twenty-one of twenty-three studies of women who took the Pill prior to having their first child showed an increased risk of breast cancer.[63] The increase was especially steep among younger women. The World Health Organization and even the companies that sell birth control pills also admit that the drug can increase a woman's risk of breast cancer.[64]

The birth control pill also has been shown to increase a woman's level of SHBG (sex hormone binding globulin),[65] which decreases the amount of testosterone available in her body. This is one reason birth control pills are sometimes prescribed to treat acne. A decrease in free testosterone in a woman's body may decrease the severity of acne. However, when testosterone is decreased, so is the woman's sex drive.

It used to be thought that this undesirable side effect would be reversible. However, research published in *The Journal of Sexual Medicine* showed levels of SHBG twice as high as normal among women a year after they went off the Pill. The authors stated, "Long-term sexual, metabolic, and mental health consequences might result as a consequence of chronic SHBG elevation." [66] In an article entitled "Can taking the pill dull a woman's desire forever?" the same scientists feared, "There's the possibility it is imprinting a woman for the rest of her life." [67]

When women take the Pill for a long period of time, their risk of heart disease may be increased even after they go off the Pill. When this discovery was made, a cardiologist from Johns Hopkins University said, "What would I tell my daughter to do? I might suggest maybe not oral contraception." [68]

Recent studies also suggest that if a woman becomes pregnant with a boy while taking the Pill, her son may be more likely to develop prostate cancer. This is because the synthetic hormones can deform the male prostate in developing baby boys. One researcher noted that the chemicals in the Pill are "extremely potent synthetic sex hormones, strong enough to completely control an adult woman's reproductive system. . . . The developing fetus is extremely sensitive to chemical disturbance . . . so exposing a male baby to them is a very bad idea." [69] Considering the failure rate of the pill and the number of women taking it worldwide, more than one million boys may be affected each year. Since this discovery is new, further research will need to be conducted in order to confirm and measure this risk.

Other studies suggest that the birth control pill can affect who you're attracted to. Here's what some scientists are saying: Many animal species have pheromones, which are odorless chemicals that can signal their availability, arousal, or sexual receptivity. This chemical can be detected by what's called the vomeronasal organ (VMO), located in the nose. You may have heard that when women live together in close proximity, their menstrual cycles often begin to synchronize. Some have theorized that pheromones may play a role in this, because they can have an effect on hormones.

In animal studies, researchers have discovered that pheromones also play a role in mate selection. For example, a female mouse tends to choose a mate that has MHC genes that are least like her own. MHC (major histocompatibility complex) is a segment of our DNA that plays a role in the immune system, and it can be detected through pheromones in mice. By selecting a mate with the MHC genes most different from her own, the offspring of the mouse is given a greater variety of MHC molecules, thus strengthening its immune system and increasing its odds of survival. It's one of nature's ways of ensuring offspring with superior immune systems.

Because of these interesting findings, scientists have set out to determine if a similar mechanism is at work in human mate selection. Preliminary findings based on a woman's preference of a man's scent show that women also prefer mates who have MHC genes that are least similar to their own.[70]

How does this all relate to the birth control pill? Women on the Pill have been shown to prefer the scent of men whose MHC genes are *most* similar to their own. So if a woman on the Pill mates with a man who has similar MHC genes, their offspring may have an inferior immune system. The explanation given for the change in the woman's preferences is that the Pill causes a woman's body to think that it is pregnant, and pregnant women tend to prefer the scents of family and relatives. Some women even reported that they felt less attracted to the men they were seeing after going off the Pill. Other researchers have proposed that because a woman's fertility is interrupted when she is on the Pill, it alters her own pheromones. This, in turn, makes her less desirable to men, or so the theory goes.[71] While such research is interesting, it is still widely debated.

According to the *Textbook of Contraceptive Practice*, the Pill causes more than 150 biological changes in a woman.[72] Some of these changes are drastic, and others are hardly noticeable. For example, one study showed that women using oral contraceptives blink 32 percent more often than nonusers.[73] The reason for this may be that the chemicals in the Pill can decrease the hydration of the woman's eye. The Pill also can cause a slight change in the shape of her eyeball, making the cornea steeper. These side effects could explain why women on the birth control pill often complain that their contact lenses have become uncomfortable. Undoubtedly science has not fully grasped the many ways in which birth control pills interfere with a woman's delicate and majestic physiology.

Despite the possible side effects, birth control pills remain the most popular form of contraception for American women.[74] In turn, they have become a lucrative business. For example, one popular pill called Ortho Tri-Cyclen registered $715 million in sales in 2003.[75] Considering that it is only one of dozens of brands available, you can imagine the immense profits being made.

## Condoms

The condom is one of the more popular forms of birth control, but few people are aware of its disadvantages and failure rate. Young people often believe that the condom has a 99 percent effectiveness rate in preventing pregnancy. This figure is partly based upon laboratory tests that calculate the size of a man's sperm as compared to the pores in a latex condom. During the laboratory testing, condoms are filled with water and air and checked for leaks. These experiments are charming, but their results are unrealistic. In fact, between 14 and 23 percent of teenage girls (and 15 percent of women in the general population) become pregnant during their first year of relying upon the condom as birth control.[76] The newly created female condom is estimated to have an even higher failure rate.[77] That's one reason why even Planned Parenthood's research institute had to admit that most high school pregnancies are caused by contraceptive failure, not by the failure to use contraceptives.[78]

Safe sex advocates argue that this high number should be blamed on incorrect condom use. It can't be denied that incorrect usage of the condom contributes to higher failure rates.[79] But considering the fact that health experts recommend up to twenty-four steps for proper condom use, it's misleading and irresponsible to tell anyone that the condom will prevent pregnancy 99 percent of the time. Is a teenager who can't remember to take his sack lunch out of the refrigerator supposed to follow two dozen safety precautions for optimum contraceptive use?

Some say that the solution is to educate youth about proper condom use. But after decades of sex ed in high schools, the results have been underwhelming. According to one university doctor, "the most recent study of heterosexual college students showed that less than half had used a condom during their last vaginal intercourse, and that was an all time high!"[80] Among those who did use "protection," the numbers are also dismal. In the journal *Sexually Transmitted Diseases*, a study showed that three out of four college men did not properly use condoms, despite the fact that more than 80 percent of them received sex education.[81]

Similar results have appeared across the globe. For example, the *British Medical Journal* published the results of a "rigorous evaluation" of a sex ed program in Scotland. The program had been in use for three years, but the scientists discovered that it did not delay sexual intercourse, improve use of contraceptives, or reduce pregnancies or abortions. However, the government decided to continue the program. Why? One reason was that the students reported feeling less regret about the first time they slept with their most recent partner.[82]

In England sex education has also flopped. In 1999 a £15 million government drive was implemented to promote sex ed. Students were offered free condoms and morning-after pills, while being taught "safe sex" in schools. However, as of March 2004, STD rates had increased by 62 percent, while teen pregnancies were also up, with some areas experiencing a 34 percent leap. Overall the greatest increases were in areas where the government had implemented its program.[83]

Those in favor of the disastrous program countered the numbers by saying that the program will take another five years to complete, because "it takes sustained action over a long period of time to achieve the societal and behavioral changes required." They added that the increased rate of pregnancies "highlights the importance of strengthening implementation of our Teenage Pregnancy Strategy."[84] In other words, "Don't bother us with the facts. We'd rather cling to our ideologies at the expense of the next generation."

Considering the fact that a woman can get pregnant only a few days out of the month, while an STD can be transmitted at any time, it is not surprising that condom distribution has not stemmed the tide of the STD epidemic. In fact, every STD in the world can be transmitted while using a condom correctly and consistently. While the condom may reduce the risk of some infections, it eliminates the risk of none.

One reason for this may be the inadequacy of the condom itself. The FDA requirements say that no more than one condom in 250 can fail a leakage test.[85] Do the math: When the United States donated eight hundred million condoms to developing nations in 1990, the condom companies could have included 3.2 million defective condoms in the batch! But it gets worse: Globally those who promote "safe sex" say that the world needs twenty-four billion condoms every year in order to be protected.[86] If they had their wish, and each government ensured that condoms were at least as reliable as those produced in America (which they are not),[87] there could be ninety-six million defective condoms being used every year.

The reliability of the condom also depends upon the manufacturer. For example, when *Consumer Reports* studied the quality of twenty-three different kinds of condoms, they discovered that Planned Parenthood, the nation's largest abortion provider, made the worst type.[88] One of their brands received the equivalent of an "F" in the two standards measured: reliability and strength. The FDA tries to prevent defective condoms from reaching consumers. However, corporations have been caught selling them to other nations after the FDA rejected them.[89]

Even if a condom is manufactured properly, it may be damaged before it reaches the consumer. Condom companies recommend that the product should be stored at room temperature (59–86 degrees), because excessive heat or cold can weaken the latex. However, some condom manufacturers have been known to leave boxes of condoms outside in freezing temperatures or in trucks where the temperature reaches well over 100 degrees.[90] Even if the consumer receives a condom that has been stored at ideal temperatures, it still has about an 8 percent chance of breaking or slipping during intercourse.[91]

While the failure rate of condoms is a common topic of debate, few people ever hear of the condom's harmful effects. In order to understand the problem with condom use, one must first understand the beneficial effects of semen for the woman's body. For example, a man's seminal fluid includes at least two dozen ingredients, including estrogens, follicle-stimulating hormone, luteinizing hormone, testosterone, transforming growth factor beta, and several different prostaglandins. During intercourse the female's body absorbs these[92] and they aid the health of the woman.[93]

Scientists from the State University of New York also discovered that women whose partners don't use condoms are less likely to be depressed. They argued that the reason for this is because several mood-altering hormones from the man, including testosterone, are absorbed into the woman's body and can be detected in her bloodstream within hours of intercourse. The scientists added that such findings are not an excuse for unprotected sex.[94] Heaven forbid!

Furthermore, when a man and woman have intercourse, the woman's body becomes accustomed to the man's sperm.[95] In medical terms, her immune system develops a gradual tolerance to the antigens on his specific type of sperm and seminal fluid. For several hours after intercourse, a woman's immune cells will collect and transfer a man's foreign proteins and entire sperm cells from her cervix to her lymph nodes, where her immune system learns to recognize his genes.[96]

However, if the couple decides to use a barrier method of birth control for an extended period of time before having children, the womb will not be accustomed to the sperm, and the woman's immune system may treat them as foreign bodies. This can disrupt the delicate balance of hormones and cause the woman's blood vessels to constrict, leading to higher blood pressure in the expectant mother.[97] This condition (preeclampsia) occurs in about 5 to 8 percent of all pregnancies and can lead to premature delivery of the baby. Unfortunately, pre-term babies are more likely to experience learning disabilities, cerebral palsy, epilepsy, blindness, and deafness. Preeclampsia can also be dangerous for the mother: it is the third leading cause of maternal death during childbirth.[98]

It has been demonstrated that a man's semen offers a protective effect against preeclampsia, because it makes the woman's immune system more likely to recognize his baby. According to *The Journal of the American Medical Association*, preeclampsia is more than twice as common in women who used barrier methods of contraception.[99] So in a certain sense, couples who use the condom are having *unprotected* sexual intercourse, because the man is not protecting the woman's body with the beneficial effects of his semen.[100]

As you can see, a woman's body is created to work with a man's in a precise way. When we tinker with God's designs, and try to flip fertility on and off like a light switch, we create more problems for ourselves.

## Depo-Provera ("The Shot") and Lunelle

Depo-Provera is an injection given to women every three months in order to prevent pregnancy. Lunelle was a drug similar to Depo-Provera, and was injected once a month. However, two short years after the FDA approved its use in 2000, Lunelle was recalled by its manufacturer (Pharmacia), and it is no longer available.

One way Depo-Provera works is by reducing a woman's chances of ovulating. However, since it changes the lining of the uterus, it also can cause early abortions when breakthrough ovulation occurs.[101] With perfect use the effectiveness of the shot in preventing pregnancy is very high—about 99 percent. But with typical use 3 percent of women become pregnant each year.[102]

Few drugs have a more controversial history than Depo-Provera. In the 1950s a scientist for the pharmaceutical company Upjohn was experimenting with the hormone progesterone, and he created depomedroxyprogesterone acetate (Depo-Provera). By 1960 the company received FDA approval for the drug as a treatment for endometriosis and habitual miscarriages. However, ten years later the FDA revoked this approval because there was no evidence that the drug worked. Instead it seemed to cause heart defects in babies. But while the drug was being tested on women in Brazil, researchers discovered that it was also able to prevent pregnancy.[103]

As a result of this finding, Upjohn decided to seek approval for the drug as a contraceptive. Studies began on rats, and results looked promising. The FDA granted the drug Investigative Drug Status. This means that it appeared safe based upon previous animal studies, and so research could continue on other animals—and humans. Despite the fact that the drug was still in the early testing phase, doctors from Jamaica to Los Angeles were already prescribing it to women as the newest contraceptive.[104]

By 1965 the drug was being tested on women in foreign countries. A few years later studies began on dogs, monkeys, and over ten thousand women in Atlanta (a disproportionate number of whom were poor and black). The dogs developed breast cancer, and the monkeys developed endometrial cancer. But as for the women in Atlanta, no annual reports were given to the FDA, as required. After eleven years investigators went to assess the situation because of "something funny going on."[105] What they discovered was that women were not given adequate information about the side effects, consent forms were absent, and women with medical conditions were given the shot despite the fact that the drug could endanger their health. Some women died of cancer, and others committed suicide (depression is now a well-known side effect of Depo-Provera). Researchers lost track of most of the women in the study, and the research was disregarded.[106]

Years later researchers studied more women from the same area in Atlanta. However, this time they followed up with the women (again, most of whom were poor and black). The scientists showed that about half of the women quit taking the shot after a year. Their main reason was that they were displeased with the side effects. Nonetheless, the summary of this research was entitled "Depo-Provera: an excellent contraceptive for those who continue to use it."[107] Today African-American women continue to be the primary targets of those who promote Depo-Provera, and they are twice as likely to use the drug as white women.[108] Likewise, the poorer a woman is, the more likely she is to be prescribed Depo-Provera.[109]

Because Depo-Provera was found to cause cancer in beagles, veterinarians stopped giving it to dogs, and the animal version of the drug (Promone) was taken off the market.[110] Testing continued on women, however. A member of the FDA's Bureau of Drugs testified, "Animal data for this drug is more worrisome than any other drug we know of that is being given to well people."[111] Unfazed, the pharmaceutical company pushed the drug overseas. According to the makers of the drug, they paid government officials, hospital employees, and others more than $4 million in the early 1970s in order to secure sales of Depo-Provera internationally.[112]

Despite urgings from those in favor of the shot, the FDA denied approval of Depo-Provera at least three times because of safety concerns for both mother and child.[113] Meanwhile, the drug was being used on millions of women in over ninety countries, such as Nigeria, Belize, Honduras, El Salvador, Costa Rica, Thailand, India, and other developing nations.[114] Reports of liver cancer, decreased bone mass, and children born with extra or missing fingers didn't help Upjohn's prospects of legalizing the drug in America.

However, in 1991 the World Health Organization published the most comprehensive research of the time, reporting no increased risk of cancer of the liver, ovaries, or cervix. It even demonstrated a protective effect against endometrial cancer. However, breast cancer risk was doubled in the first five years of use. With this new research Upjohn again asked the FDA to approve the drug in 1992. Numerous groups protested, including the National Women's Health Network, the National Black Women's Health Project, and the National Latina Health Organization. Despite their objections, the FDA approved the drug in October 1992.

At the time, the acting president of Planned Parenthood was ecstatic, calling the approval "a very exciting development that is long overdue."[115] Many women did not share his enthusiasm. Since the approval in 1992, many women's groups have united to request that the FDA impose a moratorium on the use of the shot.[116] While many women do not experience serious side effects from Depo, other women have gone off the drug, saying, "This hideous poison should never have made it out of the lab."[117]

Even after the FDA's approval of the drug, many countries were still hesitant to license it. In 1991 Canadian women's groups and various health associations petitioned their government to keep the drug out of the country. They wrote, "We urge the government to stand by their decision of 1988, and to remain committed to protecting the health and safety of Canadian women." Aware of the side effects of Depo-Provera, advocates of women's health were especially concerned about the fact that the shot was "currently being prescribed to teenagers, the physically and mentally disabled, immigrant, Native and Inuit women without their informed consent."[118]

Unfortunately, these protests were not heeded, and the drug was approved for use in Canada in 1997. But by 2005 women seeking compensation for their suffering brought a class-action lawsuit of $700 million against the makers of the drug.[119] Some of them suffered early osteoporosis and bone fractures, needed knee replacements, and complained that they were never warned about the drug's ability to thin a woman's bones. One of the attorneys involved in the lawsuit mentioned that he was defending a woman in her twenties who may need a hip replacement.

Nowadays Depo-Provera is made by the pharmaceutical company Pfizer. That name might ring a bell. Pfizer is also being sued because of the heart attacks, deaths, and birth defects attributed to other drugs they manufacture, such as Zoloft and Celebrex.

Objections to Depo-Provera span the globe. Women's groups in India requested a complete ban on the shot, which had been approved for marketing in their country before the necessary safety trials had been completed. They wrote, "In a country where a large percentage of women in the reproductive age suffer from anemia, irregular and heavy bleeding can have catastrophic consequences. Studies have shown that injectable contraceptives like Depo-Provera can also lead to osteoporosis. This can have grave consequences for poor women with low bone density due to poor nutritional status. . . . The evidence available is already damning and it would be unethical to subject more women to clinical trials with these contraceptives."[120]

According to India's *Economic and Political Weekly*, one reason the FDA approved Depo-Provera was that the U.S. was concerned with population control in third world countries, whose governments were hesitant to approve a drug that was not even licensed in the country that created it.[121] Thankfully the women's groups in India won a victory for women's health in 2002, when the Indian government cancelled its plan to introduce Depo-Provera through the government health services systems.[122]

In September 2004 the makers of Depo-Provera received more

bad news about their drug: it increases a woman's risk of contracting certain STDs. According to the journal *Sexually Transmitted
Diseases*, when a woman takes the shot, she triples her chances of
being infected with gonorrhea and chlamydia (which can sterilize
a woman).[123] The scientists speculated that the increased disease
risk might be caused by the drug's interference with a woman's
immune system or by its ability to assist the growth of infections.

Regardless of how it makes a woman more susceptible to disease, the discovery is troubling. For example, when the drug is
used in certain population control programs, many women do
not have access to modern health care services. Interestingly, the
study that discovered this STD link was funded in part by the
U.S. Agency for International Development (USAID), who provided over forty million units of Depo-Provera to developing nations, especially in Africa.[124] Undoubtedly the women who used
it were unaware of the Depo-Provera–STD connection and were
probably also ignorant of the fact that infection with gonorrhea
or chlamydia makes a woman up to five times as likely to contract
HIV, if exposed.[125]

Disappointingly, the makers of the shot deny any STD connection, stating on their Web site, "There is no proof from clinical
studies that shows Depo-Provera increases your risk of acquiring a
sexually transmitted disease."[126] Unfortunately, as of 2008, Pfizer
still has not corrected its Web site, despite the fact that the con-
tradictory research was published in 2004.

Two months after the STD connection was discovered, Depo-
Provera received more bad press when the FDA slapped a "black
box" warning on the label.[127] According to the FDA, "a 'black
box' warning is the most serious warning placed in the labeling
of a prescription medication."[128] In the case of the shot, it was
required because the medicine can cause irreversible bone loss in
women, which can lead to osteoporosis. The researchers who discovered this noticed the effects in girls as young as twelve. This
is especially problematic for young women, because the teenage
years are a critical time for bone development. After years of
receiving birth control injections as a teen, a girl in her early
twenties could have the bones of a fifty- to sixty-year-old. How-

ever, the same year that the shot received the black box warning, the makers of the drug raked in $200 million in revenue from it. [129]

Because of the concerns of bone loss, Pfizer and the FDA now say that the shot should never be used for longer than two years, unless a woman has no other option. In regard to side effects, the above information is only the beginning. According to the makers of the shot, here are some of the other potential side effects of the drug: [130]

Young women who have taken the shot in the last four years are more than twice as likely to develop breast cancer.

Children born to women on Depo-Provera are more likely to have webbed toes and fingers, and chromosomal anomalies. The boys are twice as likely to have genital deformities, and the baby girls are more likely to suffer masculinizing effects of the drug's chemicals, causing genital abnormalities. Babies conceived to women on Depo-Provera may be at an increased risk of low birth weight, which is associated with an increased risk of neonatal death. (Research not done by the makers of the shot reports that infants exposed to the shot while in their mother's wombs were 80 percent more likely to die in their first year of life.) [131]

Depo-Provera can pass through a mother's breast milk to her child. Most studies do not show adverse effects on the baby. However, one study of women who took the shot two days after the delivery of their baby showed it had substantial consequences. The babies in this group had a 75 percent higher incidence of infectious diseases visits to the doctor in their first year of life.

Women on Depo-Provera tend to experience weight gain according to how long they have been on the drug: five pounds in the first year, eight by the second, fourteen by the fourth, and over sixteen pounds by the sixth year.

Many women on the shot stop having periods after one year of use. However, when a woman goes off the shot, the menstrual period "will usually, in time, return to its normal cycle."

Many women who take the shot will be able to become pregnant soon after stopping the injections. Sometimes, there is a delay in the return of fertility. For example, about half are unable to conceive within ten months of their last injection. Seventeen percent were unable to get pregnant after fifteen months off the shot, and 7 percent were still not able to conceive after eighteen months.

Other side effects include menstrual irregularities, abdominal pain, dizziness, headache, fatigue, nervousness, backache, breast pain, leg cramps, depression, bloating, nausea, rash, insomnia, acne, joint pain, convulsions, numbness, coughing up blood, severe allergic reactions, spontaneous flow of breast milk, darkening of the facial skin, urinary infections, cysts, chest pain, anemia, artery blockage in the lung, loss of consciousness related to temporary insufficient blood flow to the brain, shortness of breath, fever, excessive sweating and body odor, dry skin, excessive thirst, blood disease, rectal bleeding, nipple bleeding, prevention of lactation (breast milk), paralysis, facial nerve damage, skin disease, excessive uterine growth, varicose veins, painful cramps, no hair growth or excessive hair growth in unusual places, and blood clots.

Depo-Provera is well known for decreasing a woman's sex drive. Because of its ability to kill a person's libido, the shot is sometimes injected into child molesters as a punishment![132] In California, the State Senate ruled that "The parolee shall begin medroxyprogesterone acetate [Depo-Provera] treatment one week prior to his or her release from confinement in the state prison or other institution and shall continue treatments until the Department of Corrections demonstrates to the Board of Prison Terms that this treatment is no longer necessary."[133] So the drug that is too dangerous for dogs but just right for sex offenders is offered to women at their local Planned Parenthood clinic!

## The Intrauterine Device (IUD) & Intrauterine System (IUS)

The Intrauterine Device is a T-shaped device inserted into the woman's uterus. Although it is not the most common contraceptive in America, it is the world's most widely used form of reversible birth control. [134] There have been several different kinds of IUDs, but only two are currently approved for use in the United States, ParaGard and Mirena. Before ParaGard was introduced in the 1980s, millions of women had used other kinds of IUDs.

One popular version in the 1970s was called the Dalkon Shield, which was owned by a company that also made flea collars and press-on nails. [135] The Dalkon Shield was a thumbnail-sized plastic device with a string dangling below it that could be used to remove it from a woman's uterus. In order to demonstrate its safety and effectiveness, a doctor from Johns Hopkins Medical School tested the product on over six hundred women. However, this doctor later admitted that the studies were intentionally skewed, and that he had a conflict of interest: he received a percentage of the profits on its sales. [136]

Its manufacturers vehemently defended the safety of the product and began marketing it in 1971, wildly exaggerating its effectiveness. Not surprisingly, it didn't take long for complaints to surface. Six weeks after sales of the Shield began, a doctor wrote to the manufacturer, "I have just inserted my tenth Dalkon Shield and have found the procedure to be the most traumatic manipulation ever perpetrated upon womanhood. . . . I have ordered all Shields out of my office and will do the same in all clinics with which I am affiliated." [137] Health experts requested that the IUD be taken off the market, but the company, A. H. Robins, refused to halt distribution, saying that such a move would "be a 'confession of liability,' and Robins would lose many of the pending lawsuits." [138] Thankfully the FDA prevailed in 1974, and the IUD was taken off the market.

Hundreds of thousands of women experienced injury from using the Dalkon Shield. Part of the problem was that the string that dangled beneath the device acted as a wick for bacteria to ascend into a woman's uterus. Injuries included life-threatening pelvic infections, hospitalization, sterility, hysterectomy, and babies born with cerebral palsy, blindness, and mental retardation. At least twenty deaths were also reported,[139] not including the thousands of babies who were miscarried or stillborn.[140]

A few years before the contraceptive was yanked off the shelves, the manufacturers knew that their U.S. market would be dwindling. So they started "dumping." This means that they began selling mass quantities of the device at wholesale prices to developing nations through a government organization, the U.S. Agency for International Development (AID). Groups that worked with AID, such as Planned Parenthood, distributed hundreds of thousands of Dalkon Shields to women across the globe.[141] However, when the makers of the device were forced to take their product off the market in the United States, AID had to issue an international recall. Unfortunately, the product continued to be used in many countries.[142]

Because of the lawsuits that began to pile up, the maker of the Dalkon Shield asked all doctors to remove any remaining ones from their patients. But the warning came too late: victims of the product were seeking justice, and over $12 billion in lawsuits were filed.[143] By the mid-1980s A. H. Robins filed for Chapter 11 bankruptcy protection, because more than 327,000 women filed injury claims against the company.[144] During the legal battles it was discovered that A. H. Robins knew that their contraceptive could cause life-threatening infections but withheld and even destroyed some of the evidence.[145] One Chief U.S. district judge, who heard over four hundred cases against the Shield in Minnesota, reprimanded the corporate leaders of the drug company and said he hoped that his statement "burns its mark into your souls."[146]

One New York woman who was accidentally sterilized for life by the Dalkon Shield recalled receiving it from Planned Parenthood as a college student. She sued and later reported in *The New York Times*, "I won the arbitration. But the victory doesn't help when we look at friends with their children and wonder what our own kids would have been like."[147] Since the drug was distributed in over eighty countries to an estimated 4.5 million women, the majority of women who suffered from the Dalkon Shield never will have had the chance to seek compensation for their pain and loss.

Because the IUD has such a sordid past, it has not been popular among American women. In the 1980s most IUD manufactures quit marketing their products in the United States because of the rising cost of lawsuits and the decreased interest in the products.[148] However, in 1984 a new IUD was approved by the FDA, ParaGard. This contraceptive is a T-shaped piece of white plastic (polyethylene) wrapped with a copper wire. It irritates the lining of the uterus, causing it to release leukocytes and prostaglandins that are toxic to the sperm and egg. This reduces the chances of fertilization. However, it does not stop the woman from ovulating. Should conception occur, the IUD can also act as an abortifacient by keeping a newly conceived baby from implanting in the womb.[149] For this reason some women have used the IUD as a form of "emergency contraception" up to five days after intercourse.

ParaGard is estimated to be more than 99 percent effective, and it is safer than the Dalkon Shield. However, it is not without its own risks. According to the patient package insert for ParaGard, if a woman becomes pregnant while using it, "you may get a severe infection or shock, have a miscarriage or premature labor and delivery, or even die. Because of these risks, your healthcare provider will recommend that you have ParaGard removed, even though removal may cause miscarriage."[150]

Other possible side effects include pelvic inflammatory disease (which can lead to infertility, hysterectomy, or even death), dizziness, nausea, ectopic pregnancy, anemia, backache, cramps, allergic reaction, perforation of the uterus (causing infection, scarring, and damage to other organs, possibly requiring surgery to repair), and so on.[151]

The ParaGard IUD can remain in a woman for up to ten years,

and a healthcare professional can remove it before then if the woman wishes. However, sometimes the device gets stuck in the woman, requiring surgical removal. Despite the possible side effects, sales of ParaGard in 2004 totaled approximately $48 million.[152]

The difference between an IUD and an IUS (Intrauterine System) is that the IUS releases hormones, and the IUD does not. The first IUD with hormones was known as Progestasert, but this was only manufactured until 2001. Now the only version available is known as Mirena, which releases a hormone called levonorgestrel into the uterus. The T-shaped device is placed in a woman's uterus and can be left there for up to five years. According to its maker, "there is no single explanation of how Mirena works. It may stop release of your egg from your ovary, but this is not the way it works in most cases. It may block sperm from reaching or fertilizing your egg. It may make the lining of your uterus thin. We do not know which of these actions is most important for preventing pregnancy and most likely all of them work together."[153] Therefore, Mirena can prevent pregnancy and may also act as an abortifacient (by thinning the uterine lining and failing to stop ovulation).

Possible side effects or complications may include ectopic pregnancy, life-threatening infection, irregular bleeding, missed periods or a cessation of periods, pelvic inflammatory disease (which can lead to infertility, hysterectomy, or death), perforation of the uterus (which can cause internal scarring, infection or damage to other organs), severe cramping, dizziness, fainting, yellowing of the eyes or skin, ovarian cysts, stroke, and heart attack.[154]

Mirena is highly effective in preventing pregnancy (over 99 percent). However, if a woman becomes pregnant while using Mirena, she may experience severe infection, premature delivery, and even death. The doctor may attempt to remove Mirena, although this may cause a miscarriage.[155]

When a woman uses Mirena while breast-feeding, some of the hormones pass through the breast milk to the baby. Existing studies do not show any adverse side effects, but the World Health

Organization notes, "there are no data evaluating the effects of progestogen exposure via breast milk on brain and liver development."[156]

Not surprisingly, Mirena was used for years on millions of women in other countries before it was approved by the FDA in 2001. Just one year later, in the U.S. alone it raked in $36 million for its makers, and sales have continued to soar.[157]

## Morning-After Pill (Plan B Emergency Contraception)

Commonly known as "emergency contraception," the morning-after pill is a high dose of the birth control pill taken within seventy-two hours of intercourse, followed by a second dose twelve hours after the first. Sometimes it works as a contraceptive by delaying or stopping ovulation or by altering the transportation of the sperm or egg.[158] However, in order for the morning-after pill to prevent ovulation, the drugs need to be absorbed through the intestines, pass into the blood stream, travel to the brain, and tell the pituitary gland not to trigger the hormonal reaction that causes ovulation. By the time this process is completed, the baby's eye color, hair color, and entire genetic code could already be determined. Although the pill can be taken three days after intercourse, fertilization can happen less than three *hours* after intercourse. But the drug is still able to work because it alters the lining of the uterus so that it can reject the implantation of the baby.[159] An early abortion takes place, without the woman's knowledge that she was ever pregnant. However, the manner in which the drug works depends upon when it is taken, when the woman ovulates, and if pregnancy even occurs.

Unfortunately, women given the morning-after pill are not told of its abortifacient potential. In fact, advertisements for the pill proclaim that "if you take Plan B and are already pregnant, it will not affect your existing pregnancy."[160] How can they get away with saying this? They redefine pregnancy as something that begins with the successful implantation of the baby, instead of with fertilization. Interestingly, even some drug companies that make contraceptives do not agree with this definition. For example, the information packet included with one form of birth control refers to the fallopian tubes as the place "where a pregnancy begins before it moves into the uterus." [161]

With regard to its effectiveness, advertisements for the morning-after pill claim that it is 89 percent effective. Studies cited by the FDA show numbers ranging from 55 to 94 percent. [162] Meanwhile, the Plan B patient package insert claims that the drug reduces the risk of pregnancy by at least 75 percent. According to one of the drug companies that makes the morning-after pill, a woman has an 8 percent risk of getting pregnant through a single act of intercourse. But if she takes their emergency contraceptive, she only has a 1 percent risk. [163] (They add that the drug is more effective if is taken as soon as possible after intercourse.) Interestingly, these statistics mean that 92 percent of the women who use the morning-after pill would not have gotten pregnant anyway. Most women who take emergency contraception will never know if they would have gotten pregnant or if they terminated the life of their newly conceived child.

For years the proponents of "emergency contraception" claimed that it would reduce the number of unwanted pregnancies and surgical abortions. However, according to a review of twenty-three studies published in a 2007 issue of the journal *Obstetrics and Gynecology*, "to date, no study has shown that increased access to this method reduces unintended pregnancy or abortion rates." [164]

According to the prescribing information of the morning-after pill, side effects of the drug may include nausea, abdominal pain, headache, fatigue, dizziness, change in menstrual bleeding, vomiting, ectopic pregnancy, and more. [165]

## Norplant and Implanon

Norplant is the name given to a series of rods or capsules that a doctor surgically inserts into a woman's upper arm. The inserts release progestin into a woman's bloodstream in order to prevent the ovaries from releasing eggs. However, this mechanism only works some of the time.[166] The contraceptive device also thickens a woman's cervical mucus, so that the movement of sperm is inhibited. Finally, Norplant also changes the lining of the uterus,[167] which can cause abortions of babies who are conceived. The implants can last for two or five years, depending upon which kind of insert is used. The rods or capsules must be surgically removed.

The effectiveness of Norplant in preventing pregnancy is about 99 percent, although this figure may decrease with time. Also, if the woman does not have the system inserted at the proper time in her menstrual cycle, she may be more likely to become pregnant during the initial weeks of use. Since the drug is placed inside the woman's body, it does not have a high "typical" (or user) failure rate.

According to its patient package insert, its potential side effects include irregular menstrual bleeding (including prolonged bleeding or no bleeding), ruptured ovarian cysts, constant headaches, fainting, ruptured liver tumors, ectopic pregnancies, heart attacks, strokes, gallbladder disease, skeletal pain, nervousness, acne, blood clots, blindness, severe depression, birth defects, weight gain, excessive growth of body or facial hair, hair loss, coughing of blood, numbness, severe abdominal pain, yellowing of the eyeballs, and death. Because the contraceptive device is surgically inserted under the skin, some women experienced nerve injury and scarring, while others suffered from the implant unexpectedly being expelled from the skin.[168]

When a woman breast-feeds while using Norplant, some of the hormones pass through the milk to the infant. Such babies are at an increased risk of respiratory and eye infections.[169] Despite all of these possible risks, population workers in developing nations are told to inform women that Norplant has "no known serious side effects."[170]

The FDA approved Norplant in 1990, but within six years over fifty thousand women sued the makers of the drug.[171] In 1999 the makers of Norplant agreed to settle for a reported $50 million to compensate thirty-six thousand women for the complications they suffered from the contraceptive system. The drug company said the settlement "was purely a business decision," and it did not admit any wrongdoing.[172] By 2002 the company stopped production of the drug, and it was phased out of the American market by 2004.

However, in 2006 the FDA approved a contraceptive method similar to Norplant, called Implanon. Instead of a series of small rods, Implanon users only need one plastic rod inserted under the skin of the inner upper arm. The insert contains a hormone (etonogestrel) that is released into the woman's body over a three year period. It can be removed at any time but must be taken out after three years.

The implant is highly effective in preventing pregnancy: over 99 percent. To accomplish this, Implanon often stops the release of eggs from a woman's ovary and changes the cervical mucus to keep sperm from reaching the egg. It also changes the lining of the uterus.[173] So if the first two methods fail, the baby can be aborted because he or she is unable to attach to the uterus. As with other hormonal methods of birth control, it is misleading to consider a drug to be 99 percent effective in "preventing" pregnancy when terminated pregnancies are considered prevention.

Implanon it is not without its potential side effects. Users may experience changes in bleeding or no bleeding at all, mood swings, weight gain, headache, acne, depression, nervousness, breast pain, viral infections, stomach pain, painful periods, back pain, nausea, dizziness, extra hair on the face and body, spotty darkening of facial skin, ovarian cysts, blood clots, heart attack, stroke, crushing chest pain, numbness, yellowing of the skin or eyes, and an increased risk of ectopic pregnancy. The insert can also break while inside the woman or be accidentally expelled from her skin. Other times the rod may be difficult or impossible to remove.[174] These complications are not common, but the makers of the drug are required to warn all patients of the potential risks. The information packet included with the drug reminds women that they should call their healthcare provider right away if they faint, cough up blood, or become blind. Details are not given as to how she should make that phone call while unconscious or unable to see.

Even though Implanon is new in the United States, millions of women in other countries have used the product since 1998. Although the drug brought in $30 million in sales in 2005, the 2006 FDA approval is expected to stimulate much greater revenue. [175]

## NuvaRing

The NuvaRing is a thin, transparent, flexible ring that is inserted by a woman into her lower reproductive tract. It slowly secretes estrogen and progestin hormones to prevent pregnancy. It is used for three weeks, removed for a week, and then replaced with a new ring for another three weeks. During the week off, the woman usually experiences a withdrawal bleed, which is similar to a normal period. This pattern of use is continued as long as the woman wishes to contracept. When used perfectly, it is over 98 percent effective in preventing pregnancy. However, with typical use, it has an annual failure rate of 8 percent. [176]

Its method of action is similar to the birth control pill. According to the makers of the ring, it inhibits ovulation, changes the cervical mucus, and changes the endometrium, which reduces the likelihood of a baby implanting in the uterus. [177] So while it can act as a contraceptive, it also can work as an abortifacient.

Side effects of the ring include heart attack, blood clots, stroke, liver tumors, gallbladder disease, breast cancer, partial or complete loss of vision, retinal lesions, swelling of the optic nerve, forward displacement (bulging) of the eyes, double vision, headache, bleeding irregularities, ectopic pregnancy, yellowing of the skin or eyes, fluid retention, weight gain, emotional disorders, depression, toxic shock syndrome, respiratory tract infection, nausea, infected or inflamed sinuses, elevated blood pressure, bloating, cramps, facial skin discoloration, temporary infertility following treatment, fatigue, difficulty sleeping, rash, yeast infection, change in corneal curvature (steepening of the external eye), increased

PMS, cataracts, inflammation with lumps and reddening of the skin below the knees, skin eruptions, excessive hair growth in unusual locations, loss of scalp hair, impaired kidney function, acne, inflammation of the colon, coughing blood, crushing chest pain, problems with speech, numbness in limbs, fainting, or death.[178]

The hormones released by the ring also increase a woman's sex hormone binding globulin (SHBG). This side effect is likewise caused by birth control pills, and may cause permanent damage to a woman's sex drive.[179] While the makers of the ring admit that the drug will increase a woman's SHBG, they do not explain what this could mean for the patient.[180]

If a mother breast-feeds a child while she uses the ring, it may decrease the quality and quantity of her breast milk. Contraceptive steroid hormones also will pass to the baby through the milk. Adverse side effects for the infant include breast enlargement and jaundice (yellowing of the skin and eyes). Therefore, nursing mothers are advised not to use the drug until the child is weaned.[181]

Based on their research on hamsters and rats, it appears that the ring will not have a long-term negative impact on a woman's fertility.[182] But because the ring is new, its long-term side effects are uncertain. The makers of the ring assume that the complications will be similar to those that occur in women who use combination birth control pills (estrogen and progestin). Because of the absence of research, however, the drug company simply says that there is not enough data available to determine if the ring is more or less dangerous than the Pill.[183] We'll just have to wait and see.

We can hope that the drug will not remain on the market for long. In February 2007 a group representing more than a hundred thousand consumers petitioned the head of the FDA to ban "third generation" birth control pills that contain the same hormones in the ring, because of the increased risk of blood clots.[184]

Because of deaths and other injuries caused by NuvaRing, online forums against the device have been created. On these Web sites hundreds of women express their frustration and forewarn others. Lawsuits are beginning to mount against Organon, the maker of the NuvaRing. However, the company should have no problem paying off any claims, because Organon has made hundreds of millions of dollars in profit from their two contraceptives, NuvaRing and Implanon. [185]

## The Patch

The birth control patch (Ortho Evra) is a sticker that a woman applies to her body weekly. It is considered a "transdermal contraceptive" because the hormones in the patch pass through a woman's skin and into her bloodstream. Its mechanism to avoid pregnancy is similar to that of the birth control pill, so it too can prevent pregnancies or abort newly conceived babies. [186] With perfect use it is 99 percent effective in preventing pregnancy. However, with typical use it is estimated to have a failure rate of about 8 percent. [187]

When a woman receives the Patch from her doctor, she also receives a patient package insert that outlines many of the potential side effects. The Ortho Evra insert mentions that users of the patch may experience heart attack, stroke, blood clots, gallbladder disease, liver tumors, breast cancer, nausea, headaches, depression, weight gain, loss of scalp hair, and a host of other ailments. [188] It also mentions in passing that the estrogen in the drug will raise a woman's SHBG levels. As discussed above on the birth control pill, this may cause a long-term decrease in a woman's sex drive. [189]

Occasionally the manufacturer or the company that sells a particular drug will announce new warnings as they discover the need for them. For example, in November 2006 (five years after the patch was approved by the FDA), Johnson & Johnson, the company that sells the Patch, announced that women need to make sure they don't expose the Patch to heat. This could cause an unexpected surge of estrogen to be released from the product, which could lead to blood clots. If a blood clot reaches the brain, it can cause a stroke; if it reaches the heart, it can lead to heart attack; and if it reaches the lung, it is called a pulmonary embolism.

Since its approval in 2001, the Patch has stirred up enormous controversy. Headlines in 2004 reported that a New York fashion student using the patch suddenly collapsed in the subway and died. The medical examiner's office revealed that she died of a blood clot, caused by the hormones in Ortho Evra. In November of the same year, an eighth-grade girl from Wisconsin died from a blood clot in her pelvis caused by the Patch.[190]

Sadly, the drug company that manufactures the drug knew of these risks but preferred not to look into the matter. In 2003 the company refused to fund a study that would have compared the Patch to a pill it also makes. An internal company memo noted that the study was declined because of concerns there was "too high a chance that study may not produce a positive result for Evra" and there was a "risk that Ortho Evra may be the same or worse than Ortho-Cyclen."[191] Sure enough, women who use the Patch were later discovered to be more than twice as likely to develop dangerous blood clots as women who take the birth control pill.[192] Even though the drug company was not interested in publishing the shortcomings of their product, some caring gynecologists took the initiative. One doctor in California sent a note to several thousand patients recommending they get off the Patch.[193]

Eventually, Johnson & Johnson issued a warning to millions of women that the hormones released by the product may increase their risk of blood clots. This may be due to the fact that users of the Patch are exposed to about 60 percent more estrogen in their blood than women on birth control pills that contain thirty-five micrograms of estrogen.[194] After the label on the drug was changed, the makers of the Patch noted in their annual report to shareholders that, regrettably, the label change and the negative media coverage probably would have a negative impact on sales.[195]

The year of this shareholders' report, a nineteen-year-old named Amanda Bianchi developed a ten-inch blood clot in her brain and suffered two strokes. Her doctors said it was a direct result of using the Patch for three months. She told CNN, "I don't want any other woman to have to go through what I'm going through."[196]

In July 2005 the Associated Press reported details of one woman's death:

> Kathleen Thoren's family gathered around her in the intensive care unit, unable to speak to their beloved sister, daughter, wife, or even stroke her hands. The slightest stimulation might create a fatal amount of pressure on the twenty-five-year-old woman's swollen brain, warned the doctors. "We were horrified, but we tried to just quietly be with her," said her sister Erika Klein. "In the end, it didn't help." The mother of three died last fall, just after Thanksgiving, after days of agonizing headaches that the coroner's report said were brought on by hormones released into her system by Ortho Evra, a birth control patch she had started using a few weeks earlier. [197]

This woman's death was not an isolated event. The Associated Press reported in 2005 that it petitioned the FDA for a database containing sixteen thousand reports of adverse reactions to the Patch. Within the reports were twenty-three deaths associated with the Patch, seventeen of them clot-related. [198] However, the FDA admits that it receives reports of only between 1 and 10 percent of serious reactions. So the death toll may be significantly higher. In September 2006 a lawsuit was brought against Johnson & Johnson, pointing out that in a period of thirty-three months, Johnson & Johnson received notice of 27,974 adverse events associated with the Patch. [199]

Reading such information makes one understand why so many people are urging the FDA to take the drug off the market. One attorney pointed out, "The amount of estrogen in the Patch is comparable to a form of contraceptive pill that was banned by the Food and Drug Administration in 1988." [200]

To see a snapshot of the chaos the Patch has caused, all one needs to do is Google the terms "Ortho Evra" and "lawsuit" on the Internet. One will immediately find a litany of lawyers eager to represent injured women. Even a former executive of the company is suing them for firing him because he tried to recall the flawed product over safety concerns. [201] When handling Ortho Evra cases, many attorneys offer their services on a "contingency fee" basis. This means that you don't pay a dime unless they win your case.

It's no surprise that the attorneys are having a field day with the makers of the Patch. In August 2006 Johnson & Johnson told its shareholders, "There are approximately 500 claimants who have filed lawsuits or made claims regarding injuries allegedly due to Ortho Evra."[202] Three months later, the number of lawsuits had doubled to a thousand.[203] By the end of 2007, it reached approximately 4,000.[204] Johnson & Johnson mentioned, "The damages claimed are substantial, and . . . the Company is confident of the adequacy of the warnings and instructions."[205] In other words, when Johnson & Johnson arrives in court, it can tell the women: "We told you this could happen. Didn't you read the nine pages of prescribing information that came with your drug? You know —the one with over nineteen thousand words?"

The report to shareholders stated, "However, the Company believes that if any liability results from such cases, it will be substantially covered by existing amounts accrued in the Company's balance sheet and, where available, by third-party product liability insurance."[206] What this means is that despite all the money being lost by Johnson & Johnson in legal settlements, it is far more profitable for it to continue selling the Patch. In 2004, when about a dozen women on the Patch died from blood clots,[207] sales of the patch reached $420 million.[208] If you include its other contraceptives, Johnson & Johnson sold $1.3 billion worth of hormonal birth control in 2004![209] Including all forms of hormonal birth control, the contraceptive market is worth more than $6 billion.[210]

Despite the enormous profits being made, the litigation fees have pharmaceutical companies concerned. According to *The New York Times*, "fear of product liability suits has driven most companies out of research directed toward development of new birth control products."[211]

## RU-486 (Abortion Pill)

RU-486, technically known as Mifeprex, is a dose of pills that can be taken by a woman up to forty-nine days after the beginning of her last menstrual cycle in order to abort her baby. The drugs work by blocking the action of progesterone, which is necessary for sustaining a pregnancy. If the abortion has not already been confirmed within thirty-six to forty-eight hours after the woman takes her first three pills, she is given another two, called Cytotec (misoprostol). This completes the abortion by softening the cervix and causing uterine bleeding and contractions.

Before leaving the doctor's office after this second visit, the woman is given the name and number of the doctor who will be handling any emergencies caused by the drug. Two weeks after the initial visit, the doctor completes the treatment by confirming that an abortion has occurred. The makers of the drug say that "the existence of debris in the uterus following the treatment procedure will not necessarily require surgery for its removal."[212] The "debris" they mention includes the remains of the child. However, between 5 and 8 percent of women who take the drugs will require surgery to end the pregnancy or stop excessive bleeding.[213]

RU-486 is over 90 percent effective when used during the first seven weeks of pregnancy. If it fails, the woman is encouraged to have a surgical abortion. Should the baby survive the drug and the woman opt against a surgical abortion, the child often suffers mental or physical defects because of the chemicals in the drugs. These may include facial malformations, skull defects, delayed growth, and limb defects. Animal studies also showed that offspring exposed to the drug while in the womb experienced malformation of the ovaries, delayed puberty, deficient male sexual behavior, and other side effects.[214] The effect of the drug on breast-fed babies is unknown.

Sometimes RU-486 also takes the life of the mother. For example, a teenage girl named Holly Patterson was given the drug by Planned Parenthood in California and died of septic shock. Several days after taking the drug, she went to the hospital. The staff assured her that "her pain and bleeding were normal, and she was sent home with painkillers."[215] Three days later she returned to the hospital, where she died. Her father told reporters, "There's no quick fix for pregnancy, no magic pill. . . . They told her it was safe, and it killed her."[216] Following her passing, her parents wrote, "We will never be able to forget those last moments of her life when she was too weak to talk and could barely squeeze our hands in acknowledgment of our words of encouragement. 'We love you, Holly,' 'Just hang in there, the whole family is coming,' 'You fight this Holly, you can do it.' "[217] Holly died in September 2003, and by mid-2005 at least three other women in California were killed by the drug[218]—three of the four having received it from Planned Parenthood.[219] Deaths also have been reported in Canada, Sweden, and the United Kingdom.[220]

So far the only thing to change is the label of the drug (twice). In 2004 the FDA also issued a warning about the risks of RU-486, because it had received reports of 676 "adverse events" linked to the drug since its approval in 2000.[221] But the makers of the drug, Danco Laboratories, stand by their product. They acknowledge that abortions can increase a woman's chance of infections but say, "We do not believe that the Mifeprex and misoprostol regimen presents any special risk of infections."[222]

Holly Patterson died from sepsis, which is a severe illness caused by infection of the bloodstream. But RU-486 can have a number of lethal complications. For example, three months before Holly's death, a teenager in Sweden bled to death after taking the abortion drug. She didn't go to the hospital because she was told to expect her bleeding to last for two weeks. Meanwhile, an Iowa woman narrowly escaped death after losing one-half to two-thirds of her blood volume after the medical abortion.[223] Women also can die as a result of ruptured ectopic pregnancies. The family of one such woman in Tennessee is suing her abortion clinic for malpractice, claiming that they could have prevented her death had they diagnosed her correctly.[224]

In Canada the drug trials of RU-486 were suspended after it

killed a woman in 2001. Unfortunately, the United States has yet to ban the drug. Therefore, many citizens are pushing for the government to pass "Holly's Law," which would withdraw FDA approval of RU-486 and subject the drug to a thorough review, which it never received. According to Congressman Chris Smith of New Jersey, "RU-486 was rushed to approval for political purposes . . . and as a result numerous safety concerns were suppressed, trivialized and overlooked." [225] In 2006 Smith pleaded to Congress, "How many deaths, investigations and warnings will it take before RU-486 is properly labeled as lethal and removed from the market?" [226]

Advocates of the drug are quick to remind others that the number of deaths caused by the drug is small compared to the number of women who have used it. However, according to *The New England Journal of Medicine*, women who use RU-486 are approximately ten times as likely to die as women who undergo surgical abortions at the same time of pregnancy. [227]

Other side effects of RU-486 are common. In fact, the makers of the drug say, "Nearly all of the women who receive Mifeprex and misoprostol will report adverse reactions, and many can be expected to report more than one such reaction." [228] These may include heavy bleeding (which can last for a month or more, and sometimes necessitates blood transfusions), fatal septic shock, abdominal pain, cramping, nausea, headache, vomiting, dizziness, fatigue, back pain, uterine hemorrhage, viral infections, shaking, stomach pain, insomnia, leg pain, loss of consciousness, heart pounding, pelvic inflammatory disease, pelvic pain, hives, and more. No long-term studies have been done to assess the drug's cancer-causing potential.

Perhaps one of the worst complications from the abortion pill is the emotional toll it takes on the expectant mothers. Since a woman can take the drugs up until her seventh week of pregnancy, a woman who uses RU-486 sometimes experiences traumatic emotional consequences when the baby passes out of her body. Many of the women express resentment that they were not prepared for what they saw. On post-abortive support Web sites, users of RU-486 express their heartbreak. One woman said, "[I] wish someone had said there was a chance I would see it clearly and that I should prepare myself for what I was going to do."

Another woman grieved, "It's been a year and a half, but I can still remember how it looked and felt. . . . I held my baby in my hand. . . . Head, eyes, nose, arms, fingers. . . . I cried over it, kissed it. . . . (sigh) That was the worst part of all . . . I knew what she was. I couldn't fool myself. I stared at her for the longest time . . . felt like eternity. I will never forget that sight as long as I live."

Other women share her remorse, saying things such as, "I saw every feature perfectly. . . . It was very, very tiny . . . just stared at it . . . was in shock. . . . It's what I see when I go to bed . . . can never un-see what I saw . . . can't lose the image . . . don't know how to deal with this . . . haven't told anybody . . . horrifying . . . nightmares . . . lots of nightmares." At the sight of their unborn babies, other mothers stared in shock, not knowing what to do with the remains: "I . . . wrapped her in a piece of tissue . . . wish I'd taken her and buried her properly. . . can't forget just flushing my baby away. . . . I will never forgive myself for this, never ever." [229]

After one reads such accounts, one can only hope and pray that these women have indeed forgiven themselves and found healing in the tender and unconditional mercy of God. He knows the difficulties and fears that influenced their decisions. He was present with them during those terrible moments, and he alone can make them whole again.

## Spermicides

Literal "sperm killers," spermicides are chemicals that are used to immobilize and kill a man's sperm before it reaches the woman's egg. Spermicides are one of the oldest forms of birth control. An Egyptian papyrus dating from 1850 B.C. describes a mixture of dough and crocodile dung that was inserted into the woman in order to prevent pregnancy.[230] It would block the sperm and, because of its acidic nature, perhaps also act as a spermicide. In second-century Rome the writings of an ancient gynecologist named Soranus of Ephesus describe up to forty different spermicidal concoctions that could be created by mixing various fruits and nuts.[231] In the early 1930s, women's magazines even recommended using Lysol as a spermicide! To boost sales, some companies that manufactured athlete's foot medicine went so far as to recommend that women could use it as a contraceptive![232]

Nowadays the most common active ingredient in spermicides is nonoxynol-9 (which is also found in some household cleaning supplies and laundry detergents). Initially it was hoped that spermicides could help to prevent the spread of AIDS.[233] However, the opposite has proven to be the case. The FDA announced in 2003 that nonoxynol-9 can damage the female reproductive tract by causing microabrasions, thus making her more likely to contract HIV or other STDs.[234] Because of the impact it has in the woman's reproductive system, she is also more likely to have vaginal infections.

In a 2005 press release, Senator Tom Coburn said: "the FDA ignored scientific data that condoms and other contraceptives containing the spermicide nonoxynol-9 (N-9) increase HIV infection risk and actually recommended their use for HIV prevention. The new FDA recommendations finally correct this medically inaccurate and dangerous claim that the agency has long made regarding N-9."[235]

In preventing pregnancy, spermicides have an annual failure rate of 18 percent with perfect use. However, their typical failure rate in preventing pregnancy is even higher—about 29 percent.[236] They are often used in combination with another form of birth control, such as a condom or diaphragm. Some condom manufacturers include spermicides on their products. However, in 2005 *Consumer Reports* said that such products "have no additional benefit in preventing pregnancy, have a shorter shelf life, and may cause urinary tract infections in young women."[237] According to the World Health Organization, these products should no longer be promoted.[238] Spermicides can also cause itching, burning, irritation, urinary tract infections, yeast infections, and bacterial vaginosis.

## Sterilization Surgeries

Sterilization is a form of birth control that is intended to be permanent. The sterilization surgery for men is called a vasectomy. This is a procedure in which the tubes that transport a man's sperm (the vasa differentia) are surgically removed, severed, or clamped shut. Such procedures are highly effective in preventing pregnancy: over 99 percent.

Following a vasectomy, a man's testes will continue to produce millions of sperm each day. However, because the vasa differentia have been severed or blocked, the sperm have no natural way to be released. If the tubes are blocked, the pressure of backed-up sperm often causes a "blowout" of the epididymis, the tubes that hold sperm, which can be very painful. Inevitably sperm cells enter the bloodstream, where antibodies must be created to destroy them.

Post-vasectomy pain is a complaint among some men. Such pain can last for weeks or even years. Various treatments may provide relief. Some men receive another operation to remove the epididymis or testicles. Sometimes the vasectomy is reversed in order to lessen the pain. One man wrote, "I have lived the nightmare of chronic pain and autoimmune reactions since my own vasectomy in August of 1999. Nineteen surgeries and nerve blocks, 197 medications and other substances, and dozens of therapies that I have pursued in the interim have not resolved the pain I experience on a daily basis."[239] Most men do not experience such severe consequences from the operation. However, men who have vasectomies may be two-and-a-half times as likely to develop kidney stones.[240]

It is not uncommon for men who have vasectomies to regret their decision. Reduced marital satisfaction and feelings of remorse often follow the operation, and sometimes last indefinitely. Thankfully, many men are able to have the operation reversed. Unfortunately, the reversal procedure is far more expensive than the vasectomy.

A woman's sterilization surgery is more involved. Commonly referred to as having her "tubes tied," a tubal ligation means that the woman has her fallopian tubes severed and sealed. Other methods involve clamping the tubes shut (tubal occlusion), burning them (tubal cauterization), or entirely removing them (salpingectomy). Depending upon which type of sterilization is used and how much damage has been done to the woman's reproductive system, the procedure may or may not be reversible. Even when the operation is reversed, the woman is more likely to suffer an ectopic pregnancy in the future because of the damage to the fallopian tubes. These types of sterilizations have a very high rate of effectiveness in preventing pregnancy: over 99 percent.

Since these forms of female sterilization involve surgery, the risks are different than for other forms of birth control. For example, the woman may experience complications from the surgery, such as severe bleeding or pelvic infection. Sometimes the sterilization surgery can be fatal. According to Planned Parenthood, "the rate is about two deaths per 100,000 women who have a sterilization procedure performed."[241] Other resources, such as the *Encyclopedia of Medicine*, place the death rate at four per hundred thousand.[242] Female sterilization is the most common form of birth control in the world, with over a hundred million women having had the surgery.[243] So in order for a hundred million women to be sterilized, at least two thousand have died. The number is probably higher, because the "two deaths per 100,000" statistic is based on available data from the most recent and safest procedures, which have not always been available and even now are not always offered to women in developing nations (who are more than twice as likely to resort to sterilization).[244] These numbers also do not include deaths caused by sterilization-related ectopic pregnancies. Despite the fact that female sterilization surgeries are more expensive, invasive, and potentially dangerous than male vasectomies, sterilization procedures are between three and six times more common for women than men.[245]

Besides the physical complications, women who undergo sterilization often suffer from the guilt and regret of mutilating their bodies. They often experience reduced marital satisfaction.

Interestingly, the more education a woman receives, the less likely she is to sterilize herself. For example, the Centers for Disease Control studied women who used contraception and were between the ages of twenty-two and forty-four. They discovered that 55 percent of the contracepting women who did not finish high school chose to be sterilized! However, among contracepting women who graduated from college, only 13 percent resorted to sterilization.[246]

A more modern form of sterilization for women was approved by the FDA in 2002, and it is called Essure. In order to prevent future pregnancies, "microinserts" are passed through a woman's reproductive tract and placed in her fallopian tubes. "Microinsert" is the pharmaceutical company's polite way of describing a four-centimeter-long device that resembles a spring or coil and is made of polyester fibers, nickel-titanium, and stainless steel. Once these are in place, they expand and lodge themselves into the ends of the fallopian tubes, partially dangling into the uterus. Over a period of three months, they cause tissue growth (scarring), creating a barrier that prevents egg and sperm from joining. At the end of three months, the woman's uterus is injected with a dye, and a specialized X-ray is used to make sure the fallopian tubes are sealed.

At times the efforts are unsuccessful. According to Essure's patient information, about one in seven women do not achieve placement of both microinserts in the first procedure.[247] Even when both are inserted, they may not be in the correct positions. For example, they may be too far into the fallopian tubes or may have fallen out. Sometimes they poke through the wall of the fallopian tube or uterus (perforation). Other potential side effects of the device or its insertion include pain, cramping, nausea, fainting, profuse perspiration, pelvic inflammatory disease, bloating, back pain, shakiness, headache, severe cramps, abdominal pain, heavier periods, tubal pregnancy, inflammation or infection of the fallopian tubes, or death.

If a woman using Essure decides that she wants the device removed, surgery is required to reconnect the fallopian tubes to her uterus. However, such a procedure would have a poor chance of success.[248] According to the makers of Essure, "There are no data on the safety or effectiveness of surgery to reverse the Essure procedure. Any attempt at surgical reversal will likely require utero-tubal reimplantation. Pregnancy following such a procedure carries with it the risk of uterine rupture and serious maternal and fetal morbidity and mortality . . . and possible hysterectomy."[249] Therefore, any woman who uses Essure should consider it to be permanent. Not surprisingly, young women are particularly likely to experience regret following a sterilization procedure.[250]

When the device is successfully placed, it is 99 percent effective in preventing pregnancy. However, since the product is new, data does not exist regarding its long-term effectiveness. Should a woman become pregnant while using Essure, the makers of the implant say "the risks of the Micro-insert to the patient, to the fetus, and to the continuation of a pregnancy are also unknown."[251] But one can suspect that a pair of coiled metallic wires hanging into the uterus would not be healthy for a developing baby.

## 70

*I take the Pill for ovarian cysts, and my friend uses it to regulate her cycle, but neither of us is sexually active. Is that a sin?*

Although it is wrong to use the birth control pill in order to prevent conception, it has other medical applications. For example, it is often prescribed to treat such conditions as endometriosis, ovarian cysts, irregular cycles, and painful cramps.

It should be noted that these conditions often have alternative remedies without the adverse side effects of the Pill, including the contraceptive effect. If an alternative therapy exists that avoids these side effects, it should be preferred to the Pill. The Pope Paul VI Institute for the Study of Human Reproduction specializes in such alternatives, so you may wish to contact them at naprotechnology.com. You can also find a list of physicians in the "NFP Directory" at the Web site of One More Soul, omsoul.com.

You mention that your friend is using the Pill to "regulate her cycle." She should know that technically the birth control pill does not do this. It may give what appears to be a regular cycle, but it is actually causing her to have a "withdrawal bleed" rather than a regular menstruation.

Here's how it works: You'll notice in most packages of birth control pills that some of the pills are of a different color. These are called sugar, blank, or placebo pills. Unlike the other pills, they contain no hormones. When the hormones are withdrawn from a woman's body, it begins to return to normal, and her period resumes. If she never took the sugar pills but instead continued with a new pack of pills, her period would not return. But the scientists who invented the birth control pill figured that women would be more likely to use it if they still felt as if they were having their monthly period.[252] So they threw in the empty pills. The woman on the Pill is not having a normal cycle. Her body thinks that it's pregnant three weeks of the month. She returns to normal for a week and then resumes the chemical pregnancy for three more weeks.

If your friend needs to menstruate regularly, there are other ways of accomplishing this, such as nutritional methods, which a doctor can recommend, or the use of progesterone. If your friend is using the Pill for medical reasons, she also should be fully informed of its side effects, risks, and potential alternatives.

## 71

*When so many people are dying of AIDS in Africa, isn't the Church being cruel by not helping to distribute condoms?*

Billions of condoms have been shipped to Africa in order to prevent the spread of HIV.[253] However, countries that have relied on such "protection" to curb the epidemic are not seeing any great decline in the virus.[254] One nation that clearly demonstrates this problem is Botswana.

For over a decade Botswana has relied upon widespread availability of condoms in order to combat AIDS. Campaigns for abstinence and fidelity were not emphasized. Instead, billboards about "safe sex" lined the streets, while schoolchildren learned songs about condoms. According to *The Washington Post*, "The anti-AIDS partnership between the Bill & Melinda Gates Foundation and drugmaker Merck budgeted $13.5 million for condom promotion—25 times the amount dedicated to curbing dangerous sexual behavior. But soaring rates of condom use have not brought down high HIV rates. Instead, they rose together, until both were among the highest in Africa."[255]

Unfortunately, Botswana was not the only nation to make this mistake. The journal *Studies in Family Planning* pointed this out in their article "Condom Promotion for AIDS Prevention in the Developing World: Is It Working?" Its authors noted that "in many sub-Saharan African countries, high HIV transmission rates have continued despite high rates of condom use. . . . *No clear examples have emerged yet of a country that has turned back a generalized epidemic primarily by means of condom promotion.*"[256]

However, there is a clear example of an African nation turning back the epidemic of AIDS by other means. In the late 1980s Uganda was viewed as the worst nation in the world in terms of HIV/AIDS infections.[257] In 1991, 22 percent of people in the country were infected with HIV. By 1999 the number had dropped to 6 percent.[258] Ugandan President Yoweri Museveni insists that their unique success among African countries is due to their behavioral approach. He said, "In comparison with other countries per capita expenditure on condoms, we spend far below other developed countries, which emphasize use of condoms in their fight against the disease."[259] Instead of placing the primary emphasis on condoms, they emphasized abstinence and faithfulness first. As a result, they have experienced the greatest decline in HIV in the world.[260] According to the *Journal of International Development*, it was "the *lack* of condom promotion during the 1980s and early 1990s [that] contributed to the relative success of behavior change strategies in Uganda."[261]

Some "safer sex" advocates attempted to claim credit for the success of Uganda's AIDS decline. But Dr. Edward Green, a Harvard senior research scientist, ruled out such a connection, since "Uganda shows a significant decline in STDs in the absence of a male condom prevalence rate over 5 [percent]."[262] In fact, condoms were not widely used in Uganda until after much of the HIV decline had already taken place.[263] The real reason for the drop in HIV is that between 1989 and 1995 casual sex in Uganda declined by 65 percent.[264] Some of the sharpest declines took place within the teenage population, which the experts said "took many of us by surprise, since we believed that teenagers are driven by 'raging hormones,' therefore abstinence is an unrealistic or impossible objective."[265] In the words of Dr. Green, who has over two decades of experience in Africa and had previously advocated widespread condom distribution, "Weren't 'we' supposed to teach 'them' how to prevent AIDS?"[266]

Unfortunately, the success in Uganda has been undermined in recent years. According to *The Washington Post*, "The Ugandan turnaround was well underway by the time foreign AIDS experts began to arrive in the early 1990s, bringing with them the Western public health approaches—and values. They began to retool Uganda's AIDS prevention efforts away from abstinence and fidelity—goals that many Westerners felt were unrealistic. As condom use increased, the percentage of young singles having sex rose from 27 percent to 37 percent between 1995 and 2000."[267] It seems that only sex-saturated Westerners (who have no handle on their own STD epidemics) are naive enough to expect that condoms will solve the AIDS problem.

Some people ridicule the idea that abstinence education is a realistic way to deal with the AIDS crisis in developing nations. However, the evidence in favor of such an approach is becoming increasingly difficult to ignore.[268] In his testimony before the U.S. House of Representatives, Dr. Green said, "Many of us in the AIDS and public health communities didn't believe that abstinence or delay, and faithfulness, were realistic goals. It now seems we were wrong."[269] In a *Washington Post* article entitled "Let Africans Decide How to Fight AIDS," he added, "Billions of dollars and the lives of countless men, women, and children will be wasted if ideology trumps proven health policy."[270]

Lest anyone think that such an emphasis on abstinence is the result of conservative religious leaders placing their ideologies above science, Green noted, "I'm a flaming liberal, don't go to church, never voted for a Republican in my life."[271] His appreciation for the effectiveness of promoting abstinence comes from witnessing its results. Had South Africa implemented Uganda's emphasis on self-control, one scientist noted, "3.2 million lives would be saved between 2000 and 2010."[272] The effectiveness of the Ugandan approach has led scientists to consider it a "social vaccine" against HIV.[273]

Why has the behavioral approach of reducing sexual partners been so much more effective than condom distribution? There are a number of reasons.

One reason is that most people do not use the condom consistently and correctly, even after being given sex education. In one study of over five hundred couples who were repeatedly advised by their clinicians to use condoms, only 8 percent of them used it consistently, *despite the fact that they knew one partner had herpes and the other did not!*[274] In studies of relationships where one partner was infected with HIV and the other was not, only about 50 percent of them always used a condom![275] If those couples were not motivated enough to use the condom consistently, it's hard to imagine that perfect condom use will ever be seen in the general population.

Some might assume, "Well, at least some protection is better than none." This would seem to be a logical argument. After all, condom use can reduce the odds of HIV transmission during an act of intercourse. However, one study of over seventeen thousand people in Africa showed that inconsistent condom use was not protective against HIV.[276] In the presence of an epidemic, unless a person changes his or her behavior, it may be only a matter of time before he or she is infected. For this reason Dr. Norman Hearst said that he feared that we are "raising a generation of young people in Africa that believe that condoms will prevent HIV."[277] While condoms may reduce the risk of HIV transmission, they do not "protect" against AIDS. When people are not taught the difference and are left thinking that risk reduction equals protection, they are more open to taking risks that they cannot afford.

A second reason why the "safe sex" message has failed to curb AIDS is that the "protection" offered by the condom decreases with repeated exposures.[278] A study funded by the Centers for Disease Control followed sexually active young women (most of whom had a steady boyfriend) to assess condom effectiveness over time.[279] The study found that those who used condoms consistently and correctly were not statistically less likely to acquire at least one STD than the girls who used condoms inconsistently or not at all. According to Dr. J. Thomas Fitch, "This study illustrates what happens over time with numerous acts of sex with an infected partner even when a condom is used."[280] Similar observations have been seen in Africa. Edward Green remarked, "Twenty years into the pandemic there is no evidence that more condoms leads to less AIDS. . . . Over a lifetime, it is the number of sexual partners [that matter]. *Condom levels are found to be non-determining of HIV infection levels."*[281]

A third reason why condoms have failed to stop AIDS is that when a person is infected with other STDs, they are up to five times as likely to get HIV if exposed. There are several reasons why this occurs.[282] One reason is that many STDs cause sores that can serve as portals of entry for the virus. For example, a woman's reproductive tract is often able to protect her from HIV.[283] However, this natural barrier is compromised when she is infected with certain STDs.[284] Considering that the number one determinant of STD infection is multiple sexual partners, any strategy to stop HIV that does not reduce sexual activity will have limited effect.

This is why one AIDS researcher remarked that safe sex "has not been safe in the UK, and in Africa it has been positively dangerous."[285]

One final reason why condoms have not stopped HIV is that those who are promiscuous more easily catch the virus. In fact, if people practiced six months of abstinence between sexual partners there would be a massive decline in the sexual transmission of HIV. This statement might sound absurd to anyone unfamiliar with the infectivity rates of HIV. The infectivity rate of a disease or virus measures the likelihood of its transmission. For HIV it is estimated to be .001, meaning that, on average, the odds of being infected with HIV through a single act of intercourse (without a condom) is about one in a thousand.[286]

However, when a person is first infected with HIV, he or she is highly contagious.[287] If this person were to get tested for HIV right away, the test would show that he or she is HIV negative, despite the fact that he or she does have the virus and can easily transmit it!

Here's why: Technically the HIV test does not look for HIV, but for antibodies against the virus. Antibodies are what your body produces to fight off intruders. But viruses are smart and they are often able to avoid being detected. HIV can hide in your body for months before your immune system recognizes it (and years before you know of it). So if your body does not know that you have been infected with HIV, it won't produce antibodies to attack the virus. According to Dr. Harvey Elder, a professor of HIV/AIDS Epidemiology and Care, "The patient's 'HIV' test becomes positive 4–24 weeks after exposure."[288] But if the HIV test doesn't find the antibodies, the doctors will tell you that you're HIV negative.

Meanwhile, inside the body of a newly infected person, the HIV plasma viral level is very high, especially in the genital fluids (semen and cervical-vaginal fluids), because antibodies haven't been produced to reduce their levels. Since the viral load is extremely high, and the person is shedding viruses, the infectivity rate soars in the early weeks of infection. Dr. Harvey continued, "During the first few months, a person infects 20–30 percent of sexual contacts but [the] HIV test is negative. When the test is positive, 0.2–0.3 percent of sexual contacts become infected [if there are no other STDs present]."

This means that if people abstained from sex at least six months between partners, the odds of HIV transmission would be decimated. Therefore, countries that encourage monogamy and self-control enjoy much greater success in preventing HIV than countries that simply hand out condoms.

A key example of this is in the Philippines, where condoms are rare, and so is HIV. A *New York Times* article entitled "Low Rate of AIDS Virus in Philippines Is a Puzzle" reported that the Church in the Philippines is "conservative and politically powerful." As a result, "the government has no AIDS-awareness program of its own and restricts the public campaigns of independent family-planning groups."[289]

But, the article reported, "public health officials say they are stumped by a paradox in the Philippines, where a very low rate of condom use [4 percent] and a very low rate of HIV infection seem to be going hand in hand." In this conservative Catholic country that shuns condoms, about twelve thousand of the eighty-four million residents are infected with HIV. Jean-Marc Olive of the World Health Organization said that he's not sure why this is, but he thinks they're "lucky." One gets the impression that "experts" would rather look puzzled than be forced to give credit to a chaste culture.

To appreciate the wisdom of the Filipino approach to halting the spread of HIV, contrast their efforts with the "safe sex" program implemented in Thailand. Both countries reported their first case of HIV in 1984. By 1987 there were 135 cases in the Philippines, and 112 in Thailand. The World Health Organization predicted that by 1999, 85,000 people would die of AIDS in the Philippines, and 70,000 in Thailand. In an effort to prevent this tragedy, Thailand enacted a "one hundred percent condom use program" and promoted widespread availability of condoms.[290]

Meanwhile, the Filipino government backed the Church's plan to prevent the epidemic. By 2005, Thailand's HIV rate was fifty times as high as the Philippines (580,000 vs. 12,000).[291]

But because Thailand's rate of new HIV infections is not as high as it used to be, it is hailed by "safe sex" experts as the model of how to protect a country against HIV. Health officials warn that an HIV epidemic has "the potential to explode" in the Philippines, but they are slow to acknowledge that if Filipinos hold fast to their morals, they'll have nothing to fear.[292] Compared to Western culture, Filipinos have a delayed sexual debut and a reduced number of partners.[293] They are living proof that self-control always trumps birth control.

While some people see the Catholic Church as an obstacle to HIV prevention, the *British Medical Journal* noted, "The greater the percentage of Catholics in any country, the lower the level of HIV. If the Catholic Church is promoting a message about HIV in those countries, it seems to be working. On the basis of data from the World Health Organization, in Swaziland, where 42.6 percent have HIV, only 5 percent of the population is Catholic. In Botswana, where 37 percent of the adult population is HIV infected, only 4 percent of the population is Catholic. In South Africa, 22 percent of the population is HIV infected, and only 6 percent is Catholic. In Uganda, with 43 percent of the population Catholic, the proportion of HIV infected adults is 4 percent."[294] In the Philippines, over 80 percent of the population is Catholic, and only .03 percent of the population has HIV![295]

The Catholic Church, like any good mother, wants what is best for her children. If your son or daughter had the chance to be sexually active with a person infected with HIV, what message would you give him or her? Would you entrust your child's life to a piece of latex? Would you buy him or her a package of condoms, and then attempt to deliver a convincing abstinence message? Odds are, every loving parent would deliver an uncompromised message about abstinence. Why then would the Church do any less for her children?

Some argue that the Church's opposition to condoms isn't realistic because "some people are going to do it anyway." But who are these "some people" who are incapable of being reached with the message of self-control? When I played college baseball, we were expected not to use steroids. Sure, some athletes do it anyway, but no coach would walk into the locker room and say, "We want you all to abstain from using performance-enhancing drugs. But since we know some of you will do it anyway, we'll have a basket of free, clean syringes in the dugout." Odds are, his players would not be inspired by his lack of confidence in them. If the coach truly cared about his players and wanted only the best for them, he'd motivate and empower them to make the best choice. In the same way, the Church will not give up on any human being but will continue to deliver the safest and healthiest message: chastity.

All of these considerations should offer more than enough evidence that the Church's stance on contraception does not stem from naïve traditionalism. It comes, in the words of one Vatican reporter, "from a profound analysis of the need to integrate sexuality in an exclusive and permanent relationship open to life in the context of marriage. The wisdom of this view is becoming increasingly clearer."[296]

Critics may belittle the Catholic Church now, but as the saying goes, "All truth passes through three stages. First, it is ridiculed. Second, it is violently opposed. Third, it is accepted as being self-evident."[297]

## 72

*What does the Church teach about in vitro fertilization, artificial insemination, fertility drugs, and stuff like that?*

Medical technology exists to promote the proper functioning of our bodies. Men as well as women can be infertile, but some of the reproductive methods you are asking about focus on women. Since infertility can be a dysfunction of a woman's reproductive system, the use of fertility drugs that counter this condition and promote the healthy functioning of the reproductive system is morally acceptable. But these must be used responsibly. If they are not, a woman's ovaries may release too many eggs, which may be dangerous to the mother and the child or children.

While reproductive technology may assist the sexual act, it must never replace it. This is partly why the Church does not permit the use of in vitro fertilization (IVF) and artificial insemination. These procedures do not help the marital act but substitute for it, bringing about conception through a means other than intercourse. In the words of Archbishop Charles Chaput of Denver, "Whether to prevent a pregnancy or achieve one, all techniques which separate the unitive and procreative dimensions of marriage are always wrong." [298] In other words, as contraception tries to make love without making babies, IVF and artificial insemination attempt to make babies without making love. Neither act is moral, because life and love are inseparable. As John Paul II said in an address to President George W. Bush, man must be "the master, not the product, of his technology." [299]

However, there is another, even more serious moral problem with both in vitro fertilization and artificial insemination: not only do these processes seek to create life in a morally unacceptable way, but they also create *many* "excess" lives that will inevitably be destroyed in their earliest stages. In vitro fertilization (IVF) is a process that involves conceiving life in a laboratory and transferring that into a woman's womb. It is not an easy process, so extra embryos are often frozen and kept for a later attempt or donated or experimented on. Since many eggs are fertilized during the procedure, a good number of them are destroyed. Commonly the effort will be a failure and none of the eggs will implant. It is obviously immoral to create and destroy so many lives in an attempt to create one life.

Artificial insemination is a different process. It involves taking the sperm from a man and injecting it into the uterus or placing it in the woman's cervix. This too is a difficult method, and it is not uncommon that the process needs to be repeated six or more times in order for it to be successful. Many states do not require

STD testing for sperm donors, so HIV and other viruses can be spread during the process.

Even without these problems, both of these methods are incompatible with the dignity of a child and the marital act. Each child should be brought into being by an act of love between his or her parents, not by a lab technician tinkering with cells in a petri dish, as in IVF, or a doctor injecting sperm into a uterus, as in artificial insemination. When the sperm are taken from a man other than the husband, it also infringes upon the child's right to be born of a father and mother known to him, and it betrays the spouses' marital pledge to become a father and mother only through each other.

Today couples can even purchase donated sperm and eggs from strangers. In order for a couple to acquire someone else's sperm or eggs, they contact a sperm bank or fertility clinic. Many of these companies advertise to college students, offering them large sums of money for their DNA.[300] Some students ignore the moral implications and seize the opportunity to pay off student loans. In turn, the companies market their genetic material with such labels as: "Blond hair, blue eyes, 5'7", athletic, with 2200 SAT score!" Potential parents can browse the Internet and pick the features they want.

If the mom-to-be does not wish to deal with pregnancy and childbirth, she can buy eggs and sperm and pay a surrogate mother to carry the child for her. One couple did just this and then decided to divorce shortly before the baby was born.[301] The would-be-adoptive dad didn't want the baby and refused to pay child support. The surrogate mother didn't want the child to end up in a divorced family, so she wanted to keep the baby. The man who donated the sperm and the woman whose egg was used never agreed to the arrangement in the first place! However, each of them was willing to take the baby if no one else would. So whose child is it? Not surprisingly, increasing numbers of children who were conceived through anonymous sperm donors are seeking out their biological fathers.

Because the practice of sperm donation is so widespread, some experts are beginning to fear that the children conceived in this manner may go on to marry their half-siblings unknowingly.[302] After all, some sperm donors may have several dozen children, and according to the journal *Nature*, children born through anonymous sperm donation "are likely to be of similar ages and to grow up in same area. A significant percentage of couples may, unknowingly, be closely related."[303]

Sometimes a couple will successfully conceive through IVF treatment but will have leftover embryos that are never implanted. To keep them alive, the couple needs to pay a clinic to store them. One husband and wife decided that upon reaching their desired family size, they no longer wished to have this expense. After receiving another bill, the wife explained:

> The bill was for Vial Number 2988—our third child. Well, not actually our third child—our embryo, in frozen storage at the in vitro clinic. Vial number 2988 was the final result of $12,000 worth of IVF treatment: fifty hormone injections, twenty-seven blood draws, sixteen sick days from work and at least one day where the whole process made me feel suicidal. The result: two beautiful children, one boy and one girl, eighteen months apart and both still in diapers, and across town, a cluster of cells in limbo. . . . Growing up liberal, I always believed in a woman's right to choose and that an embryo . . . wasn't actually a child. Yet, I couldn't help but think of this third embryo (which was frozen at five days' development) as a child, especially because both of the other embryos I had created eventually became children.[304]

Sadly, instead of completing the pregnancy or giving up the embryo for adoption, she chose to have the unborn baby thawed. Such bizarre scenarios show how little respect our culture has for the dignity of life.

Because of contraception and reproductive technologies, we have separated what God has joined together: sex and babies. You may ask, "Well, if these methods are immoral, then why does God let conception occur?" God has entrusted us with the gift of sexuality, and He will not prevent us from abusing that freedom. For example, if a child is conceived out of wedlock, the act is immoral, yet God still allows life to come forth from it. Just because conception occurs does not mean that the methods to achieve it were good. There are many ways to bring life into the world, including marital love, fornication, adultery, rape, incest, IVF, and artificial insemination. Only one, marital love, is consistent with the dignity of the human person.

Many believe that IVF and artificial insemination are the only options available to an infertile couple hoping to have a child of their own. This is not the case. There are many doctors who specialize in determining the cause of infertility and healing it, instead of replacing fertility with technology. See naprotechnology.com for more information.

# 8

# Sexually Transmitted Diseases

## 73

*Won't a condom protect you from getting an STD?*

In 2000 the National Institutes for Health (NIH) published the first thorough review of the scientific research on condom effectiveness.[1] The study examined eight STDs and demonstrated that condoms reduce the risk of contracting or transmitting two of them: HIV and gonorrhea (in men). The studies revealed that, when consistently and correctly used, condoms provide an 85 percent risk reduction for the transmission of HIV in males and females and a 45 to 75 percent risk reduction for the transmission of gonorrhea in males.

While the condom may reduce the likelihood of contracting HIV, yearly cases of this virus are much less than 1 percent of all the yearly STD cases.[2] Gonorrhea is a much more common problem, but there was not sufficient evidence to determine how much protection condom use offered women. This is not good news for women, because they suffer much greater consequences from being infected by this disease. It can lead to ectopic pregnancy, pelvic inflammatory disease, and infertility.

In regard to the other diseases, the report stated that "there was no evidence that condom use reduced the risk of HPV infection."[3] Furthermore, the data were unable to determine how effective the condom is in reducing the risk of the other STDs. In spite of all the talk today about condoms and safe sex, they could not say what degree of protection condoms offered for most of the STDs reviewed! This is troubling, considering that these diseases infect millions of people each year and can make them at least two to five times as likely to transmit HIV.[4]

While the NIH study does not prove that the condom is useless in protecting against the STDs mentioned above, it does mean that twenty-eight expert panel members scouring through 138 peer-reviewed studies on condom effectiveness were unable to determine its effectiveness. Since the publication of this study, others have determined that the condom use reduces STD risks only by about half.[5]

In the wake of the NIH report, politicians who favor promotion of "safe" sex were livid, arguing that the publication of such information could contribute to a rise in STDs because it undermines public confidence in the condom.[6] What they didn't want to admit was that the outdated message of "safe sex" causes people to be overconfident in the condom. One scientist noted:

> Some fear that informing the public of how little we know about condom effectiveness would lead to nonuse of condoms. Although it is improbable that any scientific evidence supports this hypothesis, the question remains. Is it ethical for health care professionals, including physicians and pharmacists, to hide the truth from the public? As in every other area of health care, we must give accurate data as we attempt to steer our patients toward the healthiest and safest choices. Ultimately, each individual must decide how much risk he or she is willing to take. But such a decision can be made responsibly only if individuals are accurately informed about the degree of risk they face (or may face) if they choose to be sexually active.[7]

Determining the effectiveness of condoms in preventing STDs is a complicated matter. For example, some STDs, such as chancroid or gonorrhea, transmit very easily, while others, such as HIV, are not as contagious. Some STDs, such as herpes, change their infectivity over time. One week the person could be shedding the virus, and a week later, not shedding. Factors such as gender, stress, drug interactions, pregnancy, and the presence of another STD also play a role in STD transmission. In fact, each person's immune system is unique in how well it resists infections. For all of these reasons and more, it is difficult to pinpoint a precise level of condom effectiveness for STDs in general.

When determining the effectiveness of the condom in preventing the spread of STDs, it's enlightening to examine how well the condom prevents pregnancy. According to the research institute of Planned Parenthood, the failure rate of the condom in preventing pregnancy is 15 percent during the first year of use.[8] Considering that a woman can get pregnant only a few days of the month and STDs can be contracted any day, the condom is by no means adequate protection. No matter what STD we are speaking about, the condom does not guarantee protection even when used consistently and correctly. On the other hand, chastity guarantees 100 percent protection.

But the bottom line is this: There is no condom for the heart —or the soul. Whatever we may do to protect our bodies from STDs, if we misuse God's gift of sexuality, our hearts and souls will not escape the consequences. But if we are faithful with our sexuality, there is no need for protection of any kind, for there is nothing to fear. The very idea of wanting to make sex "safe" is a contradiction in terms. Sex is meant to be a total gift of the self, holding nothing back. Concerns about "safety" should not enter into the equation. You protect yourself from your enemies; you give yourself to your beloved.

## 74

*How do you know if you have an STD?*

Some of the symptoms of STDs include blisters, warts, lesions, painful urination, itching, swelling, and unnatural bleeding or discharge. However, many STDs have no obvious symptoms, and *eight out of ten people who have an STD are currently unaware of their infection.*[9] If you have had any genital contact, you should get tested. Many STDs may remain dormant and undetectable for some time, so you could test negative for STDs and still be infected. This is why clinicians recommend that women (and some men) who have been sexually active in the past get tested annually, regardless of their current sexual activity.

Doctors administer different tests to determine the presence of an STD, depending upon the person's symptoms and sexual history. If you have ever had intercourse, you should receive all of the following tests: 1) Pap test (for women) and perhaps HPV screening by means of an HPV DNA detection test; 2) cervical cultures for gonorrhea and chlamydia (for women); 3) vaginal swabs for trichomonas and bacterial vaginitis (for women); 4) culture of any ulcers or sores (herpes and syphilis); 5) blood tests for HIV, hepatitis profile, and syphilis.[10] You may also be tested for other infections by means of a urine sample. Oral (and anal) sex can transmit virtually every STD,[11] and hand-to-genital contact can transmit some as well.[12] Therefore, even virgins can get STDs, including oral cancer from HPV.[13]

When one STD is diagnosed or suspected, there are likely to be more. Since some STDs can lead to sterility in men and women —and even death—you should treat any possible STDs as soon as possible. For a free, anonymous, and helpful tool for STD diagnosis, visit stdwizard.com.

## 75

### If I think I have an STD, what should I do? Can I get tested without having to tell my parents?

You should get tested as soon as possible, and since testing can usually be done on a confidential basis, it is not *necessary* to go with your parents. If you call a local hospital or (800) 672-2296, they'll be able to direct you to a clinic in your area.

Regarding your parents: You may think, "What Mom and Dad don't know can't hurt them. If I did tell them, my mom would cry for a week, and I would probably be grounded until my forty-seventh birthday." As difficult as this may be, put yourself in your parents' shoes. Imagine you had a child who was sexually active. You would want your child to be able to come to you and be honest about whatever was going on in his or her life.

The sooner you get a real relationship with your folks, the better. Sure, your parents will be upset, but under that hurt are two hearts that want only what is best for you. Perhaps we do not like to tell our parents stuff because of our pride. If we had listened to them in the first place, we would not be in trouble! Swallow your pride, and do what you would want your own child to do. Even if you refuse to tell them, make sure to get tested. Some STDs can be easily cured but may lead to infertility if they are not treated.

## 76

*I heard that an incurable STD called HPV has killed more American women than AIDS. If this is true, what is it, and why aren't teens told about it?*

What you heard is correct. Human papillomavirus (HPV) is the most common STD in the world, infecting more than 440 million people.[14] There are over one hundred different types of HPV, and about thirty to forty of them cause genital infections.[15] While most people who contract HPV will not suffer serious consequences from the virus, it does cause 99.7 percent of cervical cancer, and this kills approximately 288,000 women annually.[16]

In the United States the annual death toll from cervical cancer is fewer than four thousand. The reason for the relatively low figure is that HPV is often treated before it leads to cervical cancer. Unfortunately, women in developing nations often lack adequate health care and routine Pap testing. Therefore they are much more likely to suffer the full consequences of the virus.

HPV can also cause genital skin cancer, which has killed more than thirty thousand people in the United States.[17] Finally, HPV can cause genital warts, but only 1 percent of sexually active people experience this symptom.[18]

Unfortunately, the virus can impact the health of children born to infected mothers. For example, I know of parents who took their infant to the doctor because she had a sore throat. The doctor examined her and told the parents that the child had genital warts growing on her larynx. This condition, recurrent respiratory papillomatosis (RRP), is uncommon but still infects over two thousand children each year.[19] Since there is no cure for HPV, children with RRP often require laser surgeries to remove the warts. Sadly, the average child with RRP needs surgery every three months for several years; such a child will have more than twenty surgeries over the course of his or her lifetime.[20]

Because the virus usually does not show symptoms, most people who have HPV are unaware of their infection. Also, HPV can remain latent in a person's body for a considerable amount of time. For example, some women have contracted the virus as teens and not suffered health effects from the infection until their thirties or forties. Also, when a woman gets checked for signs of HPV, the doctor's colposcope may fail to detect genital wart infestations. Doctors may also give a woman a Pap test to see if there is any abnormal cell growth in her cervix caused by HPV. However, this is not technically an "HPV test." In fact, one study of more than three hundred sexually active teen girls discovered that 62 percent of the girls were infected with HPV, despite the fact that most of them had normal Pap test results![21]

Because the Pap test can sometimes fail to detect HPV, many doctors recommend a yearly test for any woman who has been sexually active, even if she is now abstinent. HPV DNA tests are now available as well. Through an HPV DNA test, a woman who has HPV can know which type (or types) of the virus she is infected with. Doctors can then tell her if she is in a high or low risk category and can follow up with her accordingly.

Recently scientists have developed a vaccine against HPV for women. Although it only prevents a few types of HPV, which infect only 3 percent of women,[22] those few types are responsible for causing most cases of cervical cancer and genital warts.

Men can be infected with HPV as well, but because they are less likely to develop cancer from it, they are often considered "vectors" for the virus. For example, when a husband is infected with HPV, his wife is five times as likely to get cervical cancer.[23] Unfortunately, most men with HPV who get tested for STDs will not learn of their infection unless they have visible genital warts. HPV DNA testing does exist for men, but it is expensive and usually only used for research purposes.

How common is the virus among males? One way to know is to consider how quickly women are infected. According to the *British Journal of Obstetrics and Gynecology,* 46 percent of teenage girls acquire HPV from their first sexual relationship.[24] Such high rates of infection are widely reported, and scientists now estimate that over 50 percent of sexually active men and women have been infected with one or more types of genital HPV.[25] Such high numbers seem almost unbelievable. But one must remember that most people with HPV will not show symptoms or suffer as a result of it.

Although HPV is incurable, this does not mean that it is permanent, like herpes. In fact, HPV will usually go away within a few years.[26] So despite the fact that most women have been infected with HPV,[27] only 27 percent currently test positive for the virus.[28]

Young women are most at risk for HPV infection. For example, 40 percent of sexually active girls between the ages of fourteen and nineteen are currently infected with HPV. The numbers are even higher for women aged twenty to twenty-four (49 percent!).[29] Among all women this age bracket has the highest rate of HPV.

The prevalence of HPV also varies according to marital status. For example, only 17 percent of married women are currently infected. However, nearly half of all women who are living with their boyfriends are infected with the virus.[30]

One reason why the virus is so common is that HPV can spread by any genital contact (genital, oral, or by means of the hands).[31] The virus can also be present, without symptoms, on a person's abdomen or thighs.[32] Therefore condoms are not very effective in preventing its transmission.

This is perhaps one reason why we don't hear more about HPV. It is the Achilles' heel of the "safe sex" campaign. For example, researchers followed hundreds of college girls without HPV and discovered that 60 percent of them contracted the virus by the end of the study. According to the researchers, "always using male condoms with a new partner was not protective [of HPV]."[33] One has to wonder if these women would have made different choices if they knew the limitations of the condom.

In the summer of 2006, *The New England Journal of Medicine* published a study that showed that condom use could reduce one's risk of contracting HPV. Countless news agencies announced the discovery, and hailed it as a victory for safe sex. But most reports of the study failed to mention that the research only included 82 women, and nearly 40 percent of them contracted HPV, despite using the condom every time![34]

In order to educate the public about HPV, Congress passed Public Law 106-554. Among other things, this law required government health agencies to make sure that educational materials are "medically accurate regarding the overall effectiveness or lack of effectiveness of condoms in preventing sexually transmitted diseases, including HPV."[35] Condom labels were to be reexamined for medical accuracy, and the Centers for Disease Control (CDC) were directed to create a report that outlined the best strategies to avoid HPV.

The CDC finally published their report three years later, admitting, "The available scientific evidence is not sufficient to recommend condoms as a primary prevention strategy for the prevention of genital HPV infection."[36] While condom use may reduce the risk of HPV-related diseases, the CDC explained earlier that "studies which have attempted to assess male condom benefit for women have generally found no evidence of protection against [HPV] infection."[37]

As soon as the CDC released its report, Congressman Mark Souder wrote a letter to the commissioner of the Food and Drug Administration:

> A meta-analysis reviewing "the best available data describing the relationship between condoms and HPV-related conditions" from the past two decades published in the November 29, 2002 edition of the journal *Sexually Transmitted Diseases* found, "There was no

consistent evidence of a protective effect of condom use on HPV DNA detection, and in some studies, condom use was associated with a slightly increased risk for these lesions." Three years after Public Law 106-554 was signed by President Clinton, condom labels still do not warn consumers about the lack of protection against HPV infection. The Subcommittee urges FDA to act on the release of CDC's HPV prevention report and *immediately relabel condoms to alert consumers that condoms do not provide effective protection against HPV infection.*[38]

Because of the inadequacy of the condom in preventing HPV, many people contract the virus while engaging in what they mistakenly believe to be "safe sex." Senator Tom Coburn, who has been working for years to encourage the FDA to correct condom labels, testified, "It is a cruel distortion of the word 'prevention' to tell women and young girls that the tremendous physical, emotional and financial costs of treatment for HPV infection are a cost worth bearing as a consequence of federal health agencies' intentional distortion and cover-up of scientific data related to HPV."[39] The financial impact he mentioned is the fact that Americans spend up to $6 billion each year treating HPV.

While some government officials have urged the FDA to update condom labels, other politicians want it left alone. Congressman Henry Waxman, a long-time opponent of abstinence education, argued, "We want to be sure that we do not end up with an unintended effect of confusing people about the situations where condoms do work. . . . [Condom labels] that include information on HPV can result in so much information on such a small package that it reduces the effectiveness of any information."[40] Therefore he believes that undermining the public's confidence in the condom will have "serious public health consequences." He added, "Are condoms perfect? Of course not. But reality requires us not to make a public health strategy against protection, but rather to ask a key question: compared to what?"[41]

Unfortunately, since Waxman thinks purity is unrealistic, his only option to stop STDs is to exaggerate the effectiveness of condoms in hopes that more people will use them. Some health "experts" concur, saying they we don't want to "create an epidemic of panic, fear, and anxiety in adolescents and young adults who are embarking on their sexual careers."[42] One leader in the sex ed movement tried to put an optimistic spin on the issue by saying, "I don't think we, in any way, want to do anything that will frighten people from using condoms. . . . The bottom-line message always needs to be that most STDs are treatable."[43]

In the midst of the debate, the FDA has not done a great deal. It said that it is "certainly committed to *looking* at this and making the requisite changes."[44] It added that it is "*preparing* new guidance on condom labeling," "*exploring* new opportunities to best inform condom users about important limitations of the device," and "*proposing* to amend the classification regulations for condoms."[45] In other words, not much has changed.

The lack of clarity from government agencies has contributed to confusion within the contraceptive industry. For example, the makers of LifeStyles condoms issued a press release "encouraging people to have a love affair with condoms."[46] In it the manufacturers claimed that safe sex reduces the risk of HPV transmission. When asked for the scientific proof to back up their claim, they admitted that their public relations firm "mistakenly included HPV among the diseases for which latex condoms provide protection."[47]

In 2005 the FDA took a step in the right direction and drafted a document with proposed language for a new condom label. As a result of this document, the commissioner of the FDA said the agency "received roughly four hundred comments on the proposed rule. Almost all comments suggested the proposed labeling language was confusing and difficult for consumers to understand. As a result, the agency intends to undertake additional labeling comprehension studies to help insure that the final labeling recommendations issued by the agency are understandable to users."[48]

While the FDA is undertaking its condom "labeling comprehension studies," millions of people are being infected with HPV while overestimating the effectiveness of so-called "safe sex."

## 77

*How many STDs are out there, and can you describe some of the really common ones?*

In the 1960s gonorrhea and syphilis seemed to be the only well-known STDs, and both of these could be treated with penicillin. Today there are over twenty-five different STDs, and some of the most common ones are without cures.[49] Among the STDs that can be cured, some are becoming increasingly resistant to modern antibiotics.

Most people who have an STD are unaware of their infection and contagious state.[50] This should especially alarm young people, because of the nineteen million new STD infections each year, nearly half of them are among people between the ages of fifteen and twenty-four.[51] According to the Centers for Disease Control, the direct medical cost associated with STDs in the United States is $14.1 billion each year![52]

Some of the most common STDs include HPV, chlamydia, herpes, gonorrhea, and trichomoniasis. The four STDs that are incurable are HPV, HIV, herpes, and hepatitis. All of the others can be cured. I already discussed HPV, so let's take a look at some of the others.

### Chlamydia

Chlamydia is the most commonly *reported* infectious disease in the United States. It is caused by the bacterium chlamydia trachomatis. In 2005 nearly a million cases were reported, but most cases go undiagnosed, and so the CDC estimate that about three million infections occur each year in the United States.[53]

The disease is found primarily among teenage girls and young women. In fact, nearly three out of every four cases of chlamydia in women are found in girls between the ages of fifteen and twenty-four.[54] It is estimated that 40 percent of sexually active single women have been infected at some time with chlamydia.[55] (However, since the disease is curable, this does not mean that 40 percent of women are currently infected.) The disease is so common that there are more cases of chlamydia reported than all cases of AIDS, chancroid, gonorrhea, hepatitis (types A, B, and C), and syphilis combined![56] This STD can also be spread by means of oral sex.[57]

Some of the symptoms of genital chlamydial infection include vaginal or urethral discharge, burning with urination, pelvic pain, and genital ulcers. Men can experience many of these symptoms, and also tenderness of the scrotum. In many cases the man will experience no symptoms, despite the fact that the STD can damage his fertility.[58] Sometimes a chlamydial infection can lead to sterility in men, although this is not common.

As is the case with most STDs, women are more likely to suffer serious consequences of chlamydial infection. For example, chlamydia may spread to a woman's uterus and fallopian tubes, causing pelvic inflammatory disease (PID). This can lead to infertility and may become a life-threatening infection. One way it can be deadly is by increasing a woman's risk of having an ectopic pregnancy, where the newly conceived baby implants outside of the uterus. One reason this can happen is that PID can scar the fallopian tubes, making it more difficult for a newly conceived baby to be transferred through them to the womb. If the baby gets stuck in one of the tubes and the condition is not treated, it can be fatal for the mother because the fallopian tube can burst. Ectopic pregnancies account for less than 2 percent of all pregnancies, and the vast majority of these women survive. But the complications that can arise from the condition make it the leading cause of maternal death in the first trimester of pregnancy.[59]

Each year more than a million American women experience PID.[60] According to the CDC, "Up to 40 percent of females with untreated chlamydia infections develop PID, and up to 20 percent of those may become infertile."[61] Unfortunately, most women (and half of men) who are infected with chlamydia show no symptoms.[62] Consequently they may not receive treatment with the necessary antibiotics.

Additionally, the screening test for chlamydia may miss the infection, and the woman can be given what is called a "false negative" diagnosis. In other words, she is told that she does not have chlamydia, despite the fact that she is infected.[63] Even when diagnosed accurately, the antibiotics prescribed may stop the bacteria from reproducing, but the disease may reactivate later. Years after the initial infection, the disease can still be present in the woman's fallopian tubes, without symptoms.[64]

Even when the disease is treated, its effects may linger. While in a woman's body, chlamydia causes the production of heat shock protein (HSP). Especially when a woman has a prolonged chlamydial infection without knowing it, her immune system creates antibodies against the HSP. This means that her white blood cells learn to attack HSP, because they associate it with chlamydia. If the woman becomes pregnant, this creates a problem. One of the first proteins made by an embryo is a type of HSP similar to the one made by chlamydia. Because the chlamydial infection trained her immune system to be hostile to HSP, her immune system may react against her baby. This can interfere with the development of the embryo. It can also leave the embryo less protected, making the unborn child more likely to die before implanting in the uterus. Finally, it can create an inflammatory reaction in the uterus. This may cause a "spontaneous abortion" or miscarriage.[65]

In one study of 216 women with infertility problems, 21 percent of them tested positive for chlamydial HSP antibodies, despite the fact that none of them knew that they had ever been infected.[66] Larger studies of women with fertility problems estimate that between 30 and 60 percent of them have chlamydia antibodies in their serum (blood plasma), indicating that they had been infected with chlamydia at some point in the past.[67] A teenager may contract chlamydia, never show symptoms of the infection, and then experience fertility problems ten years later when she and her husband try to conceive a baby. For all of these reasons chlamydia is called the "silent sterilizer."

Because of the physical nature of STDs, the emotional consequences of the infections are often overlooked. One woman said, "Sometime during my wild college days, I picked up an infection that damaged the inside of my fallopian tubes and left me infertile. I am now married to a wonderful man who very much wants children, and the guilt I feel is overwhelming. We will look into adoption, but this whole ordeal has been terribly difficult."[68]

Should a woman contract chlamydia and conceive successfully, it is possible for her to pass the infection on to her baby. This can lead to blindness, pneumonia, or premature birth.[69] Even when a woman receives treatment for chlamydia, doctors are encouraged to follow up with her three months later.[70] This is because many girls get reinfected from their untreated partner(s).

Because of how the disease compromises a woman's immune system, women with chlamydia are up to five times as likely to become infected with HIV, if exposed,[71] and are more likely to develop cervical cancer from HPV.[72] One rare form of chlamydia is known as Lymphogranuloma Venereum (LGV). This disease may cause a person's lymph nodes in the groin to swell up to the size of a lemon and burst. LGV is not nearly as common as chlamydia, but it has been detected especially in people who engage in high-risk sexual behaviors.

Consistent and correct condom use may reduce (but not eliminate) the risk of being infected with chlamydia, but the degree of protection offered by the condom is not certain. According to the most comprehensive research on condom effectiveness for STD prevention, the National Institutes for Health reported, "Taken together, the available epidemiologic literature does not allow an accurate assessment of the degree of potential protection against chlamydia offered by correct and consistent condom usage."[73] Since the time of this report, other studies have suggested that condom use may decrease the risk of chlamydia infections by about half.[74]

## Herpes

Herpes is a virus that infects the skin and mucous membranes such as the mouth and genitals. Herpes type one (HSV-1) infects 58 percent of people and primarily causes oral infections, such as cold sores.[75] Most people with HSV-1 do not have it as a result of sexual contact. However, it can be transmitted to and from the genitals via oral sex. Due to the increasingly common practice of oral sex, certain populations—such as high school and college students—are seeing a steep increase in genital HSV-1 infections.[76] Type two (HSV-2) mostly causes genital herpes, and it also can be transferred to the mouth from the genitals.

Unlike certain STDs that are spread only by means of bodily fluid, herpes is most often spread by skin-to-skin contact. Not only a person's genitals but also his or her abdomen, thighs, hands, and other areas can be infected. Herpes can be picked up through contact with these areas and transmitted by a partner who shows no symptoms.

Since herpes is easily transmitted and incurable, it is the most common STD in terms of the number of individuals currently infected. In other words, it is the most *prevalent* STD. While it is unknown how many people are infected with genital HSV-1, about one in six people are infected with genital HSV-2.[77] Among sexually active singles, the percentage of those infected with herpes is even higher: between 30 and 40 percent![78] While these numbers may seem astoundingly high, one must realize that nine out of ten people who have genital herpes are unaware that they are infected.[79] This is especially worrisome since people with herpes are at an increased risk of contracting and spreading HIV.[80] Women with HSV are also more susceptible to cervical cancer from HPV.[81]

Within a week of contracting herpes, a person may have preliminary symptoms including fever, headache, and muscle aches.

Lesions may then appear where the virus was contracted. The lesions usually begin as small blisters before breaking and becoming ulcers. Other symptoms include itching, burning with urination, vaginal discharge, and swollen lymph nodes in the groin area. Since herpes is incurable, it is not uncommon for infected people to have recurrent outbreaks of lesions for the rest of their lives.

Thankfully, it is uncommon for a mother to pass the virus on to her newborn child. But if this occurs, it can be fatal for the baby. To avoid such a tragedy, women with active herpes infections usually give birth by means of a caesarean delivery.[82]

Although there is no cure for herpes, antiviral medications can shorten and sometimes prevent outbreaks. Regarding prevention of the virus, studies show that if a person uses a condom consistently and correctly, it will decrease the risk of herpes transmission by only about half.[83] Therefore, do not expect a condom to protect your future spouse and children from the effects of this STD.

## Gonorrhea

Gonorrhea is the second most commonly reported infectious disease in the United States.[84] According to the CDC, "African-Americans remain the group most heavily affected by gonorrhea, with a rate in 2005 that was eighteen times greater than the rate for whites."[85] Worldwide, about sixty-two million cases occur each year.[86]

Gonorrhea is highly contagious, especially for women. Through a single act of intercourse with an infected partner, the male has a 20 percent chance of contracting it from an infected female, but the female has about a 70 percent chance of being infected from a man who has the disease.[87] When a person is infected with one STD, it often makes his or her body more likely to be infected with others. In the case of gonorrhea, the infected person is three to five times as likely to get HIV if exposed.[88] Furthermore, men with a history of gonorrhea are twice as likely to develop bladder cancer.[89]

When a person is infected, his or her symptoms vary, depending upon the individual and what part of the body is infected. Some experience a discharge from the genitals and painful urination. Women can suffer from abnormal bleeding, and men from swelling around the testicles. This may be a sign of epididymitis in the male, a condition that can lead to infertility if not treated.

In a woman gonorrhea may spread to the uterus and fallopian tubes, leading to PID, which can cause infertility. Infected mothers may also pass the disease to their babies during birth, which can lead to blindness, joint disorders, and a life-threatening blood infection in the child. However, if a woman receives treatment for gonorrhea, she can reduce the risk of infecting her baby.

The majority of infected men will show symptoms of the disease within days of contracting it. However, many women will experience no initial symptoms.[90] For men and women alike, the disease can remain undetected even though the person's mouth may be infected. If the disease is detected, it can be treated with antibiotics.

Doctors have noticed, however, that gonorrhea is becoming increasingly resistant to the antibiotics used to treat it. One specialist remarked, "Gonorrhea has now joined the list of other superbugs for which treatment options have become dangerously few."[91] According to the CDC, "Resistance is especially worrisome among men who have sex with men (MSM), where resistance was nearly eight times higher than among heterosexuals (29 percent vs. 3.8 percent)."[92]

Gonorrhea can be transmitted by means of intercourse, oral sex, and anal sex. The National Institutes of Health reported that condom use reduces the risk of gonorrhea for men. But "the available epidemiologic literature does not allow an accurate assessment of the degree of protection against gonorrhea infection in women offered by correct and consistent condom use."[93] Studies published since the NIH report estimate that the condom can reduce the risk of gonorrhea by about half.[94] Therefore, even correct and consistent condom use does not eliminate the risk of contracting the disease.

The findings are especially dismal for those who report inconsistent condom use. According to one medical journal, "Inconsistent condom use was not protective against HIV and STDs, and significantly increased the risks of infections such as gonorrhea and chlamydia. Inconsistent condom use may actually be an 'enabling' process allowing individuals to persist in high-risk behaviors with a false sense of security."[95]

This study is not the only one to show that those who use condoms less than perfectly are *more* likely to contract STDs than those who do not use condoms at all.[96] The reason for this, as the journal explained, is that those who report condom use may be more likely to engage in risky behavior (such as having multiple sexual partners). According to one researcher, "The number-one determinant of whether a person will catch a sexually transmitted disease is the number of lifetime sexual partners. We seem to go out of our way as a government and a nation to avoid telling people that, but we hand out a lot of free condoms."[97]

## Trichomoniasis

Trichomoniasis is a protozoan parasite that infects the genital tract. In North America it infects about eight million people each year. Worldwide the annual total is 170 million. According to the CDC, it is the most common curable STD among young women.[98]

However, most people who are infected with trichomoniasis do not have symptoms, especially males. When symptoms are present, they may include genital irritation and burning with urination. For women the parasite can cause vaginitis, cervicitis, abnormal bleeding, swelling, itching, discharge, abdominal pain, and other symptoms. When a woman is infected with trichomoniasis, she is also more susceptible to contracting HIV, if exposed.[99] Although uncommon, an infected mother can pass the parasite on to her baby through childbirth. If she is infected while pregnant, the baby also has an increased risk of being born early and having low birth weight.

In regard to condom effectiveness in preventing the spread of trichomoniasis, the National Institutes of Health reported, "One limited study demonstrated a 30 percent protective effect for women. The [lack] of epidemiologic studies on condom effectiveness for trichomoniasis does not allow an accurate assessment of the reduction in risk of trichomoniasis offered by condom usage."[100]

When considering the potential impact of STDs, we should remember the words of former U.S. Surgeon General C. Everett Koop: "When you have sex with someone, you are having sex with everyone they have had sex with for the last ten years, and everyone they and their partners have had sex with for the last ten years."[101] This is frightening for many to learn, considering the fact that people can get tested for STDs, be told that they are clean, and then transmit dormant STDs that the tests did not detect. Most tests today pick up the majority of the infections they are testing for. The problem is that many people believe they have been tested for all STDs when, in reality, they have been tested for only a few.

Recently a high school girl contacted me because she was considering sleeping with her boyfriend. She was a virgin, but he had been with eleven girls. If his previous partners were as sexually active as he had been (and depending on the types of STDs), she could be exposing herself to the possible infections of more than two thousand people if she slept with him once.[102] Wisely, she chose not to take the risk.

## 78

*I have heard that teenage girls are at a high risk of getting STDs. Why is that?*

Women are more susceptible to STDs than men because of the nature of their reproductive organs. Many STDs survive best where it is dark, moist, and warm. Because the woman's reproductive system is mostly interior, her body is more easily infected. Compared to a man, she also has a larger surface area of tissue that certain STDs might affect. Furthermore, a woman's body is exposed to infectious diseases for a longer amount of time after intercourse. These biological differences make women more likely to catch certain STDs.

The risk of infection is greater for young women because the cervix of a teenager is immature. In what is known as the "transformation zone" of her cervix, young women have what is called "cervical ectopy." This means that the cells from within the cervical canal extend out toward the opening of the cervix. Such cells are sensitive to infections, and so their exposure makes the women more vulnerable to certain STDs. The rapid cell changes within the cervix also make a young woman more susceptible to certain diseases. When a woman reaches her mid-twenties, the cervix will have matured and some of its tissue been replaced by a different type that is more resistant to infections from STDs.[103]

The birth control pill also increases a young woman's chance of contracting certain STDs because it interferes with her immune system.[104] The Pill also causes the production of a certain type of cervical mucus that makes it easier for cancer-causing agents to have access to a woman's body.[105]

All this research only confirms the fact that a woman's body is like her heart: she is not designed for multiple sexual partners. She is made for love.

# 9

# Purity Renewed

## 79

### *Can God forgive you if you have had premarital sex?*

Yes. Not only *can* God forgive you, He longs to forgive you. The Bible says that even the angels in heaven rejoice when people return to God (Luke 15:10). Elsewhere, the Scriptures say, "To the penitent He provides a way back, He encourages those who are losing hope! . . . Turn again to the Most High and away from sin" (Sir. 17:19, 21, *NAB*). If we repent He will forgive any sin, including premarital sex.

In the Gospel of John, a crowd wanted to kill a woman who was caught in sexual sin. In his book, *The Love That Satisfies*, Christopher West points out: "It is in the midst of this feeling of emptiness and shame that she meets Christ. The anxious crowd was ready to stone her. Christ said whoever was without sin could cast the first stone. According to His own words, Jesus could have thrown a stone. But Jesus came not to condemn. He came to save."[1] After Jesus sent the people away to think about their own sins, He asked, " 'Woman, where are they? Has no one condemned you?' She said, 'No one, Lord.' And Jesus said, 'Neither do I condemn you; go, and do not sin again' " (John 8:1–11). This personal encounter with the love of God is what each person needs when their heart is weighed down with the burden of sin.

Scripture repeatedly reminds us of the mercy of God. Psalm 103:12 reads, "As far as the east is from the west, so far does He remove our transgressions from us." Lamentations 3:22–23 states, "His mercies never come to an end; they are new every morning." God holds no grudges and does not look down on you because of the past. On the contrary, He says, "I have swept away your transgressions like a cloud, and your sins like mist; return to me, for I have redeemed you. . . . I will not remember your sins" (Is. 44:22, 43:25).

Many people assume that they need to become perfect in order for God to love them. The story of the prodigal son shows that this isn't the case. When the son who deserted his father decided to return to him, the father saw him "while he was yet at a distance" and ran to him (Luke 15:20). There is no mention of the son's running. This seems to imply that the father covered most of the distance between them. In the same way, as soon as you turn your heart back to God, He is already there waiting for you with open arms. In fact, your desire to return to Him is itself a sign that He is with you.

When you come to Him in prayer, He will not be thinking, "Oh, here comes that kid who did all that stuff at that party." Instead He is thinking the same thing He was thinking thousands of years ago: "Fear not, for I have redeemed you; I have called you by name, you are mine. . . . Behold, I have graven you on the palms of my hands" (Is. 43:1; 49:16). The greatest sin you have ever committed is like a grain of sand next to the mountain of His mercies.

Jesus instituted the sacrament of reconciliation to bring the gift of His forgiveness to us. After He rose from the dead, He came to the apostles, gave them His peace, and then breathed on them. The only other place in the Bible where God breathes on anyone is at the moment of creation. So we know something big is happening here. Jesus then said, "If you forgive the sins of any, they are forgiven; if you retain the sins of any, they are retained" (John 20:21–23).

For two thousand years the Church has made this healing gift from Jesus available to us, so that we can hear the consoling words of absolution: "God, the Father of mercies, through the death and resurrection of His Son has reconciled the world to Himself and sent the Holy Spirit among us for the forgiveness of sins; through the ministry of the Church may God give you pardon and peace, and I absolve you from your sins in the name of the Father, and of the Son, and of the Holy Spirit."

So do not run from mercy. Come to the great sacrament of reconciliation, and receive the gift of God's forgiveness.

## 80

*I have been with a lot of guys in high school, and I have a horrible reputation. I'm going to college in the fall, and I'm looking forward to starting with a clean slate. Is it possible to become innocent again?*

I had a friend in college who looked up to a young woman I will call "Rachel." She was a resident assistant (RA) in my friend's dormitory and was a campus leader. More importantly, Rachel seemed to reflect the love of Jesus to everyone who crossed her path. My friend always admired her purity and innocence. One night this RA shared her testimony with my friend. Rachel had been sexually active throughout high school but chose to accept God's invitation and turn her life around. My friend was astonished as Rachel opened her heart and revealed how Christ had made her a new creation. Now Rachel is married to a great man of God, and they have begun to raise a beautiful family.

This young woman is living proof of Saint Paul's words: "There-fore, if any one is in Christ, he is a new creation; the old has passed away, behold, the new has come. All this is from God, who through Christ reconciled us to Himself" (2 Cor. 5:17–18). Notice that Saint Paul says that this is from God, not from us. All we can do is come to the Lord in our woundedness and allow Him to work His miracles.

Do not let yourself fall into despair, thinking, "I already gave my virginity away, so what does it matter now? Once it's gone it's gone. What use am I to God, and what good guy would want me now?" One young woman said that after she lost her virginity, "I've never hated myself more. But it was done. My virginity was gone. Never could I get it back. It didn't matter after that, so sex

became an everyday occurrence. My only fear was losing Bobby
—he was the first—and even if he treated me badly (and there
were those times), I was going to do anything I could to hang on
to him."[2] Christ is there for you now, and He calls you to cling
to Him. He still has a plan for your life.

Remember when Jesus fed the multitudes in the Gospel of
Matthew? He asked how much food they had and they brought
Him five loaves and two fish—not much if you need to feed five
thousand, not counting women and children. He took what little
they had, multiplied it, fed the thousands, and had enough left
over to fill twelve baskets (Matt. 14:13–21). We can learn from
this that it does not matter how little we have to give Him. What
matters is how fully we give what little we have. He will take care
of the miracle in you. You just come to Him to be loved by Him
as you are. Jesus will take your sins of scarlet and in their place
paint an image of His mercy for the world to see. In the words of
the prophet Isaiah, "Though your sins are like scarlet, they shall
be as white as snow; though they are red like crimson, they shall
become like wool" (Is. 1:18).

The question is not whether Christ can make you a new creation but whether you have faith that He will. He says to you as
He said to the blind men in the Gospel of Matthew: "Do you
believe that I am able to do this?" (Matt. 9:28). Say yes, and pray
as David did in the Psalms, "Create in me a clean heart, O God,
and put a new and right spirit within me" (Ps. 51:10). And remember that Jesus said, "Whatever you ask in my name, I will
do it" (John 14:13). God will give you this clean slate, a purity
that you can guard and build on.

## 81

*I have made some big mistakes in the past, but I do not know how to
bring this up with the guy I am seeing right now, or even if I should.
What would you recommend?*

Do not feel that you should tell a guy all about your past just
because you are in a relationship with him. If the relationship is

serious and possibly heading toward marriage, then it is good to be honest with him regarding these issues. However, pray about the timing of this, and do not feel pressured to pour everything out. Be general, and admit that you made some mistakes in past relationships and that you really want this relationship to be pure and focused on God. As time progresses and you feel comfortable and the timing seems right, you may want to disclose more.

If and when this happens, keep the following in mind: Do not be overly explicit in explaining everything that happened. These details could harm the guy you are seeing. Without being in any way dishonest, be prudent about how much you disclose. You might not end up marrying this man, and if you have shared every single memory and hurt, then the emotional bond you have created could make it difficult to break things off. Also, it would be troubling to know that this man who is not your husband knows things about you that only your husband should know.

If you do end up marrying him, reassure him of how much he means to you. A study of 130 couples with strong marriages found that most of the husbands reported that their wives knew how to make them feel good about themselves.[3] Do not talk a lot about how intimate you have been with other men. Simply reaffirm in his heart that he is your man. Frequently the previous intimacies of one spouse will cause feelings of pain, inferiority, or resentment in the other partner. So love him all the more to quell any discomfort he may have about feeling compared to others.

Finally, since you may not have the gift of your virginity left to give him, here is a suggestion. A young woman I know lost her virginity during high school and experienced more than one broken sexual relationship. Instead of giving in to despair that she would have nothing left to give her future husband, she came up with a beautiful idea. She went to confession, made a commitment to reclaim her purity, and wrote a letter of encouragement to herself to stay firm in this resolve. She listed all the reasons she would no longer lead a promiscuous life. She included in this letter all the things she hoped for in a future husband and promised to wait for God to bring them together. Whenever she felt tempted to return to her former life, she pulled this letter out and reminded herself that true love was possible and that she should save herself for her future husband. Each time she read the letter, she added to it, and she wrote to her future husband. This letter was a constant support for her, and each time she added to it she became stronger in her convictions. By the time of her wedding, she had a large envelope filled with many pages that she waited to give to her husband on their honeymoon.

I know all these details about her, because I am the husband who received those letters. What a comfort and a blessing it was for me to see that, although she made mistakes, she turned her life around and saved herself for me. She could have said, "It's too late for me. Once your virginity is gone it's gone. I might as well forget about ever being pure again." Instead she trusted in the Lord and had faith that He had a plan for her life.

Therefore it is never too late. Have courage and trust in God for a godly husband. You are worth it.

### 82

*I am dating someone with a sinful past who has made an incredible conversion and is really pure now. The problem is that what this person did keeps haunting me. Any suggestions on how to get beyond this?*

One reason why these thoughts keep coming to mind is probably because you are trying to push them down and out of your mind without dealing with them. Sweeping them under the rug will allow them to keep coming back to bug you. As I see it, the solution is not to repress these thoughts but to deal with them by accepting them and lifting them up. Whenever you have these troubling thoughts, do three things.

First, if the relationship is heading toward marriage, do not be afraid to talk to your boyfriend or girlfriend about the struggle you are having. If you do not feel ready for this, perhaps you can speak with a priest or some other counselor you respect. How-ever, remember that good relationships require open and honest communication. Also, it is better that these issues come to the surface before marriage instead of within marriage. When you bring up your concerns, make sure not to blame him or her for the past but rather express the fact that you want to work through this issue together. Share your insecurities, fears, or hurts, and allow the other person to love you. This will require some vul-nerability on your part and some patience and empathy from him or her. If your love is strong and forgiving, the two of you will be able to overcome this difficulty. In the meantime, do not fear that these haunting thoughts of the past will never diminish. Over the course of time, you should feel greater peace as your love deepens.

Second, do not dwell on the past, but offer those thoughts to Jesus and His Mother when they come to mind. Give thanks that the Lord has brought your date away from that lifestyle. Then offer that pain in your heart as a prayer for the person's healing, for your date's former partners, and for all those who are living in sin. Anytime the memories bother you, use that as a reminder to pray for these intentions. Because of Christ's sufferings, our trials in life have redemptive value when we accept them with faith and offer them up to Him. In other words, Jesus can use your suffering to bring grace to others. You need to realize the good that the Lord can do through it.

Finally, resolve never to lead your date into sin. The Lord will heal you both as He knows best. In the meantime, let the pain become a prayer.

## 83

*A guy I barely knew raped me at a party. What should I do, and how do I heal from this emotionally?*

I am so sorry to hear what you have been through. I have several friends who have been through the same thing, and I have learned from them that there are a number of things you can do.

First of all, a man who forces himself on a woman has committed a crime as well as a sin. If you have been raped, you should discuss it with your parents. As difficult as this may seem, you need their comfort and consolation during this difficult time. When a woman suffers any form of sexual abuse, part of her healing process involves showing her wounded heart and receiving validation. Without this she may come to blame herself or simply grieve in silence.

If you feel that it is impossible to tell your parents, at least work on improving your relationship with them, so that you will be able to open up to them one day. In the meantime find some adult with whom you can speak about this, such as a priest, teacher, counselor, or youth minister. You are not alone in this, and they are there to give you the help that I cannot. Among the things you need to talk about are the possibilities of getting counseling and pressing charges; after all, the guy may do the same thing to someone else. By standing up to him, you have the opportunity to protect others from him. Speaking of date rape, Wendy Shalit said, "A man who did not respect female modesty wasn't more manly—he was less of a man. . . . [He] wasn't displaying his masculinity, only his immaturity. He was announcing, in effect, that he didn't understand what it meant to be a man." [4] So if you can press charges against this guy, you'll not only be bringing him to justice; you'll also give him a much-needed lesson on how *not* to treat a lady.

In order to find peace in your suffering, you will need to learn to let go of any hatred, so that bitterness will not take root in your heart. When painful memories come back to you, learn to transform that pain into prayer. Since Jesus said to pray even for our enemies, pray for the man who hurt you. The more anger or hatred you feel toward him, the more you will need to conquer that anger and hatred—for your sake as well as his. Pray that he may encounter Christ and that he may realize what it means to be a man. By praying for him as Jesus prayed for those who put him to death, you will be practicing the essence of forgiveness: namely, continuing to will the other person's good. Forgiveness does not mean that you ignore what he did to you or that you do not press charges. It means that you allow Christ's love rather than your own pain and anger to determine your attitude toward this man.

Increase your prayer time as well, since God is a healer of wounds seen and unseen. As the healing process begins, do not think that no guy will ever love you. This man took from you, but you still have yourself to give. Remember, you did not give yourself to him.

Also, know that being raped is not a sin. Where there is no consent, there is no sin.

Finally, take a look at your social group and see if this is the best bunch for you. Check out church youth groups in your area, because solid friends are priceless. In the words of Sirach, "A faithful friend is a sturdy shelter: he that has found one has found a treasure" (6:14).

## 84

*What can I do in the future to prevent being raped?*

Here are a few practical tips for how to avoid being a victim of rape. Do not allow yourself to become isolated with a guy you do not know or trust. Choose good friends—both male and female. The male friends will be gentlemen, and your good female friends will not want to hang out with men who are not. If you are at a party, stick close to your friends, and look out for each other.

Drugs and alcohol are factors that make rape and sexual mistakes much more common, so stay clear of these. If you are of age to drink, know your limit and do not leave your drink unattended. If someone hands you a drink that is already opened, do not take it.

If you are on a date with a guy, be straightforward about your boundaries. Of course, a gentleman should always respect your no or "Stop" no matter what, but too much intimacy creates sexual momentum, and even a guy who intends to respect your wishes might not always stop when he should. So play it safe and respect yourself by saving sexual arousal for marriage.

## 85

### *Is it OK for a girl to have an abortion if she was raped?*

A few years ago in the former Yugoslavia, a group of soldiers broke into a convent and raped a nun named Sister Lucy Ver-trusc. As a result of the rape, she became pregnant. Sister Lucy was faced with a decision: do I keep this child, whose face will be an icon of the man who raped me? She chose life and said, "I will be a mother. The child will be mine and no one else's. . . . Someone has to begin to break the chain of hatred that has always destroyed our countries. And so, I will teach my child only one thing: love. This child, born of violence, will be a witness along with me that the only greatness that gives honor to a human being is forgiveness."[5] She knew that the baby did not deserve the death penalty for the crime his father committed.

Women who abort children who were conceived by rape often say that it took longer to recover from the abortion than from the rape. In general, post-abortive women often experience depression, and they are six times as likely to commit suicide than women who gave birth.[6] When a woman has been raped, has she not suffered enough emotional pain? Will she be comforted when the suffering of the rape is compounded with the guilt of knowing that she took her child's life? Has she not been violated enough? Now is the time when she needs to be immersed in love and supported, so that some good can come from the tragedy of the rape.

Aside from the emotional consequences, when a woman gets an abortion, she faces numerous health risks, such as perforation of the uterus, septic shock, sterility, and sometimes even death. This is no way to treat a woman who has suffered enough because of rape.

If you or someone you know is pregnant and unmarried, call 1-800-866-4666 to find a local crisis pregnancy center that can help. The people who work for these organizations will offer hope, healing, encouragement, and practical support—not to mention plenty of love.

## 86

*I want to start over, but I can't give up sex. What should I do to get back on track?*

I recommend six steps to get back on track:

1. *Recognize* your mistakes and admit your faults, but do not let yourself get preoccupied with them. Like everyone else, you are not perfect, so give yourself the freedom to forgive yourself and then decide to overcome your weakness. You have to want it for yourself.

Recognizing your faults is one side of the coin, but recognizing that you deserve respect is the other. Many people who have fallen into sexual sins have lost all self-respect. They feel that there is no point in turning back, but even if they wanted to turn back it would be impossible, and that even if it were possible, no one would love them after all they have done. You do deserve respect, but you have to respect yourself first. When we commit sexual sin, we lose respect for our bodies and for the bodies of others. When this happens it becomes easier and easier to fall into un-healthy physical relationships. Only you can choose to break out of this. It is important that you know from the get-go that the healing process will demand work and sacrifice on your part.

2. *Repent.* You have realized that you do have a problem, so come to God as His child, asking for His grace. Ask Him to for-give you and heal you, not only of this area of weakness but also of any other wounds or vulnerabilities, however deep or old they might be, that might have contributed to your problem in this area. As Jesus said, "Apart from me you can do nothing" (John 15:5). You are wholly dependent upon God to get out of this,

and He is wholly capable of finishing the good work that He has begun in you. The Holy Spirit is already alive in you, moving you to recognize your problem and seek a new beginning. God is at work in you; He has not abandoned you.

Come to Him in the great sacrament of reconciliation and experience His mercies. He forgives, heals, restores, and encourages us, but we must come to Him with sincere hearts: "A broken and contrite heart, O God, you will not despise" (Ps. 51:17).

3. *Resist* the temptation to give in to destructive thinking: "I'm a bad person, I don't deserve real love, and I need sex. I'm addicted—I can't help myself." None of those things is true! Sexual addictions can be real, but more often than not people tell themselves that they are addicted to things like sex in order to make themselves feel as if they do not have any control over their behavior. In their minds they have no choice but to keep indulging in it. But this is not true. You do have control, and you do have dignity. You are not a "bad person." You are a son or daughter of God. That is your identity. Sure, you have made mistakes. But do not identify yourself by them.

Take to heart the consoling words of Pope John Paul II to the youth of the world:

> Although I have lived through much darkness, . . . I have seen enough evidence to be unshakably convinced that no difficulty, no fear is so great that it can completely suffocate the hope that springs eternal in the hearts of the young. . . . Do not let that hope die! Stake your lives on it! We are not the sum of our weaknesses and failures; we are the sum of the Father's love for us and our real capacity to become the image of His Son.[7]

You *are* worthy of love, because that is what God has created you for. When you make mistakes, you do not forfeit your worthiness to receive love. Also, you do not "need" sex. Perhaps you have formed an attachment to the pleasure of sex or to its emotional intimacy. Perhaps sex has become for you a way to avoid genuine relationships. Instead of using sex to express intimacy, you may be using it to escape intimacy. God's grace is stronger than those chains, and He will give you a greater love if you cling to Him. Your desires will not disappear when you come to Him, but He will give you His love so that you will be able to overcome the temptations.

4. *Refrain* from bad relationships, and make a clean break from any unhealthy relationships. These drive you deeper into loneliness. Sometimes breaking them off is easy; the hard part is not running back to them. This is when you must run to God instead.

When we use sex to feel secure, we end up feeling more insecure than ever, and we may be tempted to jump into sexual acts to deal with our fear of not being lovable. It becomes a vicious cycle. It is then that you must come back to God with all your heart. Do not let fear stand in the way, and do not run elsewhere to find the fulfillment and wholeness that only He can give.

5. *Resolve* to live in purity. Part of the process is moving away from bad situations, but the other half is moving into good ones. Make that decision that no one else can make for you. You have to want it for yourself, so set your guidelines, write them down before you enter a relationship, and stick by them.

Josh McDowell said, "After interviewing thousands of young people, I am convinced that many teens and young singles are sexually active not because they really want to be, but because they don't have any deep personal reasons for waiting until they are married."[8] You need a vision of real love, a hope that will make it easier for you to forego the passing traps of lust in favor of a better and more beautiful kind of life and love. It does exist. So go for purity, and make a conscious effort to do things differently in the future.

For starters, change the way you approach relationships. It is a sign of maturity to seek the advice of older and wiser people, particularly our parents. If your parents are unwilling or unavailable, go to a good priest, youth minister, relative, or other mentor to get input on your relationships.

Also, look at your selection of friends, music, magazines, movies, and other things that influence you. If you need motivation to persevere in purity, browse through the videos, links, and articles at chastityproject.com. Also, see if you can get involved in a local youth group, Bible study, or prayer group at school or church. This may be stepping out of your usual social circles, but you need that support and fellowship. In addition, find a good priest or counselor with whom you can speak openly and regularly about your struggles. A wise counselor will be able to discern the extent of your problem and lead you on the path to purity. Lastly, as a reminder to yourself and a sign to others of your commitment, you could wear a ring to symbolize your commitment to chastity.

6. *Renew* yourself through prayer. It is essential to know that you are deeply loved by God, so set a time for prayer each day. He will work wonders in you. As a friend of mine once said, "Hold nothing back from God. What He can do through the soul that gives itself utterly to Him! Limitless!" He has so much He is waiting to tell you and so much He wants to give you. The best is yet to come (Jer. 29:11–14). If you are serious about wanting true love, a new path awaits, but only you can make that decision to be generous with God.

## 87

*I have gone to confession, but I can't forgive myself for what I did.*
*How do you get over the feelings of guilt and regret and forget the*
*bad experiences?*

As you are realizing, sin often leaves deep wounds in the heart. During this difficult time when you may want nothing more than to move on and feel forgiven, keep the following points in mind.

Consider the story of the prodigal son. He returned home to his father and said, "I have sinned against heaven and before you; I am no longer worthy to be called your son" (Luke 15:21). Look at the father's reaction. He welcomed him with open arms, threw the finest robes on him, put rings on his fingers, and threw a party. The son stopped moping and accepted the father's merciful love. He did not sit outside the celebration but allowed his father to rejoice that he had returned. The father's joy embraced the son. This parable not only tells us of God's mercy; it also shows us how to accept His forgiveness. We might feel as if our sins make us unworthy to be a child of God, but when we repent the Father looks into our eyes and sees His own life within us. He sees His own Son within us.

Nevertheless, it is true that sexual wounds take time to heal. Be patient and do not beat yourself up. All of us must come to terms with the parts of our past we wish we could erase. We are all sinners, and God's work of restoring us to wholeness is one that will unfold in time. As He works to heal you, these feelings of remorse are bound to come to the surface.

In some ways, forgiving yourself for your own mistakes is similar to forgiving someone else who has hurt you. Forgiveness does not necessarily mean that you do not feel the pain anymore. In the words of the *Catechism of the Catholic Church*: "It is not in our power not to feel or to forget an offense; but the heart that offers itself to the Holy Spirit turns injury into compassion and purifies the memory in transforming the hurt into intercession."[9] The pain you feel over your own failures can be transformed in the same way. You actually can use the bad memories and wounds of sin that rush back into your mind as a way to heal the past.

Because the past sometimes hurts, we try to suppress the memories and shove them to a place in our mind where they will stop haunting us. There is a better way. When the hurts of the past weigh upon your heart, take those pains and offer them as a prayer for all who may have been hurt in these past experiences —including yourself. When the flashbacks happen, take that as a reminder to offer up a prayer for healing.

In time God will heal the past, and you may think about it less often. Let Him work on that. Your task is to accept His forgiveness and to draw close to Him. Do not give in to despair, thinking that you are of no use to God because you made some mistakes. Look at Rahab in the Old Testament. She was a prostitute who turned back to God, and Jesus was her descendant.

Also realize that God wants to purify you not only for your sake but for the sake of those you will lead to Him. The Lord will be able to use you and your past to reach and heal others who are going through the same difficulties that you have been through. You are in a position to reach hearts that no one else could reach. Listen to God's voice if He calls you to help others in big or small ways in the apostolate of purity. By ministering to others in this way, you will regain a sense of wholeness and peace. You will see for yourself that God can write straight with crooked lines.

It is also good to recognize that *living purely in future relationships will begin to heal the past*. Relationships can actually be healing, not scarring. To get relationships off in the right direction, be up front with regard to your values, and do not wait for an intimate moment to decide or announce your guidelines.

Finally, remember that forgiveness is not a feeling. Sometimes feelings of consolation are present, but when they are not, we need to trust that God has still forgiven us. His mercy is a free gift from a good God. Hannah Arendt wrote: "Without being forgiven, released from the consequences of what we have done, our capacity to act would, as it were, be confined to a single deed from which we could never recover; we would remain the victims of its consequences forever."[10] Thankfully, because of the death and resurrection of Christ, the debt of our sins has been paid, and we are free to call God our *Abba*, Father. Your worth rests in God, and He loves you.

## 88

*I have been through a lot of really bad relationships. How can I learn to trust a guy again?*

Begin by jumping headlong into an intense, intimate relationship with a trustworthy guy—Jesus. The more you get to know Him, the more you will be able to recognize guys that resemble Him and guys that do not. Recognize that the ones who are most like Him are most worthy of trust, but do not be quick to give your heart away. The Lord can heal anything, but the healing of wounds and the rebuilding of trust is a process that takes time.

Also, do not think that you always need to be in a relationship
—especially if you are in high school. Take some time for just you
and God. Having alone time with the Lord is part of the healing
process. In addition, having God-centered relationships will help
to mend the wounds of the past. To find the healing and love
that you truly deserve, turn to God and follow His lead in your
relationships.

In the future keep the following four considerations in mind
when choosing your companions: *First*, take your time before entering a relationship. Instead of worrying about trusting boyfriends
in the future, begin to build innocent friendships with decent guys.
This safe environment will help you to see that there are plenty
of good guys out there. *Second*, do not date someone if you cannot
see yourself marrying him. *Third*, do not marry someone unless
he loves God more than he loves you. *Fourth*, do not carry on a
relationship with a guy who is unable to resist temptation. If he
is unable to refuse temptation before marriage, how will he resist
temptation within marriage? What woman wants to marry a guy
who cannot say no to sex?

## 89

*What if I feel that I don't deserve a good guy? Will someone still love
me even if I made some mistakes and am carrying "baggage"?*

You may think that the holier a guy is, the less likely he would be
to accept you with your "baggage." Actually, the opposite is true.
The Bible speaks repeatedly of God as the Bridegroom and His
people as the bride. When Israel turned away from God in the Old
Testament, it was described as an act of spiritual adultery. In the
book of Hosea, it is written, "The land commits great harlotry by
forsaking the Lord. . . . She . . . decked herself with her ring and
jewelry, and went after her lovers, and forgot me, says the Lord"
(Hos. 1:2; 2:13). Even so, the Lord took her in: "I will espouse
you for ever; I will espouse you in righteousness and in justice,

in steadfast love, and in mercy. I will espouse you in faithfulness; and you shall know the Lord" (Hos. 2:19-20).

When a "good guy" loves and accepts a girl who has a bad past, it is an act of love in imitation of the heavenly Father. God loved Israel even when she was impure, and a "good guy" is able to love a woman even if she has an impure past. Through the work of redemption God purifies His bride, "that He might present the Church to Himself in splendor, without spot or wrinkle or any such thing, that she might be holy and without blemish" (Eph. 5:27). Similarly, by living purely with you, a godly man can help you heal your memories. The more a man is like God, the more He will be able to love you as God loves all of us, despite our "baggage." He loves us where we are, but loves us too much to leave us there.

None of us deserve the gifts that God bestows upon us. His generosity is unimaginable. Scripture says, "No ear has ever heard, no eye ever seen, any God but you, doing such deeds for those who wait for Him" (Is. 64:34, *NAB*). "Shall I not open for you the floodgates of heaven, to pour down blessing upon you without measure?" (Mal. 3:10, *NAB*).

The truth is, we all have made mistakes. Even good guys have their imperfections. Suppose, though, that you met a young man who had a less-than-perfect past. Would you refuse to accept him? If you would accept such a man, then why would a good guy refuse to accept you? Besides, if he holds your past against you, is he really that good a guy?

Keep hope alive, and may the following words from a husband to his wife (who had slept with another man before marriage) be a comfort for you: "I was always held to a higher standard by you than by any other girl I ever dated. You were strong, uncompromised, and pure. That's all I know of you. That's all that matters to me." [11] Do not be afraid that you will not find a good guy or that you will not have a successful marriage. The absence of virginity does not doom marriages, but the absence of the virtue of chastity does.

# 10

# How to Stay Pure

## 90

*What can my girlfriend and I do on dates so that we don't end up going too far?*

Step number one begins before a date: if you are serious about the virtue of chastity, then pray often for the grace to be pure and to avoid temptations. As Mother Teresa said, "To be pure, to remain pure, can only come at a price, the price of knowing God and loving him enough to do his will. He will always give us the strength we need to keep purity as something beautiful for God. Purity is the fruit of prayer."[1]

In the words of Scripture, "How can a young man keep his way pure? By guarding it according to your word. With my whole heart I seek you; let me not wander from your commandments! I have laid up your word in my heart, that I might not sin against you" (Ps. 119:9–11). Stay near to Christ, since He is the source of purity. Couples who draw near to Jesus allow His love to flow through them to each other. In fact, the closer they get to God, the more they will be able to love each other. They get out of the way and let Him provide the love that exists between them. This is purity of heart, a life of intimacy with God.

Prayer is our first priority. After that we need to set guidelines in order to avoid temptations. If you are alone at home and kissing your girlfriend on the couch, it is not the best time to start thinking about your boundaries. Know them in advance, because your judgment will be anything but objective during a passionate moment.

What should you do during a date? Here is a great way to get going in the right direction (a friend of mine at San Diego State

University went on a date like this and recommended it to me). Pick up your girlfriend on a Saturday afternoon and head off to church. Go to reconciliation, and then take some time to talk about your relationship. Prayerfully set some firm boundaries regarding intimate behavior. Talking about these things will open up communication and contribute to a healthy relationship. Often couples who establish these boundaries and goals feel a new sense of freedom, peace, and security in the relationship.

While discussing your boundaries, you may realize that the two of you are wired differently. For example, a woman needs to realize that a man's body works differently than hers. She might be content snuggling with a guy, but the guy's body is working at a much faster pace. Be honest with yourself and with each other, and make your resolutions clear. Men respond and work best when they have a concrete goal and feel they are needed for a task. If it is clear to you that she trusts you in leading her toward God, it will be easier for you to accept the challenge.

After your talk, sit there in church and write each other a love letter promising to lead one another to purity and to God. Vague resolutions do not stand well, so do not just say, "I promise to be more pure." This kind of resolution is worthless. Be specific. Exchange the letters, read them, and go buy a pair of chastity rings as a reminder of your commitment to God and to each other. (Tell your parents about this. I am sure your mom or dad would be more than willing to fork over some money for a chastity ring!) After buying the rings, go back to your place (with your parents or roommate home), and cook her dinner. Even if you don't know how to cook, give it a shot. You'll at least make her laugh.

I consider this romance without regret. By striving toward God together, you will find a unique bond that is known by few couples. You'll also begin to see why married couples "who frequently pray together are twice as likely as those who pray less often to describe their marriages as highly romantic."[2]

Besides the chastity ring and love letter date, I recommend going on group dates, since you are less likely to get into tempting situations with good friends around you. Be careful about spending too much time alone. Even if you do not group date, people are so stuck on going to dinner and a movie that dates can get pretty monotonous. Get creative, and do some service work together for a change. Maybe the two of you could buy groceries, make lunches, and pass them out to poor people downtown. If you are into sports, then try some sport together that you have never done.

The important thing is to plan ahead for a date, especially if it will be in the evening. When a couple has not put any effort into it, it is easier for boredom to set in, and they may become sexually intimate since they cannot think of anything else to do.

Lastly—and perhaps most importantly—avoid places where the two of you have fallen in the past. If you have a favorite scenic overlook, do not expect to drive there late at night with her and end up playing Scrabble. If the two of you always seem to go too far when you are at her house alone, go somewhere else or wait for her parents to get home before you visit. Likewise avoid alcohol and drugs, since these are the gateway to many regrets.

I just rattled off a bunch of useful guidelines, but it is important to recognize that guidelines do not create purity of heart. They create a safer environment in which the virtue of purity can grow. The actual development of purity comes about through prayer. Through our interior life with God, He reveals our calling and mission. This is essential for a guy, because the key to glorifying God in our relationships is to know what our task is with a girl.

Some men go to great lengths to plan a night so that they say and do all the right things to get a woman to hop in bed with them. They know their goal, plan ahead, and achieve what they set out to do. We Christian men have a great deal to learn from these guys—not in regard to their goal but in regard to their focused determination. Before spending time with a young woman, we must have a premeditated agenda and deliberate plans to bless the girl. Instead of being determined to take from the girl—to "get some"—we are called from the cross to empty ourselves and to direct our creativity, skill, and passion toward selfless love instead of selfish lust.

Bluntly, God invites us to come and die. As Christ said, "If any man would come after me, let him deny himself and take up his cross and follow me" (Mark 8:34). It is through this emptying of ourselves that we find our manhood.

## 91

*If you are on a date and things are going too far, how do you stop suddenly and tell him no?*

Most situations of impurity can be avoided if you think ahead and avoid people and places that are likely to endanger your purity. But if you are already in a situation where you need to cool it off, there are a number of things you can say. Everyone seems to recommend different approaches.

For starters, do not underestimate the direct approach: simply saying, "We need to stop—we're going too far," may do the trick, especially if it is already understood that you are committed to chastity. Include yourself as well as him—say, "*We* need to stop," instead of, "*You* need to stop"—to indicate that you are not blaming him, just putting on the brakes. This may be hard, but consider it a learning experience so that you do not let things get to that point again.

On the other hand, some prefer the humorous approach: "Here's my cell phone. Call my dad, and if he says it's OK for us to do what you want, then I'll do it." Or, "You've got protection? Good. You are going to need it if you don't get your hands off me." And then there is, "Everyone's doing it? Then you shouldn't have trouble finding someone else."

These may be entertaining, but I do not know how realistic they are. It might be more practical to give him a compliment—guys love that—such as, "I really like you, and I have so much fun when we're together, but this is the kind of stuff I want to save for marriage." Also, feel free to blame your parents for your decision: "My mom would kill me if she ever found out we were doing this. We need to stop."

Another reason to skip the humorous approach is that this is not a time for jokes but for witnessing to the truth of love. Be humble but clear, confident, and firm, and see this as a teachable moment. Use a verbal no *and* a no with your body language. If you are lying with him on a couch and whispering a halfhearted "no," he probably will not take you seriously, since you do not take your commitment to purity seriously. Also, when a girl is unable to say no, she is less attractive. Wendy Shalit described a "deadness" in girls' demeanor "that comes from inauthenticity, from giving away too much," from not knowing how to set limits and having the character to stand by them.[3] To avoid this deadness, pray to God for the strength to maintain and grow in your purity.

Even if you don't convince your date to live purely in his own life, that's OK. It's more important that you do what is right than it is for you to convince another. You should not have to play the chastity cop. In fact, both people in a relationship should be mutually accountable. The responsibility to blow the whistle should not rest entirely on one person. Also, you do not owe your date a thirty-minute presentation on why chastity is important to you, and you certainly do not owe him sexual favors. If he does not accept a simple no, then he does not love you.

Let the guy go, and look for a man who knows how to honor a woman. Most importantly, do not be afraid. One teenage girl wrote to me and said, "I really like him, but I do not know why I have sex, like sometimes I am scared to say no." There are worse things in the world than not being asked out again by a guy who only loves himself. If he dumps you over this, then he did not deserve your attention to begin with. Could this be embarrassing? Perhaps. But regret lasts much longer than embarrassment.

It also might not be embarrassing at all. One high school girl said to me, "I know a lot of guys who act like they want sex just because they think they have to think that. But really, on the inside they are not like that at all." Sometimes it is a relief for a guy when a girl is clear about her boundaries and has strong values. It may take the pressure off a guy who assumes that you expect him to act like the rest of the guys. The numerous stories of sexual conquests that guys overhear in the locker room may make a good guy think that he is less of a man if he does not try to go as far with a woman as his classmates have. Also, some men are afraid that women will consider them unmanly or reject them if the men do not try to have sex with them. Your date may be trying to go too far with you in order to avoid appearing less of a man. Your character will serve to remind him of real manhood.

If you think that temptations make it almost impossible to say no, remember that you have the ability to tell your body what to do. It will obey you. If a married couple were in bed together and their house caught on fire, do you think they would say, "Oh, no! We can't say no to sex. We're going to die!" Or do you think they would stop their actions—no matter how intimate and exciting —and save their lives? In the same way, remember that you have the capacity to sacrifice the pleasures of the moment for a greater good—to save your spiritual life.

When things are going too far, value yourself enough to say no. Unfortunately, many young women use physical intimacy as a way of giving themselves value. The embraces feel like an affirmation of their worth, and perhaps because of mistakes they have made in the past, they do not understand the tremendous value of their bodies. Your purity is a treasure, so have the confidence to respect yourself. When the two of you work to preserve purity, it will keep an element of mystery and excitement in your relationship that is lost when couples do not bother to keep anything secret and sacred.

## 92

*The life of chastity seems so hard. How am I supposed to resist with all the pressure out there from the other guys, and how do I tell my girlfriend that I want to be pure without feeling like a geek?*

A heart filled with love rises to the greatest challenges. In college I used to wake up at 5:00 in the morning twice a week to meet with the young woman I was seeing. Then we would drive to Pittsburgh in the freezing weather in order to do pro-life work together. I am not a morning person, and since I was born in Florida and raised in Arizona, I am not real big on snow either. But the sacrifice of getting up in the cold did not seem to matter because of the joy of being together. In the same way, the sacrifices you make to live chastely seem light when they are done for the sake of love. In the words of Saint Josemaría Escrivá, "When you decide firmly to lead a clean life, chastity will not be a burden on you: it will be a crown of triumph." [4]

When we lose sight of why we are sacrificing, the challenges of love seem heavy. You may be tempted to think, "No one's going to get hurt from a little fun on a date. Maybe I should just give in." That is when you must look into your heart and remember why—or more specifically, for whom—you are waiting. What is worth more: a few moments of pleasure or giving your bride the lifelong joy of knowing that you saved yourself for her? Always remember that love for a woman and the exercise of chastity go hand in hand. *Chastity cannot exist without love, and love cannot exist without chastity.*

When it comes to love and lust, one will be in control. Either love will overpower lust and your passions will be under your control, or lust will dominate and corrupt any love that was once present. It is your choice.

I will admit that a life of chastity involves times of trial and even heroic struggle. This is because struggle cannot be separated from love. The kind of love that endures and makes you happy is not easy. "Chastity is a difficult, long term matter," Pope John Paul II said. "One must wait patiently for it to bear fruit, for the happiness of loving-kindness which it must bring. But at the same time, chastity is the sure way to happiness." [5] Did you catch that? *Chastity is the sure way to happiness.* Love can be demanding at times, but it is precisely because of that challenge that true love takes on such a rare beauty.

In regard to what to say to your girlfriend so that you do not feel like a geek, how about something along these lines: "I have so much fun when we're together, and I really like being with you . . . so I don't want to mess this up by doing things we could regret. I want to fall in love with you for all the right reasons."

Trust me, when you say that, "geek" will not be on her mind. But if she, or any of the guys, look down on you for having this much love, so be it. You care more about your God, the heart of your future spouse, and the health of your future children than you do about the passing pleasures of prom night and the opinions of an adolescent locker room. She is worth waiting for—even if you are the only one who seems to realize it. So wait for the woman God has in mind for you, and when you get married your bride can spend the entire honeymoon telling you how much of a geek she thinks you are for waiting for her. Sometimes being a geek is excessively romantic.

If others pressure you, some adults advise that you forget the insults and mockery. I advise the opposite. Remember the names that you are called for living a chaste life, and remember the jokes. Then when you stand before the altar and lift your bride's veil, listen. Listen carefully. Where is the laughter? There is only silence, because you have won. You are the victor; the guys who mocked you would pay a million bucks to be in your shoes right now.

True love is a great gift because it is costly. As Mother Teresa said, "Love, to be real, it must cost—it must hurt—it must empty us of self." [6] It might cost you your reputation. It might even cost you certain friendships. But this is precisely why true love is such a rarity today. Those who have the goal of true love should prepare their hearts for sacrifice. God knows the path is challenging, but He would not call us to this lifestyle without providing us the graces to live it.

Sure, the mockery is not fun while you are going through it, but think about *why* they are pressuring you. It is not because their lifestyle is so fulfilling and they want what is best for you, but because your life of chastity sets the standard high. This probably makes others feel guilty. Their consciences would bug them less if you made the same mistakes they are making. Believe me, you are not missing out on anything by not having a series of broken sexual relationships.

Withstand the abuse also for the sake of men. You see, we guys have a reputation as jerks and we bear a particular responsibility for the many wounds caused to women. There is a certain balance of love between the sexes that needs to be restored. Pope John Paul II wrote: "The man has a special responsibility, as if it depended more on him whether the balance is kept or violated or even—if it has already been violated—reestablished."[7] So I commend you for being willing to stand for virtue when it is anything but popular.

You may feel that you stick out in a bad way, but without self-mastery we do not stick out at all. We become dull beasts, and there is nothing unique about us. With purity we can become radiant, clear, and alive with a uniqueness that women will not fail to see. Sin dulls our individuality. So if we wish to be most unique and most fully ourselves, we will find our identity in Christ. God and women are both searching for men with backbone.

For God's sake, may we be such men. The world today desperately needs men who are not afraid to be gentlemen, men who understand what it means to be a man and are willing to take up that yoke of responsibility, men who will guard a woman instead of seeking ways to empty her of her innocence.

## 93

*How do you control sex drives? They can be a real pain sometimes —for girls as well as guys!*

It is not wrong to have sexual desires. It is what we do with them in our thoughts, words, and actions that can be good or bad. So here are some tips for training.

Step number one is prayer. Set a daily prayer time and stick to it. I also recommend the frequent reception of the sacraments, especially Mass and reconciliation. The Eucharist is the fountain of purity, so take advantage of those graces. Going to Mass will not take away all your temptations, but it will give you the grace of charity. In the Eucharist Christ gives Himself fully to us so that we might give ourselves fully. This is the foundation of chastity, because love motivates us to live for others instead of for ourselves. Make time for daily Mass and go whenever possible. If there is a church in your area that has a Eucharistic Adoration chapel, make frequent visits to Jesus there. In other words, *make your life intensely Eucharistic.*

There are many devotions that can strengthen your life. For example, pray a rosary every day. This takes only fifteen to twenty minutes, so set some time aside for that. Praying the stations of the cross is another source of tremendous power that people tend to overlook. For a simple prayer, quietly and devoutly say the names of Jesus, Mary, and Joseph. Take up a devotion to your guardian angel, who is always there to help you resist temptation. Turn to the Bible, because it is a great source of grace and consolation whenever we need it. For starters, read 1 Peter 5:6–10. Also find a good spiritual director. As they say, "He who has himself as a guide has a fool for a disciple."

Besides prayer, do not place yourself in relationships or situations where you know mistakes will happen. Sometimes we march right into tempting situations and then blame God that the temptations were too strong to resist. Surround yourself with good friends, because as Saint Paul said, "Bad company ruins good morals" (1 Cor. 15:33). We may have heard our parents say that before, but research backs it up: when most of a teen's friends are sexually active, that teen is thirty-one times as likely to get drunk and twenty-two times as likely to have smoked pot compared with teens who don't hang out with sexually active friends.[8] Other researchers have noted, "only 4 percent of young people whose friends were not sexually active were sexually active themselves. Amongst those whose friends *were* sexually active, the figure was 43 percent."[9]

If you watch MTV or vulgar sitcoms or if you read *Cosmopolitan*, *Seventeen*, or other things that you know to be impure, get rid of them. Consider them love pollution. Also avoid being idle. This is the chief means by which we end up falling into sin. Keep yourself occupied with friends, service work, sports, hobbies, and similar activities.

This all requires a determination for purity. But consider how people deny themselves to get the perfect body. If Americans spent one-tenth that time caring for their souls, we would be a nation of saints. No one thinks a man is repressive if he eats healthy food to prepare for a marathon. In the same way, what you are preparing for—love and holiness—requires serious training. You will not be repressing your sexual desires but redirecting that energy toward selfless love.

You are not alone in your struggle with temptation. In fact, even the saints endured similar battles. In the words of Saint Paul, "I do not do the good I want, but the evil I do not want is what I do. . . . But I see in my members another law at war with the law of my mind, making me captive to the law of sin that dwells in my members" (Rom. 7:19, 23). During this struggle, remember that God's grace is sufficient, for His power is made perfect in our weakness (2 Cor. 12:9). Ask God for the wisdom to avoid temptation and the grace to please Him. He will give these spiritual gifts—and many others—to those who ask for them. In the words of a wise priest, "The one obstacle that can turn our lives to misery is the refusal to believe that God will give us the victory of perfect chastity." [10]

## 94

*I don't understand the deal with modesty. If a guy has a bad imagination, that should be his issue and not mine. Why should I have to dress a certain way for his sake?*

If you are fed up with the way guys often treat women and wonder what can be done to restore a sense of respect, modesty is the solution. The problem is this: Many men today do not know how to relate to women. Part of the remedy for this ailment lies in the hands of women. Wendy Shalit said, "Ultimately, it seems that only men can teach other men how to behave around women, but those men have to be inspired by women in the first place; inspired enough to think the women are worth being courteous to."[11]

How will this happen? Well, many young women are aware that they have the power to seduce a man, but few girls are aware that their femininity also has the power to educate a guy. The way a girl dresses (not to mention the way she talks, dances, and so forth) has an extraordinary ability to help shape a man into a gentleman or into a beast.

I have read tens of thousands of pages of theology, counseling, and information about relationships and human sexuality, but I never learned how to treat a woman until I dated one who dressed modestly. It was captivating, and I realized for the first time that immodest dress gets in the way of seeing a woman for who she is. Immodest outfits might attract a man to a girl's body, but they distract him from seeing her as a person. As one man said, "If you want a man to respect you, and perhaps eventually fall in love with you, then you must show him that you respect yourself and that you recognize your dignity before God."[12]

A woman who dresses modestly inspires a guy in a way that I am not ashamed to admit I cannot explain. I suppose it is safe to say that it conveys your worth to us. When a woman dresses modestly, I can take her seriously as a woman because she is not constantly begging for attention. She knows that she's worth discovering. Such humility is radiant. Unfortunately, many women are so preoccupied with turning men's heads that they overlook their power to turn our hearts.

Sometimes femininity is confused with weakness, but nothing could be further from the truth. A woman who is truly feminine is well aware that she could dress like a collection of body parts and receive countless stares from guys. But she has the strength to leave room for mystery. Instead of dressing in a way that invites guys to lust, the way she dresses says, "I'm worth waiting for." She trusts God's timing, and she knows that she does not need to make boys gawk in order to catch the attention of the man God has planned for her.

In his letter on the dignity of women, Pope John Paul II said: "The hour is coming, in fact has come, when the vocation of women is being acknowledged in its fullness, the hour in which women acquire in the world an influence, an effect and a power never hitherto achieved. That is why, at this moment when the human race is undergoing so deep a transformation, women imbued with a spirit of the Gospel can do so much to aid humanity in not falling." [13]

So what is modesty? It is not about looking as ugly as possible. It is about taking the natural beauty of womanhood and adorning it in a way that reflects one's true identity. When a girl knows that she is a daughter of the King of heaven, she does not allow her outfits, conversations, and mannerisms to distract from this. She is aware that her body is sacred because it is a temple of the Holy Spirit. This brings about a certain humility of the body, since humility is the proper attitude toward greatness. In this case it is the greatness of being made in the image and likeness of God.

This is not an "I am woman, hear me roar!" bit, but a serene sense of not needing to grope for attention. Sure, guys will gawk at a woman who dresses provocatively, but in your heart do you long to be gawked at or to be loved? You want real love. When a girl dresses immodestly, she often does not realize that she robs herself of the intimacy for which she yearns. When a girl wears outfits that could not be any tighter without cutting off her circulation, guys will think she is trying to tell them, "Hey, boys, the greatest thing about me is my body!" They will stare and will probably agree. But if her body is the greatest thing about her, it must be all downhill from there. If that is the best she has to offer, why should they get to know her heart, her dreams, her personality, and her family? They want to get to know her body.

Dressing immodestly also harms a girl's chances of being loved. The type of guys who will be drawn to her will not be the type of guys who will treat her as a daughter of God. No matter how a woman dresses, she sends out an unspoken invitation for men to treat her the way she looks. For example, consider a magazine I recently saw at an airport newsstand. On the cover was a woman wearing a short skirt that could be mistaken for a wide belt. Her airtight top was scarcely the size of an unfolded napkin, and in big bold letters across the cover was "Suzie [or whatever her name was—I don't remember] wants men to respect her!" I wished her the best of luck and walked on to my gate, after covering up the magazine with a few issues of *Oprah*. (I consider this a corporal work of mercy—clothing the naked.) Although a girl deserves respect no matter what she wears, a guy can tell how much a woman respects herself by how she is dressed. If she does not respect herself, the odds are that guys will follow her lead.

In the heart of a woman, there is no desire to be a sex object. Is there a desire to receive attention, affection, and love? Certainly. But is there a desire to be reduced to an object? No girl wants to go there, but many do for the sake of receiving emotional gratification. When a girl puts on a belly-button-showing, spaghetti-strap shirt, she is not thinking about how she hopes to lead men to sin. She's probably thinking, "That's a cute top, and it will look perfect with my shoes." But beneath this simple desire to be attractive is a deeper desire to be accepted. If a girl understands how visual guys are when it comes to sexuality, she may look at the outfit as a means to receive attention. She may see the scantily-clad mannequin and think, "That outfit turns heads. If I wear it, guys will look at me. Maybe I'll even meet a nice one." But her logic will not pay off.

Assume that a girl dresses provocatively and she comes across a genuinely good man. The man is no better off because of her outfit. Men are more visually stimulated than women, and immodesty can easily trigger lustful thoughts. When men harbor these impure ideas, lust separates us from Christ, the source of unconditional love. Does a woman really want to separate men from the source of the unconditional love she seeks? If not, then why not opt for the more modest outfit? There is nothing wrong with wearing things that make you look cute, but seductive and sexy outfits should not be part of a Christian woman's wardrobe.

If your heart is saying, "Is this too short?" or "Does this look too tight?" listen to that voice. It has already answered your question.

Listen to this voice for your sake and for ours. For your sake, realize that as a moat surrounds a castle, modesty protects the treasure of chastity. For our sake, remember when Cain killed Abel back in Genesis? When God asked Cain where his brother was, Cain replied, "Am I my brother's keeper?" In the same way, it is all too easy for guys and girls alike to shrug off the responsibility we have to help one another maintain purity. Adopt the attitude of Saint Paul, and live in a way that does not cause your brothers to stumble (Rom. 14:21).

Some girls spend more energy trying to make guys notice them (even if they have no interest in the guys) than they spend trying to focus young men's attention on God. As a woman of God, use your beauty to inspire men to virtue. Again, there is no problem with looking cute. Problems arise, however, when clothing (or the lack thereof) is worn in a way that is immodest, or when a person falls into vanity and excessive concern about looking perfect. Your body is precious in the sight of God, and you do not need to look like an airbrushed *Cosmo* model to deserve love.

## 95

*Is it bad to always be thinking sexual stuff about girls? If it is, what am I supposed to do?*

To begin with, your sexual attraction toward women has been stamped into your heart by God, not by the devil. There is nothing sinful about being sexually attracted to a girl. It is normal and healthy. Do not feel guilty about sexual attraction because it is not the same thing as lust. Just because you have strong desires, this does not mean that you are impure.

Lust is a different matter because it is a conscious act of the will to allow your mind to imagine illicit sexual acts. Lust treats the person as an object—a thing to be used for your pleasure. Therefore it is a distortion of love, and it will never satisfy. Illicit sexual acts such as premarital sex—or imagining premarital sex —are always incomplete.

Jesus wants us to have the fullness of love and not sell ourselves short with lust. So He warned us that whoever looks lustfully at a woman has already committed adultery with her in his heart (Matt. 5:28). By saying this, Jesus is not condemning us but is calling us. Work as Saint Paul did to "take every thought captive to obey Christ" (2 Cor. 10:5).

In regard to what to do with tempting thoughts, I recommend what I have recommended elsewhere: If you have impure magazines, videos, and music, get rid of them. Become a man of prayer. Be patient with yourself. Impure thoughts are bound to come. Take it one day at a time, one minute at a time, and one thought at a time. Do not get overwhelmed. Purity of heart does not mean that you are never tempted and that you cease to be sexually attracted to others. Some people even think that they are pure just because they do not have strong desires or because they never had the opportunity to do something impure with a girl. This is not purity. To be pure requires an act of the will to love, not the absence of sexual desire.

One way to grow in purity is to be grateful for the beauty of women. Lust and true gratitude cannot coexist. So when you see an attractive woman, instead of thinking of her as a mere temptation, give thanks to God for making women so amazing. All beauty comes from God. Therefore, allow the beauty of every woman to remind you of the infinitely greater beauty that awaits you in heaven if you persevere in faith. By doing this you turn your heart toward God when you otherwise may be tempted to turn away from Him. Now, I'm not recommending you gawk at a woman and offer a twenty minute prayer of thanksgiving, or you seek out gorgeous women for the sake of having more reasons to be thankful. Rather, be grateful for a woman's beauty when you notice it, and then move on.

All that God asks is that you be faithful to Him as He reveals Himself to you in the present moment. He loves you and will give you the grace you need to maintain your purity. As you grow in control over your mind, you will have greater control over your body. "No temptation has overtaken you that is not common to man. God is faithful, and He will not let you be tempted beyond your strength, but with the temptation will also provide the way of escape, that you may be able to endure it" (1 Cor. 10:13).

## 96

*How can I promote this message of chastity at my school?*

I would recommend three things. First, pray and fast for your school. In the Gospel of Mark, Jesus spoke about how some people could only be healed of their spiritual illness through other people's prayer and fasting for them (9:29).

Second, one of the most effective things you can do to spread the message of chastity is to live it. This is because the virtue of purity is more easily caught than taught. As Saint Francis said, "Preach the gospel always. When necessary, use words." Your silent example comes first. If you are in a dating relationship, make sure that God is the center of it so that your classmates will see what joy a godly relationship can bring. Even if you are not dating anyone, your witness of purity is just as powerful. To quote Saint Paul, "Let no one despise your youth, but set the believers an example in speech and conduct, in love, in faith, in purity" (1 Tim. 4:12).

The world seriously doubts that chastity can exist in the lives and relationships of modern couples. It refuses to believe that two young people madly in love with one another can resist temptation. What the world does not see is that as long as the couple have a motive—true love—it is very possible. Not only is it possible, but Mary Beth Bonacci observed that couples who live chastity "were having an easier time getting out of bad relationships. They were making better marriage decisions. They were happier."[14] Therefore, be a light to the world. Your school needs to see that we do not embrace chastity because we're afraid of venereal infections or unwanted pregnancy.

Everyone is aware of the sexual messages that bombard us on every television channel and radio station. The message of "sexual liberation" surrounds us. Unfortunately, to curb this permissiveness, the message of purity has often been couched in terms like "Just say *no*," "True love *waits*," "*Abstain*." All of these slogans are good, but they can create the impression that purity is nothing more than a system of restraints. This may not appeal to a person who only knows the immediate "love" and affection of purely physical relationships. Because of this, the message of chastity needs to be rehabilitated so that everyone will be able to see the clear and obvious link between true love, total freedom, and purity. It is not about avoiding STDs. It is about having a better kind of love. Most importantly, it is about wanting heaven for the person you love.

Third, to get this message out, I would recommend starting a chastity club at your high school or college. This is not an abstinence bereavement group but an apostolate to spread the message of chastity courageously. Through the club, you can connect with students who share your passion for purity and launch any number of projects and activities to transform your campus. Some of the projects involve visiting local high schools or junior highs to spread the message of chastity to younger students. Considering that there are over sixteen million high school students in America, there is much work to be done.[15] If your school is Catholic, another goal of the club can be to start up Eucharistic Adoration on your campus, with the help of the chaplain or campus minister. This has an unspeakable power to sanctify the students (and faculty) because you are bringing Christ Himself into their midst. In the words of Pope John Paul II,

> The Eucharist is the secret of my day. It gives strength and meaning to all my activities of service to the Church and to the whole world. . . . Let Jesus in the Blessed Sacrament speak to your hearts. It is He who is the true answer of life that you seek. He stays here with us: He is God with us. Seek Him without tiring, welcome

Him without reserve, love Him without interruption: today, tomorrow, forever. [16]

Go to my Web site (chastityproject.com) to learn how to spread the message of chastity. The site explains how to begin a club, launch projects, give a chastity talk, and obtain low-cost books and CDs to share with your school or church.

One girl said after hearing a talk on sexual purity, "I agree with everything you say. I know most of my friends would, too. It all makes so much sense. It's just that no one else I know is actually doing it. I don't know if I'm strong enough to be the first one. Maybe if a group of us all started together." [17] This is your job —to create a culture in which it is easy to be good, a climate favorable to purity. In the words of Saint Catherine of Siena, "If you are what you should be, you will set the world on fire." [18]

# II

# Vocations

## 97

*How do I know if God is calling me to be a priest, or get married, or whatever?*

Some people hear the call to religious life when they are in first grade. Others seem to receive the call after they have spent a decade in a professional career. Each calling is a bit different. But whether you hope to get married, be ordained, or live a life offered to God through religious vows, all are ways of serving God. Some people also serve God in the single life. We can know what God is calling us to if we learn to listen to him.

Here are several things you can do to listen to him. Set a daily prayer time and stick to it. To hear God's calling, you must listen. To listen to God, we must learn to pray. To learn to pray, we must make time to pray and ask the Holy Spirit to teach us how. Listening to Him involves patience and obedience, so be still in your prayer time and allow God to speak in the silence of your heart. This takes practice, but like any good relationship, your relationship with God will deepen according to how much effort you put into it. Sin damages this relationship, so work toward holiness. Though we may not associate chastity with discernment, it is an essential virtue if we hope to hear our calling. When a young man or woman is indulging in sexual sin, the mind seems to be filled with such dull and heavy thoughts that he or she can hardly recognize the voice of God.

Also, it is wise to find a holy priest who can act as your spiritual director. He probably has been listening to God's voice since before you were born, so you can benefit from His sanctity. Also speak about your vocation with people whose holiness and joy you admire. Pope John Paul II advises: "In the first place I say this: you must never think that you are alone in deciding your future! And second: when deciding your future, you must not decide for yourself alone!"[1] "Confidently open your most intimate aspirations to the love of Christ who waits for you in the Eucharist. You will receive the answer to all your worries and you will see with joy that the consistency of your life which He asks of you is the door to fulfill the noblest dreams of your youth."[2] "The search and discovery of God's will for you is a deep and fascinating endeavor. Every vocation, every path to which Christ calls us, ultimately leads to fulfillment and happiness, because it leads to God, to sharing in God's own life."[3]

If you are considering the priesthood, it is beneficial to spend some time on a good discernment retreat, if one is available. One other method of discernment is to reflect on your life: look at what doors the Lord has opened or shut in your life, and look at what talents He has given you and what desires He has placed in your heart. Often we complicate the discernment process more than we need to, and we lose our peace. Whatever vocation God calls you to, this will be the place where you will have the most joy. Each vocation will have plenty of suffering as well, but all vocations are ways that we can become holy.

Some guys assume, "I think women are beautiful, so God must not want me to be a priest." But this is not sincere discernment. I know of a mother superior of nuns who gave some surprising advice to a group of young men who were discerning the priesthood. She lovingly said to the seminarians, "If you have no desire to be a father and a husband, we don't want you here. Good-bye."

In other words, in order to be a good priest, a man *must* long to become a father and a spouse. If those urges are not within his heart, how can he become a spiritual father? How can he give himself fully for his bride, the Church? When a man becomes a priest, he is not annihilating those desires. He is fulfilling them in a different way. Instead of giving himself to a woman in order to bring children into this world, he gives himself to the Church in order to bring us into eternal life.

During this time of discernment, be patient. Often God does

not want us to know His will regarding the future. That may sound strange, but we grow in the times where He seems silent. His will is our holiness, and trusting in Him during this time of uncertainty may be all He is calling you to right now. In the meantime I recommend that you pray one Hail Mary each day for your vocation. May Our Lady guide you to hear the voice of her Son and give you the courage to respond generously. In the words of Pope John Paul II: "My desire is for the young people of the entire world to come closer to Mary. She is the bearer of an indelible youthfulness and beauty that never wanes. May young people have increasing confidence in her and may they entrust the life just opening before them to her."[4]

## 98

*I am going to a university in the fall, and I'm setting my heart on meeting someone there. If not, I think I may have to become a priest. Is this being too harsh on myself?*

I would not plan on becoming a priest simply because you do not meet the right person within your time frame. When we try to force our vocation into a timetable, we are acting out of impatience and saying to God, "You've got X amount of months to accomplish my will." Often God's ways are not our ways, so pray that God will make it clear if He calls you to the celibate life. If you accept any vocation, it should be out of generosity, love, and courage, not frustration.

Sometimes we decide what we want in order to be happy, and then we wait until we get it to become pleased with life. This is a recipe for unhappiness, because God gives us what we need, not always what we want. Though this time of singleness may seem like a problem, perhaps you need to look at it differently. Mother Teresa used to say that there are no problems in life; there are only challenges in love for Jesus. She also remarked that the world sees everything as a "problem." Why not use the word *gift*?

Why a gift? Well, the vocation that God has in mind for you is where you will have the most joy. You do not want a marriage that He has not willed, and you do not want to have a marriage before God wills it. The Bible repeatedly says in its love poem, Song of Songs, "Do not stir up love before its own time" (Song 2:7; 3:5; 8:4 *NAB*). You may feel that love's time is long overdue, but trust that the Lord will act, and know that His timing is perfect.

Take one day at a time. His faithfulness and kindness reach to the skies, and God has glory in what He conceals. He wants you where you are right now, so embrace His will as it is revealed to you in the present moment in order to grow in sanctity. Also, remember that a vocation is not the ultimate purpose for our existence. Holiness is. God may not be calling you to know your vocation today, but He is calling you to holiness.

I understand that this time of loneliness is difficult, but allow the words of Scripture to console you and encourage you to persevere:

> My son, when you come to serve the LORD, prepare yourself for trials. Be sincere of heart and steadfast, undisturbed in time of adversity. Cling to Him, forsake Him not; thus will your future be great. Accept whatever befalls you, in crushing misfortune be patient; For in fire gold is tested, and worthy men in the crucible of humiliation. Trust God and He will help you; make straight your ways and hope in Him. You who fear the LORD, wait for His mercy, turn not away lest you fall. . . . Study the generations long past and understand; has anyone hoped in the LORD and been disappointed? . . . For equal to His majesty is the mercy that He shows (Sir. 2:1–7, 10, 18, *NAB*).

## 99

*I have thought about the priesthood or religious life, but I can't imagine not having sex at least once in my life. Wouldn't God understand if I had it once for the sake of experiencing it?*

Seven centuries ago a young man named Thomas Aquinas felt a call from the Lord to join the Dominican order. However, his family had other plans in mind. So they hired a prostitute to seduce him. When she attempted to distract him from his vocation, he chased her out of the room with a hot firebrand. Imagine if this great saint, whom we know as "The Angelic Doctor of the Church," had succumbed to her invitation.

In the same way that a man who is planning on getting married and becoming a father begins reevaluating his life in light of the responsibilities and expectations of fatherhood, so a young person thinking about the priesthood or religious life should be thinking about living up to God's expectations—not living down to the expectations of the world.

Besides the spiritual consequences of sex, you also have to consider the fact that one act of sex could bring a child into the world. What kind of father do you want to be? A spiritual one, or a biological one? Whichever one you choose, give yourself completely to that calling. Furthermore, what about the emotional toll this will take on you and the woman? You would be using her, as you said, "for the sake of experiencing it." This is no way to prepare to become an image of Christ in the priesthood.

As you realize, choosing the pure life is demanding. Jesus demands that *all* his followers be ready to make sacrifices: "No one who puts his hand to the plow and looks back is fit for the kingdom of God" (Luke 9:62). Persevere for Christ. "My son, hold fast to your duty, busy yourself with it, grow old while doing your task. Admire not how sinners live, but trust in the Lord and wait for His light" (Sir. 11:20–21, *NAB*).

Do not make the mistake of thinking about celibacy in negative terms. If you become a priest or religious, then the gift of your sexuality is not being wasted. Rather, you are being offered as a living sacrifice to God, for the sake of the Church. To give your virginity away to another would be like a groom losing his virginity to a stranger the night before his wedding. Make this sacrifice, as a groom waits for his bride. As Pope John Paul II said, young people "know that their life has meaning to the extent that it becomes a free gift for others."[5] If the Lord has called you to Himself, then you are His. As Saint Francis once said to his brothers, "Hold back nothing of yourselves for yourselves so that He who gives Himself totally to you may receive you totally."[6]

As a reward for such a generous donation of self, Christ

promises, "There is no one who has left house or brothers or sisters or mother or father or children or lands, for my sake and for the gospel, who will not receive a hundredfold now in this time, houses and brothers and sisters and mothers and children and lands, with persecutions, and in the age to come eternal life" (Mark 10:29–30).

Also, remember that the one-flesh union of a husband and wife is only a sign that points to an eternal reality: we all will be wedded to God in heaven. The celibacy of Catholic priests around the world is a constant witness to humanity that there is a greater reality than the daily affairs and pleasures of earth. By giving up marital intercourse in this life, you are essentially saying to God that you are skipping the sign and beginning to embrace the reality of total union with God.

100

**Don't you think that the vocations crisis would be over if priests could be married?**

This is a good question, and the answer may be a bit surprising. At the beginning of Pope John Paul II's pontificate in 1978, there were 63,882 seminarians.[7] However, by 2006 this number had grown to 114,139.[8] That's an increase of nearly 80 percent! During his papacy the number of seminarians in Africa and Asia surged by 304 percent and 153 percent.[9] In fact, vocations have increased on every continent around the globe.[10] In the United States the number of seminarians decreased for some time but is again on the rise, especially in dioceses where Catholic teaching is presented in its fullness.[11]

However, since the number of Catholics has grown to over one billion, the surge in seminarians has not filled the shortage of priests in some areas. Would the number of vocations be even greater if married men could be ordained? There is no evidence for this. For example, Eastern Orthodox churches (which allow married men to become priests) are not experiencing any greater increase in vocations.

The discipline of priestly celibacy has been with us from the earliest centuries of the Church. Although this is not an unchangeable aspect of the priesthood—it is a Church discipline that the Church has the authority to change if it sees fit—I would not look for the change to come. Celibacy is an enormous blessing to the Church, not a burden. It allows priests to serve Christ and His flock in ways that otherwise would be impossible. The Church has decided to maintain this discipline rooted in the example and the teaching of Jesus and Saint Paul.

Saint Paul recommends celibacy on the grounds that it frees people to devote their lives exclusively to serving God in prayer and service to the world, whereas marriage limits their ability to devote themselves to those things (1 Cor. 7). Likewise, Jesus speaks of "those who have renounced marriage for the sake of the kingdom of heaven." A more literal translation refers to those who have "made themselves eunuchs for the sake of the kingdom of heaven" (Matt. 19:11–12). The term *eunuch* refers to a celibate royal servant who was in charge of taking care of a king's wives. In the same way, priests have embraced consecrated celibacy in order to care for the Church, the bride of Christ—the King of Kings.

It would be unwise to do away with priestly celibacy in an effort to increase the numbers of priests. Could you imagine if the U.S. military took that approach? Imagine government leaders saying, "We don't have enough Navy Seals. Maybe we should just lighten up the requirements. Push-ups are overrated anyway. Instead of making them run for miles, let them use golf carts. Just imagine how our ranks will swell!" Just as the military needs its elite soldiers who are willing to sacrifice everything for our country, the Catholic Church needs priests who are willing to sacrifice everything for the sake of their bride, the Church.

In conclusion, I think that a vocations crisis is not the result of abstinence among clergy but of an absence of the virtue of chastity within families. In the words of one Church document,

"A lack of vocations follows from the breakdown of the family, yet where parents are generous in welcoming life, children will be more likely to be generous when it comes to the question of offering themselves to God." [12]

I also believe that our lack of prayerfulness is to blame for the lack of priests in some areas. Jesus told us to ask the harvest master to send out laborers to gather His harvest (Matt. 9:38). Have you prayed for vocations, and—more importantly—have you prayed to know your own vocation? You never know: perhaps God wants to use you to solve the vocations crisis!

**Books:**

*How to Find Your Soulmate without
Losing Your Soul*
By Jason and Crystalina Evert

This bestselling book is written for
women from the ages of 15 and 35,
and offers 21 tips on how to navi-
gate through the single years of life.

*Pure Faith: Book of Prayer*
By Jason Evert

*Pure Faith* is a hardcover devotion-
al, written and designed just for teens.
It contains prayers from the saints,
prayers for every occasion, and prayers
to help young people get the most out
of Mass, confession, and adoration.

*Theology of His Body/
Her Body*
By Jason Evert

*Theology of His Body* and
*Theology of Her Body*
are two books in one
that offer liberating an-
swers to teens' most

pressing questions about love and sexuality. Teens are encouraged to not only learn the truth about their own body, but also to discover the beauty of the opposite sex, for it is in seeing the complementarity of the two sexes that one discovers the real meaning of his or her own body.

*Theology of the Body for Teens* (Curriculum with DVD)
By Jason and Crystalina Evert and Brian Butler

*Theology of the Body for Teens* brings Pope John Paul II's teachings on human sexuality into a practical format of 12 lessons that teenagers will enjoy and understand. This program takes the two hottest topics on the planet—God and sex—and "marries" them through Pope John Paul II's compelling vision for love and life. The curriculum includes a student workbook, a leader's guide, a parent guide, and a DVD to facilitate the lessons.

**Booklets:**

*Pure Love*
By Jason Evert

In an easy-to-read Q & A format, this booklet is a great introduction to the topic of chastity. Due to its popularity in youth groups, confirmation classes, and high schools, *Pure Love* has been given to hundreds of thousands of teens at several World Youth Days. (Catholic, Spanish, and public school versions are available.)

*Pure Womanhood*
By Crystalina Evert

Every woman longs for love, but many have given up. In *Pure Womanhood*, Crystalina Evert restores a woman's hope. By her powerful testimony and blunt words of wisdom, she shows that real love is possible . . . regardless of the past. (Catholic, Spanish, and public school versions are available.)

*Pure Manhood*
By Jason Evert

Teenage boys are often told to be gentlemen and to treat women like ladies. However, they are rarely given concrete steps on how to do this. In *Pure Manhood*, Jason Evert challenges young men to look to Christ as the model of masculinity and purity. (Catholic, Spanish, and public school versions are available.)

**CDs & DVDs:**

*Love or Lust?*
(DVD & CD)
By Jason & Crystalina Evert

In this high school assembly, Jason Evert and Crystalina Evert use their humor, honesty, and powerful testimonies to provide compelling reasons to pursue a life of purity, regardless of one's past. (Catholic and public school versions are available.)

*Porn Detox*
By Jason Evert

This CD provides strategies to help men conquer their daily temptations with lust, with special emphasis on breaking free from pornography. If you, or someone you love, struggles with pornography or simply lust in general, this CD will be a blessing in your battle with temptation.

*How to Date Your Soulmate* (CD)
By Jason Evert

You like someone. Now what? Most young people have only been told what they're not supposed to do while dating. This CD offers teens ten strategies for how to practice courtship without compromise.

*How to Save Your Marriage—*
*Before Meeting Your Spouse*
By Jason Evert

Can you divorce-proof a marriage before it begins? Marriage preparation
doesn't start with the engagement. To
build the foundation for lasting love,
learn what to do before saying "I do."

*Green Sex (CD)*
By Jason Evert

First comes love, then comes marriage.
Then what? In this CD, Jason explains the
role of chastity within marriage and why
this virtue strengthens the love between
a man and a woman. This talk will help
every couple—whether newly engaged or already married.

*Parenting for Purity (CD)*
By Jason Evert

Parents are the primary sex educators for
their children, but many are uncomfortable with this responsibility because they
don't know where to begin. Jason provides
excellent tips and advice for preventing
teens from falling into damaging life-
styles. Parents will come to realize the importance of teaching their children about chastity, no matter what their age.

# Notes

[1] Pope John Paul II, address, Vigil of Prayer, Tor Vergata, Rome, World Youth Day, August 19, 2000.

[2] Pope John Paul II, address, Message of the Holy Father to the Youth of the World, Vatican, World Youth Day, June 29, 1999.


## INTRODUCTION

[1] *Sex and Disease: What You Need to Know* (New York: Planned Parenthood Federation of America, 1988). As quoted by Richard Wetzel, M.D., *Sexual Wisdom* (Ann Arbor, Mich.: Proctor Publications, LLC, 1998), 57 (emphasis mine).

[2] Sharon Begley, "Sex and the Single Fly," *Newsweek*, August 14, 2000, 44–45.

[3] *Cosmopolitan*, September 2001, cover.

[4] Pope John Paul II, encyclical letter, *Redemptor Hominis* 10 (The Redeemer of Man), (Boston: Pauline Books & Media, 1979).

[5] Letter from Karol Wojtyla (Pope John Paul II) to Teresa Heydel, December 1956. As quoted by George Weigel, *Witness to Hope* (New York: Cliff Street Books, 2001), 101.


## I. CHASTITY AND THE MEANING OF SEX

[1] Sarah E. Hinlicky, "Subversive Virginity," *First Things* (October 1998), 15.

[2] Wendy Shalit, *A Return to Modesty* (New York: Touchstone, 1999), 193.

[3] Proverbs 25:2.

[4] William Mattox, Jr., "Aha! Call It the Revenge of the Church Ladies," *USA Today*, February 11, 1999 (usatoday.com).

[5] Robert T. Michael, John H. Gagnon, Edward O. Laumann, and Gina Kolata, *Sex in America* (Boston: Little, Brown, 1994), 1.

[6] Laumann, et al., *The Social Organization of Sexuality*, table 10.5, 364.

[7] Laumann, et al., *The Social Organization of Sexuality*, table 10.7, 368.

[8] William R. Mattox, Jr., "The Hottest Valentines: The Startling Secret of What Makes You a High-Voltage Lover," *The Washington Post*, February 13, 1994.

[9] Les Parrott III and Leslie Parrott, *Saving Your Marriage Before It Starts* (Grand Rapids, Mich.: Zondervan Publishing House, 1995), 145.

[10] Elisabeth Elliot, *Passion and Purity* (Grand Rapids, Mich.: Revell, 1984), 21.

[11] *Catechism of the Catholic Church* 2339 (San Francisco: Ignatius Press, 1994).

[12] Josh McDowell, *Why Wait?* (Nashville, Tenn.: Nelson Book Publishers, 1987), 16.

[13] Thomas Lickona, "Sex, Love, and Character: It's Our Decision" (address given to assembly of students at Seton Catholic High School, Binghamton, N.Y., January 8, 1999), 10.

[14] All About Cohabiting Before Marriage, "Myths About Cohabitation," members.aol.com/cohabiting/myths.htm.

[15] Suzanne Ryan, et al., "The First Time: Characteristics of Teens' First Sexual Relationships," *Research Brief* (Washington, D.C.: Child Trends, August 2003), 5.

[16] A. B. Moscicki, et al., "Differences in Biologic Maturation, Sexual Behavior, and Sexually Transmitted Disease Between Adolescents with and without Cervical Intraepithelial Neoplasia," *Journal of Pediatrics* 115:3 (September 1989), 487–493; M. L. Shew, et al., "Interval Between Menarche and First Sexual Intercourse, Related to Risk of Human Papillomavirus Infection," *Journal of Pediatrics* 125:4 (October 1994), 661–666.

[17] R. A. Hatcher, et al., *Contraceptive Technology* (1994), 515.

[18] Peter Bearman, et al., "Chains of Affection," *American Journal of Sociology* 110:1 (July 2004), 44–91.

[19] Robert E. Rector, et al., "Sexually Active Teenagers are More Likely to be Depressed and to Attempt Suicide," The Heritage Foundation (June 3, 2003).

[20] Hallfors, et al., "Which Comes First in Adolescence—Sex and Drugs or Depression?" *American Journal of Preventive Medicine* 29:3 (October 2005), 169.

[21] Hallfors, et al., 168; Hallfors, et al., "Adolescent Depression and Suicide Risk: Association with Sex and Drug Behavior," *American Journal of Preventive Medicine* 27:3 (October 2004), 224–231; Martha W. Waller, et al., "Gender Differences in Associations Between Depressive Symptoms and Patterns of Substance Use and Risky Sexual Behavior among a Nationally Representative Sample of U.S. Adolescents," *Archives of Women's Mental Health* 9:3 (May 2006), 139–150.

[22] As reported by D. P. Orr, M. Beiter, G. Ingersoll, "Premature Sexual Activity as an Indicator of Psychological Risk," *Pediatrics* 87 (February 1991), 141–147.

[23] See also Romans 1:18; 6:12–14; 1 Corinthians 6:9–11; 2 Corinthians 7:1; Galatians 5:16–23; Ephesians 4:17–24; 5:3–13; Colossians 3:5–8; 1 Timothy 4:12.

[24] John 14:23–24.

[25] St. Augustine, *Sermons* 20:2 (*inter* A.D. 391–430).

[26] J. Kikuchi, ±á®Rhode Island develops successful intervention program for adolescents,±á~ *National Coalition Against Sexual Assault Newsletter*, Fall 1988.

[27] Henry Cloud and John Townsend, *Boundaries in Dating* (Grand Rapids, Mich.: Zondervan, 2000), 252.

[28] Hinlicky, 15.

[29] Mother Teresa, as quoted by motherteresa.com.

[30] Pope John Paul II, address, May 18, 1988, Asuncion, Paraguay. As quoted by Pedro Beteta López, ed., *The Meaning of Vocation* (Princeton, N.J.: Scepter Publishers, 1997), 18–19.

[31] Pope John Paul II, address, November 22, 1986, Auckland, New Zealand. As quoted by López, ed., *The Meaning of Vocation*, 19.

[32] Pope John Paul II, address, October 1, 1979, Boston, Massachusetts. As quoted by López, ed., *The Meaning of Vocation*, 19–20.

[33] West, *Good News About Sex and Marriage*, 29.

[34] Centers for Disease Control, "Youth Risk Behavior Surveillance—United States, 2007," *Morbidity and Mortality Weekly Report* 57:SS-4 (June 6, 2008), 22.

[35] Centers for Disease Control, "Trends in the Prevalence of Sexual Behaviors: National YRBS: 1991–2007," Fact Sheet (2008).

[36] Centers for Disease Control, "Trends in HIV-Related Behaviors Among High School Students—United States 1991–2005," *Morbidity and Mortality Weekly* 55:31 (August 11, 2006), 851–854.

[37] National Campaign to Prevent Teen Pregnancy, *America's Adults and Teens Sound Off About Teen Pregnancy: An Annual National Survey* (December 16, 2003), 17.

[38] The National Campaign to Prevent Teen Pregnancy, "The Cautious Generation? Teens Tell us About Sex, Virginity, and 'The Talk,'" (April 27, 2000), 1.

## 2. DATING AND COURTSHIP

[1] Karol Wojtyla (Pope John Paul II), *Love and Responsibility* (San Francisco: Ignatius Press, 1993), 131.

[2] McDowell, *Why Wait?*, 110.

[3] Joyce L. Vedral, *Boyfriends: Getting Them, Keeping Them, Living Without Them* (New York: Ballantine Books, 1990).

[4] B. C. Miller, et al., "Dating Age and Stage as Correlates of Adolescent Sexual Attitudes and Behavior," *Journal of Adolescent Research* 1:3 (1986), 367.

[5] Eric and Leslie Ludy, *When God Writes Your Love Story* (Sisters, Ore.: Loyal Publishing, 1999), 64.

[6] St. Thérèse of Lisieux, *The Story of a Soul* (Rockford, Ill.: TAN Books and Publishers, Inc., 1997), 2.

[7] Elliot, *Passion and Purity*, 145.

[8] Dannah Gresh, *And the Bride Wore White* (Chicago: Moody Press, 1999), 70.

[9] Anthony Stern, M.D., ed., *Everything Starts from Prayer* (Ashland, Ore.: White Cloud Press, 1998), 130.

[10] Canadian Broadcasting Corporation interview with Mother Teresa.

[11] Jay N. Giedd, "Structural Magnetic Resonance Imaging of the Adolescent Brain," *Adolescent Brain Development: Vulnerabilities and Opportunities* 1021 (June 2004), 77–85; Medical Institute for Sexual Health, "Maturation of the Teen Brain," *Integrated Sexual Health Today* (Spring 2005), 2–9.

[12] Suzanne Ryan, et al., "The First Time: Characteristics of Teens' First Sexual Relationships," 2.

[13] Hsu G., "Statutory Rape: The Dirty Secret Behind Teen Sex Numbers," *Family Policy* (1996), 1–16.

[14] Trudee Tarkowski, et al., "Epidemiology of Human Papillomavirus Infection and Abnormal Cytologic Test Results in an Urban Adolescent Population," *Journal of Infectious Diseases* 189 (January 1, 2004), 49.

[15] The National Center on Addiction and Substance Abuse, "National Survey of American Attitudes on Substance Abuse IX: Teen Dating Practices and Sexual Activity," Columbia University (August 2004), 6.

[16] Lickona, "The Neglected Heart," 7.

[17] McDowell, *Why Wait?*, 16.

[18] Cloud and Townsend, *Boundaries in Dating*, 46.

[19] Ludy, *When God Writes Your Love Story*, 109.

[20] Edward O. Laumann, et al., *The Social Organization of Sexuality: Sexual Practices in the United States* (Chicago: University of Chicago Press, 1994), 503.

[21] Wojtyla (Pope John Paul II), *Love and Responsibility*, 171, emphasis added.

[22] Pope John Paul II, general audience, December 3, 1980. As quoted by *Man and Woman He Created Them* (Boston: Pauline, 2006), 325.

[23] Pope John Paul II, apostolic exhortation, *Familiaris Consortio* 33 (The Role of the Christian Family in the Modern World) (Boston: Pauline Books & Media, 1981).

[24] Wojtyla (Pope John Paul II), *Love and Responsibility*, 172.

[25] McDowell, *Why Wait?*, 17–18.

[26] Cloud and Townsend, *Boundaries in Dating*, 251.

[27] Laura Morgan, *Marie Claire*, 2000. As re-published in "How Strong is Your Sex Drive?" *Complete Woman*, February–March 2001, 17.

[28] Shalit, *A Return to Modesty*, 97.

[29] Andreas Bartels and Semir Zeki, "The Neural Correlates of Maternal and Romantic Love," *NeuroImage* 21 (2004), 1164.

[30] "Break-up Predictors," *Reader's Digest*, April 2002, 185.

[31] Cloud and Townsend, *Boundaries in Dating*, 228.

[32] McDowell, *Why Wait?*, 63.

[33] Joe Hanley and Jack Manhire, eds., *Classic Quotes of Catholic Spirituality* (Chicago: PLS Press), 9.

[34] Mary Teresa of St. Joseph, *Mother Mary Theresa of St. Joseph*, Rev. Berchmans Bittle, O.F.M. Cap., trans. (Wauwatosa, Wisc.: Carmelite Convent, 2000), 249.

## 3. PREPARING FOR MARRIAGE

[1] For financial advice before (and during) marriage, see Philip Lenahan, *The Catholic Answers Guide to Family Finances* and *Seven Steps to Becoming Financially Free*.

[2] Wojtyla (Pope John Paul II), *Love and Responsibility*, 134.

[3] Parrott, *Saving Your Marriage Before It Starts*, 68.

[4] C. S. Lewis, *The Four Loves* (San Diego: Harcourt Brace & Company, 1960, 1988).

[5] Parrott, *Saving Your Marriage Before It Starts*, 41.

[6] Letter from Karol Wojtyla (Pope John Paul II) to Teresa Heydel, December 1956. As quoted by George Weigel, *Witness to Hope* (New York: Cliff Street Books, 2001), 101.

[7] Karol Wojtyla, *The Way to Christ* (New York: Harper & Row Publishers, Inc., 1984), 51.

[8] John Paul II, homily, "The Love Within Families," April 8, 1982. As quoted by West, *Good News About Sex and Marriage*, 65.

[9] James Dobson, *Love Must Be Tough* (Dallas: Word Publishing, 1996), 209–213.

[10] William G. Axinn and Arland Thornton, "The Relation Between Cohabitation and Divorce: Selectivity or Casual Influence?" *Demography* 29 (1992), 357–374.

[11] Cf. Bennett, et al., "Commitment and the Modern Union: Assessing the Link Between Premarital Cohabitation and Subsequent Marital Stability," *American Sociological Review* 53:1 (February 1988), 127–138.

[12] Elizabeth Thompson and Ugo Colella, "Cohabitation and Marital Stability: Quality or Commitment?" *Journal of Marriage and the Family* 54 (1992),

263; John D. Cunningham and John K. Antill, "Cohabitation and Marriage: Retrospective and Predictive Consequences," *Journal of Social and Personal Relationships* 11 (1994), 90.

[13] Koray Tanfer and Renata Forste, "Sexual Exclusivity Among Dating, Cohabiting, and Married Women," *Journal of Marriage and Family* (February 1996), 33–47.

[14] Chuck Colson, "Trial Marriages on Trial: Why They Don't Work," *Breakpoint*, March 20, 1995.

[15] Lee Robins and Darrell Regier, *Psychiatric Disorders in America: The Epidemiologic Catchment Area Study* (New York: Free Press, 1991), 64.

[16] Marianne K. Hering, "Believe Well, Live Well," *Focus on the Family*, September 1994, 4.

[17] William Mattox, Jr., "Could This be True Love? Test It with Courtship, Not Cohabitation," *USA Today*, February 10, 2000, 15A (usatoday.com).

[18] Reginald Finger, et al., "Association of Virginity at Age 18 with Educational, Economic, Social, and Health Outcomes in Middle Adulthood," *Adolescent & Family Health* 3:4 (2004), 169.

[19] G. K. Chesterton, *What's Wrong with the World* (San Francisco: Ignatius Press, 1910, 1994), 64.

[20] Wojtyla (Pope John Paul II), *Love and Responsibility*, 135.

[21] *Catechism of the Catholic Church* 2350.

[22] Elliot, *Passion and Purity*, 179.

## 4. HOW FAR IS TOO FAR?

[1] Elliot, *Passion and Purity*, 131.

[2] Karen S. Peterson, "Younger Kids Trying It Now, Often Ignorant of Disease Risks," *USA Today*, November 16, 2000, 1D (usatoday.com).

[3] Lalle Hammarstedt, et al., "Human Papillomavirus as a Risk Factor for the Increase in Incidence of Tonsillar Cancer," *International Journal of Cancer* 119:11 (December 2006), 2622.

[4] Gypsyamber D'Souza, et al., "Case-Control Study of Human Papillomavirus and Oropharyngeal Cancer," *The New England Journal of Medicine* 356 (May 10, 2007), 1944–1956.

[5] Lalle Hammarstedt, et al., 2620–2623; Justine Ritchie, et al., "Human Papillomavirus Infection as a Prognostic Factor in Carcinomas of the Oral Cavity and Oropharynx," *International Journal of Cancer* 104:3 (April 10, 2003), 336–344; Rolando Herrero, et al., "Human Papillomavirus and Oral Cancer: The International Agency for Research on Cancer Multicenter Study," *Journal of the National Cancer Institute* 95:23 (December 3, 2003), 1772–1783.

[6] McDowell, *Why Wait?*, 115.

[7] Pope John Paul II, address, April 29, 1989, Antananarivo, Madagascar. As quoted by López, ed., *The Meaning of Vocation*, 28.

[8] Tom and Judy Lickona, *Sex, Love & You* (Notre Dame, Ind.: Ave Maria Press, 1994), 74.

[9] "Dating Game," *Complete Woman*, 84.

[10] McDowell, *Why Wait?*, 172.

[11] Leon Kass, "The End of Courtship," *Public Interest* 126 (Winter 1997), 39–63.

[12] True Love Waits, "Interview with a Non-Virgin," April 15, 2001 (life way.com/tlw/tns_adv_wjjarc.asp).

[13] *Thoughts of the Curé D'Ars*, W. M. B., ed. (Rockford, Ill.: TAN Books and Publishers), 25.

[14] Pope John Paul II, Message for 2004 World Youth Day, Vatican City (March 1, 2004).

## 5. PORNOGRAPHY AND MASTURBATION

[1] Estela Welldon, as quoted in Edward Marriott, "Men and Porn," *The Guardian* (November 8, 2003).

[2] John Paul Day, as quoted in Edward Marriott, "Men and Porn," *The Guardian* (November 8, 2003).

[3] Wetzel, *Sexual Wisdom*, 72.

[4] West, *Good News About Sex and Marriage*, 84.

[5] Robert Stoller, *Porn: Myths For The Twentieth Century* (New Haven, Conn.: Yale University Press, 1993), 31.

[6] Stoller, 32.

[7] U.S. Department of Justice, *Child Pornography, Obscenity, and Organized Crime* (Washington, D.C., February 1988).

[8] Marriott, "Men and Porn," *The Guardian* (November 8, 2003).

[9] Laurie Hall, "When Fantasy Meets Reality" (pureintimacy.org).

[10] Pope John Paul II, general audience, November 24, 1982. As quoted by *Man and Woman He Created Them*, 519.

[11] Pope John Paul II, apostolic letter, *Mulieris Dignitatem* 14 (On the Dignity and Vocation of Women) (Boston: Pauline Books & Media, 1988).

[12] St. Teresa of Avila, *The Life of St. Teresa of Avila* (New York: Cosimo, Inc., 2006), 240.

[13] Karol Wojtyla, *The Way to Christ* (New York: Harper & Row Publishers, Inc., 1984), 38.

[14] C. S. Lewis, *The Great Divorce* (New York: MacMillan Publishing Company, 1946).

[15] Douglas Weiss, M.D., *The Final Freedom* (Fort Worth: Discovery Press, 1998).

[16] St. Robert Bellarmine, *The Art of Dying Well*, as quoted in R. E. Guiley, *The Quotable Saint* (New York: Checkmark Books, 2002), 135.

## 6. HOMOSEXUALITY

[1] R. McKie, "The Myth of the Gay Gene," The Press NZ, July 30, 1993, 9. As quoted by Neil and Briar Whitehead, *My Genes Made Me Do It!* (Lafayette, La.: Huntington House Publishers, 1999), 135.

[2] W. Byne and B. Parsons, "Human Sexual Orientation: The Biological Theories Reappraised," *Archives of General Psychiatry* 50 (1993), 228–239; "Gay Genes Revisited," *Scientific American*, November 1995, 26.

[3] "Nature? Nurture? It Doesn't Matter," by John Corvino (August 12, 2004), Independent Gay Forum.

[4] E. Moberly, Homosexuality: A New Christian Ethic (Cambridge, U.K.: James Clarke, 1983); G. van den Aardweg, *On the Origins and Treatment of Homosexuality: A Psychoanalytic Reinterpretation* (Westport, Conn.: Praeger, 1986).

[5] "Gay, Catholic, and Doing Fine," by Steve Gershom (pseudonym), Little Catholic Bubble.

[6] "I'm Gay and I Oppose Same-Sex Marriage," by Doug Mainwaring, Thepublicdiscourse.com; "A Gay Catholic Voice Against Same-Sex Marriage," by Mark Oppenheimer, *The New York Times*, (June 4, 2010).

[7] Ari Karpel, "Monagamish," *The Advocate*, July 7, 2011.

[8] Ellen Willis, "Can Marriage Be Saved? A Forum," *The Nation*, July 5, 2004, 16.

[9] Jean-Dominique Bunel, as quoted in "French homosexuals demonstrate against same-sex 'marriage'," by Wendy Wright, Lifesitenews.com.

[10] Rosie O'Donnell, "ABC Primetime Thursday" interview with Diane Sawyer (March 14, 2002).

[11] Eisold, B. K "Recreating Mother," *The American Journal of Orthopsychiatry* 68:3 (July 1998): 433–42.

[12] Kristen Anderson Moore, et al., "Marriage from a Child's Perspective: How Does Family Structure Affect Children, and What Can We Do about It?" *Child Trends Research Brief* (June 2002): 1–2, 6.

[13] Mark Regenerus, "How Different Are the Adult Children of Parents Who Have Same-Sex Relationships? Findings from the New Family Structures Study," *Social Science Research* 41 (2012): 752–70; *Marriage and Public Good: Ten Principles* (Princeton, N.J.: The Witherspoon Institute, 2008).

[14] Susan L. Brown, "Family Structure and Child Well-Being: The Significance of Parental Cohabitation," *Journal of Marriage and Family* 66, no. 2 (2004): 351–67; Wendy D. Manning, et al., "The Relative Stability of

Cohabiting and Marital Unions for Children," *Population Research and Policy Review* 23 (2004): 135–59; Sara McLanahan and Gary Sandefur, *Growing Up with a Single Parent: What Hurts, What Helps* (Cambridge, Mass.: Harvard University Press, 1994).

## 7. CONTRACEPTION

[1] St. Augustine, *Marriage and Concupiscence* 1:15:17 (A.D. 419), St. John Chrysostom *Homilies on Romans* 24 (A.D. 391), and others (catholic.com/library/Contraception_and_Sterilization.asp).

[2] Frank Sheed, *Society and Sanity* (New York: Sheed and Ward, 1953), 107.

[3] Cardinal Carlo Martini, *On the Body* (New York: Crossroad Publishing Co., 2000), 49.

[4] Pope Paul VI, encyclical letter, *Humanae Vitae* 17 (Of Human Life) (Boston: Pauline Books & Media, 1997).

[5] Abigail Van Buren, *The Best of Dear Abby* (New York: Andrews and McMeel, 1981), 242. As quoted in DeMarco, *New Perspectives*, 42.

[6] West, *Good News*, 122.

[7] Donald DeMarco, "Contraception and the Trivialization of Sex" (cuf.org/july99a.htm).

[8] Donald DeMarco, *New Perspectives on Contraception* (Dayton, Ohio: One More Soul, 1999), 89.

[9] Pope John Paul II, apostolic exhortation, *Familiaris Consortio* 86 (The Role of the Christian Family in the Modern World) (Boston: Pauline Books & Media, 1981).

[10] P. Frank-Hermann, et al., "The Effectiveness of a Fertility Awareness Based Method to Avoid Pregnancy in Relation to a Couple's Sexual Behaviour During the Fertile Time: A Prospective Longitudinal Study," *Human Reproduction* doi:10.1093/humrep/dem003 (February 2007), 1–10; R. E. J. Ryder, "'Natural Family Planning' Effective Birth Control Supported by the Catholic Church," *British Medical Journal* 307 (September 18, 1993), 723, 725.

[11] J. Budziszewski. Foreword. Sam and Bethany Torode, *Open Embrace* (Grand Rapids, Mich.: Eerdmans, 2002), xvi.

[12] *What's Wrong with Contraception?* (Cincinnati, Ohio: The Couple to Couple League International); Mercedes Arzú Wilson, "The Practice of Natural Family Planning Versus the Use of Artificial Birth Control: Family, Sexual, and Moral Issues," *Catholic Social Science Review* 7 (November 2002).

[13] West, *Good News About Sex and Marriage*, 179.

[14] Nona Aguilar, *No-Pill, No-Risk Birth Control* (New York: Rawson & Wade, 1980), 102.

[15] R. A. Hatcher, et al., *Contraceptive Technology, Nineteenth Revised Edition* (New York: Ardent Media, 2007).

[16] Thomas Hilgers, et al., "Creighton Model NaProEducation Technology for Avoiding Pregnancy. Use Effectiveness," *The Journal of Reproductive Medicine* 43:6 (June 1998), 495–502.

[17] Pope Paul VI, *Humanae Vitae*, 21.

[18] Charlotte Hays, "Solving the Puzzle of Natural Family Planning," *Crisis*, December 2001, 15.

[19] Cyril Jones-Kellett, "Charger Quarterback Lends Voice to Chastity Conference," *The Southern Cross* (June 21, 2007), 11.

[20] Janet E. Smith. *Contraception, Why Not.* Audiotape of lecture presented at meeting of the Catholic Physicians Guild at the Pontifical College Josephinum, Columbus, Ohio, May 1994. (Dayton, Ohio: One More Soul, 1999).

[21] The Consortium of State Physicians Resource Councils, "New Study Shows Higher Unwed Birthrates Among Sexually Experienced Teens Despite Increased Condom Use" (February 10, 1999).

[22] Jana Mazanee, "Birth Rate Soars at Colorado School," *USA Today*, May 19, 1992, 3A.

[23] Stanley Henshaw, "Unintended Pregnancy in the United States," *Family Planning Perspectives* 30:1 (1998), 24–29, 46.

[24] Rachel Jones, et al., "Contraceptive Use Among U.S. Women Having Abortions in 2000–2001," *Perspectives on Sexual and Reproductive Health* 34:6 (November/December 2002), 296.

[25] Mary S. Calderone, ed., *Abortion in the United States: A Conference Sponsored by the Planned Parenthood Federation of America and the New York Academy of Medicine* (New York: Harper and Row, 1958), 157.

[26] Malcolm Potts, *Cambridge Evening News*, February 7, 1973, as quoted in "The Connection: Abortion, Permissive Sex Instruction, and Family Planning," Life Research Institute (January 2000).

[27] Walter L. Larimore and Joseph B. Stanford, "Postfertilization Effects of Oral Contraceptives and Their Relationship to Informed Consent," *Archives of Family Medicine* 9 (February 2000), 126–133.

[28] Mother Teresa, February 5, 1994, National Prayer Breakfast, Washington, D.C.

[29] Ryder, " 'Natural Family Planning' Effective Birth Control supported by the Catholic Church," 723.

[30] Joseph D'Agostino, "Vatican Officials Discuss Solutions for European Underpopulation," *National Catholic Register* (July 15, 2006).

[31] Wetzel, *Sexual Wisdom*, 273.

[32] Wetzel, *Sexual Wisdom*, 274; "The Fizzling Population Bomb," Zenit News Agency, March 13, 2005.

[33] United Nations Department of Public Information, "World Population Will Increase by 2.5 Billion by 2050; People Over 60 to Increase by More Than 1 Billion," Press Release 952 (March 13, 2007).

[34] Mercedes Arzú Wilson, *Love & Family* (San Francisco: Ignatius Press, 1996), 192–193.

[35] Jacqueline Kasun, "Too Many People?" *Envoy*, May–June 1998, 34.

[36] Kasun, "Too Many People?" 36.

[37] Dukes, G. N. (editor of the *International Journal of Risk and Safety in Medicine*), as quoted from a letter dated January 24, 1995, to Judith Richter, author of *Vaccination Against Pregnancy: Miracle or Menace?* (London and New Jersey: Zed Books, 1996), n.p.

[38] Gail Vines, "Contraceptives?: There's a Revolution Going on in Birth Control for Men and Women. But the Drugs Companies Have All but Abandoned Research," *New Scientist* (April 30, 1994), 36.

[39] Baylor College of Medicine, "Evolution and Revolution: The Past, Present, and Future of Contraception," *The Contraception Report* 10:6 (February 2000), 15.

[40] Baylor, "Evolution and Revolution," 16.

[41] Baylor, 19.

[42] Ray Quintanilla, *Puerto Rico Herald*, "Anger At Island's 'Pill' Test Lingers," *Orlando Sentinel*, April 5, 2004.

[43] Janet E. Smith. *Contraception, Why Not.*

[44] Department of Public Health & Policy, London School of Hygiene & Tropical Medicine, "The Pill: Balancing the Risks and Benefits," *Research Briefing* 1 (May 2000), 1; Aude Lagorce, "Schering AG Storms Birth Control Market," Forbes.com (July 11, 2003).

[45] Barbara Ehrenreich, "The Charge: Genocide," *Mother Jones* (November/December 1979).

[46] Larimore and Stanford, "Postfertilization," 127.

[47] Larimore and Stanford, 127.

[48] *Physicians' Desk Reference* (Montvale, N.J.: Thomson, 2006), 2414.

[49] Larimore and Stanford, 131.

[50] Larimore and Stanford, 133.

[51] *Federal Register* 41:236 (December 7, 1976), 53,634.

[52] Larimore and Stanford, 133.

[53] Public Health Service Leaflet no. 1066, U.S. Dept. of Health, Education, and Welfare (1963), 27.

[54] Sheldon Segal, ed., et al., "*Proceedings of the Second International Conference, Intra-Uterine Contraception,*" October 2–3, 1964, New York City, International Series, Excerpta Medica Foundation, No. 1 (September 1965).

[55] College of Obstetricians and Gynecologists, "Terms Used in Reference

to the Fetus," *Terminology Bulletin* 1 (Philadelphia: Davis, September 1965).

[56] Shu-Juan Cheng, et al., "Early Pregnancy Factor in Cervical Mucus of Pregnant Women," *American Journal of Reproductive Immunology* 51:2 (February 2004), 102–105.

[57] J.A. Spinato, "Informed Consent and the Redefining of Conception: A Decision Ill-Conceived?" *The Journal of Maternal-Fetal Medicine* 7:6 (November-December 1998), 264–268.

[58] Germaine Greer, *The Whole Woman* (New York: Anchor Books, 1999), 99.

[59] Haishan Fu, et al., "Contraceptive Failure Rates: New Estimates From the 1995 National Survey of Family Growth," *Family Planning Perspectives* 31:2 (March/April 1999), 61.

[60] L. M. Dinerman, et al., "Outcomes of Adolescents Using Levonorgestrel Implants vs Oral Contraceptives or Other Contraceptive Methods," *Archives of Pediatrics & Adolescent Medicine* 149:9 (September 1995), 967–972.

[61] Haishan Fu, et al., 61.

[62] *Physicians' Desk Reference*, 2416–2417.

[63] Chris Kahlenborn, et al., "Oral Contraceptive Use as a Risk Factor for Premenopausal Breast Cancer: A Meta-Analysis," *Mayo Clinic Proceedings* 81:10 (October 2006), 1290–1302.

[64] World Health Organization, "IARC Monographs Programme Finds Combined Estrogen-Progestogen Contraceptives and Menopausal Therapy are Carcinogenic to Humans," International Agency for Research on Cancer, Press Release 167 (July 29, 2005); *Physicians' Desk Reference*, 2415.

[65] *Physicians' Desk Reference*, 2414; Julia Warnock, et al., "Comparison of Androgens in Women with Hypoactive Sexual Desire Disorder: Those on Combined Oral Contraceptives (COCs) vs. Those Not on COCs," *The Journal of Sexual Medicine* 3:5 (September 2006), 878–882.

[66] Panzer, et al., "Impact of Oral Contraceptives on Sex Hormone-Binding Globulin and Androgen Levels: A Retrospective Study in Women with Sexual Dysfunction," *Journal of Sexual Medicine* 3:1 (January 2006), 104–113.

[67] "Can Taking the Pill Dull a Woman's Desire Forever?" *New Scientist* (May 27, 2005), 17.

[68] "Study Links Birth Control Pill to Arterial Plaque," Reuters (November 6, 2007).

[69] John Pickrell, "Oral Contraception Linked to Prostate Deformities," *New Scientist* (May 2005); Barry Timms, et al., "Estrogenic Chemicals in Plastic and Oral Contraceptives Disrupt Development of the Fetal Mouse Prostate and Urethra," *Proceedings of the National Academy of Sciences* 102:19 (May 10, 2005), 7014–7019.

[70] F. Bryant Furlow, et al., "The Smell of Love: How Women Rate the

Sexiness and Pleasantness of a Man's Body Odor Hinges on How Much of Their Genetic Profile is Shared," *Psychology Today* 29:2 (March/April 1996), 38; Sarah Richardson, "Scent of a Man," *Discover* 17:2 (1996), 26.

[71] Lionel Tiger, *The Decline of Males* (New York: St. Martin's Griffin, 1999).

[72] Malcolm Potts and Peter Diggory, *Textbook of Contraceptive Practice*, 2nd ed. (Cambridge: Cambridge University Press, 1983), 155.

[73] D. P. Yolton, et al., "The Effects of Gender and Birth Control Pills on Spontaneous Blink Rates," *Journal of the American Optometric Association* 65:11 (November 1994), 763–770.

[74] William Mosher, et al., "Use of Contraception and Use of Family Planning Services in the United States, 1982–2002," *Advance Data From Vital and Health Statistics* 350, Centers for Disease Control (December 10, 2004). 1.

[75] Suzanne Shelley, "Authorized Generics' Makes for Surprising—and Controversial—Partnerships," Pharmaceutical Commerce (January 1, 2006).

[76] Haishan Fu, et al., 61; Hatcher, et al., *Contraceptive Technology, Nineteenth Revised Edition.*

[77] Hatcher, et al., *Contraceptive Technology, Nineteenth Revised Edition.*

[78] John Santelli, et al., "Contraceptive Use and Pregnancy Risk Among U.S. High School Students, 1991–2003," *Perspectives on Sexual and Reproductive Health* 38:2 (June 2006), 106–111.

[79] R. A. Crosby, "Men with Broken Condoms: Who and Why?" *Sexually Transmitted Infections* 83:1 (February 2007), 71–75.

[80] Anonymous, M.D., *Unprotected* (New York: Sentinel, 2006), 18.

[81] Richard Crosby, et al., "Condom Use Errors and Problems Among College Men," *Sexually Transmitted Diseases* 29 (2002), 552–57.

[82] M. Henderson, et al., "Impact of a Theoretically Based Sex Education Programme (SHARE) Delivered by Teachers on NHS Registered Conceptions and Terminations: Final Results of Cluster Randomised Trial," *British Medical Journal* (November 21, 2006), 4.

[83] David Bamber, "Teen Pregnancies Increase After Sex Education Classes," *Sunday Telegraph*, England (March 14, 2004).

[84] "Teen Pregnancy Rates Increase," BBCNews.com (March 5, 2004).

[85] "Perspectives in Disease Prevention and Health Promotion: Condoms for Prevention of Sexually Transmitted Diseases," *Morbidity and Mortality Weekly Report* 37:9 (March 11, 1988), 133–137.

[86] Gardner, et al., "The Condom Gap: A Health Crisis," *Population Reports*, Series H, No. 9 (Baltimore: Johns Hopkins School of Public Health, Population Information Program, April 1999), 36.

[87] Associated Press, "Study Finds Fewer Defects in Condoms on U.S. Market," *New York Times*, May 12, 1988.

[88] "Condoms: Extra Protection," *Consumer Reports* (February 2005).

[89] Catherine Carey, "Holey Condoms—Marketing Defective Condoms," *FDA Consumer* (February 1989).

[90] William B. Vesey, "Condom Failure," *Human Life International Reports* 9:7 (July 1991), 1–3.

[91] R. A. Hatcher, et al., *Contraceptive Technology*, Seventeenth Revised Edition (New York: Ardent Media, Inc., 1998), 330; M. Steiner, et al., "Can Condom Users Likely to Experience Condom Failure be Identified?" *Family Planning Perspectives* 25:5 (September/October 1993), 220–223, 226.

[92] G. G. Gallup, Jr., et al., "Does Semen Have Antidepressant Properties?" *Archives of Sexual Behavior* 31:3 (June 2002), 289–293; P. G. Ney, "The Intravaginal Absorption of Male Generated Hormones and Their Possible Effect on Female Behaviour," *Medical Hypotheses* 20:2 (June 1986), 221–231; Herbert Ratner, "Semen and Health: The Condom Condemned," *Child and Family* (1990); C. J. Thaler, "Immunological Role for Seminal Plasma in Insemination and Pregnancy," *American Journal of Reproductive Immunology* 21:3–4 (November/December 1989), 147–150.

[93] Ratner; Ney, 221–231.

[94] Gallup et al., 289–93; "Hormones in Semen Shown to Make Women Feel Good," *Reuters* (June 16, 2002).

[95] S. A. Robertson, et al., "Transforming Growth Factor Beta—A Mediator of Immune Deviation in Seminal Plasma," *Journal of Reproductive Immunology* 57:1–2 (October/November 2002), 109–128.

[96] Douglas Fox, "Gentle Persuasion," *New Scientist* (February 9, 2002); Douglas Fox, "Why Sex, Really?" *U.S. News and World Report* (October 21, 2002), 60–62.

[97] S. A. Robertson, et al., "The Role of Semen in Induction of Maternal Immune Tolerance to Pregnancy," *Seminars in Immunology* 13 (2001), 243; John B. Wilks, *A Consumer's Guide to the Pill and Other Drugs*, 2nd ed. (Stafford, Va.: American Life League, Inc., 1997), 136.

[98] A. Hirozawa, "Preeclampsia and Eclampsia, While Often Preventable, Are Among Top Causes of Pregnancy-Related Deaths," *Family Planning Perspectives* 33:4 (July/August 2001), 182; Andrea Mackay, et al., "Pregnancy-Related Mortality From Preeclampsia and Eclampsia," *Obstetrics & Gynecology* 97 (2001), 533–538.

[99] H. S. Klonoff-Cohen, et al., "An Epidemiologic Study of Contraception and Preeclampsia," *The Journal of the American Medical Association* 262:22 (December 8, 1989), 3143–3147.

[100] S. A. Robertson, et al., "Seminal 'Priming' for Protection from Pre-Eclampsia: A Unifying Hypothesis," *Journal of Reproductive Immunology* 59:2 (August 2003), 253–265; G. R. Verwoerd, et al., "Primipaternity and Du-

ration of Exposure to Sperm Antigens as Risk Factors for Pre-eclampsia," *International Journal of Gynaecology and Obstetrics* 78:2 (August 2002), 121–126; J.I. Einarsson, et al., "Sperm Exposure and Development of Preeclampsia," *American Journal of Obstetrics and Gynecology* 188:5 (May 2003), 1241–1243; M. Hernandez-Valencia, et al., "[Barrier Family Planning Methods as Risk Factors Which Predisposes to Preeclampsia]," *Ginecologia y Obstetrica de Mexico* 68 (August 2000), 333–338; Dekker, et al., "Immune Maladaptation in the Etiology of Preeclampsia: A Review of Corroborative Epidemiologic Studies," *Obstetrical and Gynecological Survey* 53:6 (June 1998), 377–382.

[101] *Physicians' Desk Reference*, 2620.

[102] Hatcher, et al., *Contraceptive Technology, Nineteenth Revised Edition.*

[103] "The Case Against Depo-Provera: Problems in the U.S.," *Multinational Monitor* 6:2–3, February/March 1985.

[104] "The Case Against Depo-Provera: Problems in the U.S."

[105] Karen Hawkins and Jeff Elliott, "Seeking Approval," *Albion Monitor*, May 5, 1996.

[106] "Depo Provera Fact Sheet," Committee on Women, Population, and the Environment (January 6, 2007); Hawkins and Elliott.

[107] M. Rosser, et al., "Depo-Provera: An Excellent Contraceptive for Those Who Continue to Use It," *Primary Care Update for Ob/Gyns* 5:4 (July 1, 1998), 172.

[108] William Mosher, et al., Advance Data From Vital and Health Statistics 350, Table 7—Supplement (CDC).

[109] William Mosher, et al., Advance Data From Vital and Health Statistics 350, Table 10—Supplement (CDC).

[110] "The Case Against Depo-Provera: Problems in the U.S."

[111] Hawkins and Elliott.

[112] "Depo Provera Fact Sheet," 2007.

[113] "The Case Against Depo-Provera: Problems in the U.S."; "Depo Provera Fact Sheet," 2007.

[114] Warren E. Leary, "U.S. Approves Injectable Drug As Birth Control," *The New York Times* (October 30, 1992); Ehrenreich, et al.; "Depo-Provera Warning for Women 14 Years Later," press release, Women's Health Action Trust (November 30, 2004).

[115] Leary.

[116] "Clinicians Clash with Consumer Groups Over Possible Depo Ban," *Contraceptive Technology Update* 16:1 (January 1995), 11–14.

[117] "Health: Depo Provera: Asking the FDA to Investigate," suite101.com.

[118] "Canadian Coalition on Depo-Provera letter to The Honorable Benoit Bouchard, National Minister of Health and Welfare" December 6, 1991.

[119] CTV.ca News Staff, "Class Action Suit Filed Over Birth Control Drug," *CTV.ca News*, (December 19, 2005).

[120] N. B. Sarojini, et al., "Why Women's Groups Oppose Injectable Contraceptives," *Indian Journal of Medical Ethics* 13:1 (January/March 2005).

[121] "Contraceptives. Case for Public Enquiry," *Economic and Political Weekly* 29:15 (April 9, 1994), 825–826 (Popline database document no. 096527).

[122] "Depo Provera Fact Sheet," Committee on Women, Population, and the Environment (January 6, 2007).

[123] Charles Morrison, et al., "Hormonal Contraceptive Use, Cervical Ectopy, and the Acquisition of Cervical Infections," *Sexually Transmitted Diseases* 31:9 (September 2004), 561–567; J. M. Baeten, et al., "Hormonal Contraception and Risk of Sexually Transmitted Disease Acquisition: Results from a Prospective Study," *American Journal of Obstetrics and Gynecology* 185:2 (August 2001), 380–385.

[124] "Depo Provera Fact Sheet," 2007; Morrison, et al., 561.

[125] Centers for Disease Control, "Chlamydia," fact sheet (April 2006); D. T. Fleming and J. N. Wasserheit, "From Epidemiological Synergy to Public Health Policy and Practice: The Contribution of Other Sexually Transmitted Diseases to Sexual Transmission of HIV Infection," *Sexually Transmitted Infections* 75 (1999), 3–17.

[126] depoprovera.com/vc-prospect-user.asp.

[127] U.S. Food and Drug Administration, "Black Box Warning Added Concerning Long-Term Use of Depo-Provera Contraceptive Injection," FDA Talk Paper (November 17, 2004).

[128] www.fda.gov.

[129] "Pfizer Contraceptive OK'd for Added Use," CNNmoney.com (March 29, 2005).

[130] Physician Information, Depo-Provera CI, Pharmacia & Upjohn Company (November 2004); Patient Labeling, Pharmacia & Upjohn Company, October 2004.

[131] "Exposure to DMPA in Pregnancy May Cause Low Birth Weight," *Progress in Human Reproduction Research* 23 (1992), 2–3.

[132] T. A. Kiersch, "Treatment of Sex Offenders with Depo-Provera," *The Bulletin of the American Academy of Psychiatry and the Law* 18:2 (1990), 179–187; California Penal Code Section 645.

[133] Assembly Bill 3339, "An Act to Repeal and Add Section 645 of the Penal Code, Relating to Crimes," California State Senate, Amended August 20, 1996; 2005.

[134] U.N. Department of Economic and Social Affairs, Population Division, "World Contraceptive Use, 2005."

[135] Michele Kort, "Fatal Contraption: The Horrifying Truth about the

Dalkon Shield," *Essence* (July 1989).

[136] "The Dalkon Shield Story: A Company Rewarded for its Faulty Product—A. H. Robins Company, Inc. Lawsuit," *Healthfacts*, May 1996.

[137] Russell Mokhiber, "The Dalkon Shield: A Deadly Product from A. H. Robins, *Multinational Monitor* 8:4 (April 1987).

[138] Morton Mintz, "A Crime Against Women," *Multinational Monitor* 7:1 (January 15, 1986).

[139] Hicks, Karen M., *Surviving the Dalkon Shield IUD: Women v. The Pharmaceutical Industry* (New York: Teachers College Press, 1994), 2.

[140] Mokhiber, "The Dalkon Shield"; Mintz, "A Crime Against Women."

[141] International Planned Parenthood Federation, "The Dalkon Shield IUD," *IPPF Medical Bulletin* 14:6 (December 1980), 3.

[142] Ehrenreich, et al.

[143] Mintz, "A Crime Against Women."

[144] Hicks, 6.

[145] "The Dalkon Shield Story," Healthfacts.

[146] Mokhiber, "The Dalkon Shield."

[147] Meryl Gordon, "A Cash Settlement, but No Apology," *The New York Times* (February 20, 1999).

[148] Baylor, "Evolution and Revolution," 18.

[149] ParaGard Patient Package Information, Duramed Pharmaceuticals, Inc. (May 2006); J. B. Stanford and R. T. Mikolajczyk, "Mechanisms of Action of Intrauterine Devices: Update and Estimation of Postfertilization Effects," *American Journal of Obstetrics and Gynecology* 187:6 (December 2002), 1699–1708; Y. C. Smart, et al., "Early Pregnancy Factor as a Monitor for Fertilization in Women Wearing Intrauterine Devices," *Fertility and Sterility* 37:2 (February 1982), 201–204.

[150] ParaGard Patient Package Information.

[151] ParaGard Patient Package Information.

[152] "Barr to Acquire FEI Women's Health," Breaking News From Pharma & Bio Ingredients, November 18, 2005 (prnewswire.com/news-releases/duramed-to-acquire-fei-womens-health-and-its-paragardr-iud-product-55388447.html).

[153] Mirena Patient Information Booklet, Bayer HealthCare Pharmaceuticals, Inc. (2004), 9.

[154] Mirena Patient Information Booklet; K. Van Houdenhouven, et al., "Uterine Perforation in Women Using a Levonorgestrel-Releasing Intrauterine System," *Contraception* 73:3 (2006), 257–260.

[155] Mirena Patient Information Booklet, 10.

[156] "Medical Eligibility Criteria for Contraceptive Use," World Health Organization, Third Edition, 2004.

[157] Aude Lagorce, "Schering AG Storms Birth Control Market," forbes.com

(July 11, 2003).

[158] Plan B Prescribing Information, Duramed Pharmaceuticals, Inc. (August 2006), 1.

[159] *Physicians' Desk Reference*, 1068; Chris Kahlenborn, et al., "Postfertilization Effect of Hormonal Emergency Contraception," *The Annals of Pharmacotherapy* 36 (March 2002), 465–470; Department of Health and Human Services, *Federal Register* Notice 62:37 (February 25, 1997), 8611.

[160] "How Plan B Works," Duramed Pharmaceuticals, Inc. (2007).

[161] Essure Patient Information Booklet, Conceptus, Inc. (2003), 6.

[162] Department of Health and Human Services, *Federal Register*, 8611.

[163] Plan B Prescribing Information, 3.

[164] Elizabeth Raymond, et al., "Population Effect of Increased Access to Emergency Contraceptive Pills: A Systematic Review," *Obstetrics and Gynecology* 109:1 (January 2007), 181–188.

[165] Plan B Prescribing Information, 6–7.

[166] Thomas Hilgers, "Norplant," *Linacre Quarterly* (February 1993), 64–69.

[167] W. Hadisaputra, et al., "Endometrial Biopsy Collection from Women Receiving Norplant," *Human Reproduction* Supplement 2 (October 1996), 31–34; L. S. Wan, "A Review of the Endometrial Changes in Norplant Users," *Annals of the New York Academy of Sciences* 828 (September 1997), 108–110.

[168] Norplant System (levonorgestrel implants) Prescribing Information, Wyeth Pharmaceuticals, Inc. (March 2005), 6.

[169] V. Schiappacasse, et al., "Health and Growth of Infants Breastfed by Norplant Contraceptive Implant Users: A Six-Year Follow-Up Study," *Contraception* 66:1 (July 2002), 57–65.

[170] "Guide to Norplant Counseling," Supplement to Population Reports, Decisions for Norplant Programs, K-4, XX:3. (Baltimore: The Johns Hopkins Center for Communication Programs, November 1992).

[171] Erica Johnson, "Medical device lawsuits," *CBC News* (April 1, 2003).

[172] "Norplant Makers to Settle," CNNmoney.com (August 26, 1999).

[173] Implanon Patient Insert, Organon USA, Inc. (July 2006), 1.

[174] Implanon Patient Insert, 2.

[175] John Bird, "Akzo Nobel/Organon: Contraceptive Hot Rods?" *Pharmaceutical Business Review Online* (July 19, 2006).

[176] Hatcher, et al., 2007.

[177] NuvaRing Physician's Insert.

[178] NuvaRing Physician's Insert.

[179] "Can Taking the Pill Dull a Woman's Desire Forever?", 17; Panzer, et al., 104–113.

[180] NuvaRing Physician's Insert.

[181] NuvaRing Physician's Insert.

[182] NuvaRing Physician's Insert.

[183] NuvaRing Physician's Insert.

[184] "Petition to the FDA to Ban Third Generation Oral Contraceptives Containing Desogestrel Due to Increased Risk of Venous Thrombosis" (Health Research Group, Publication #1799), February 6, 2007.

[185] Theresa Agovino, "Schering-Plough to Buy Akzo Nobel's Pharmaceutical Division for $14.4 Billion," Associated Press (March 12, 2007).

[186] *Physicians' Desk Reference*, 2402.

[187] Hatcher, et al., *Contraceptive Technology, Nineteenth Revised Edition*.

[188] "Ortho Evra (norelgestromin/ethinyl estradiol Transdermal Contraceptive)," Ortho McNeil Pharmaceutical, Inc. (September 2006).

[189] Panzer, et al., 104–113.

[190] "Parents Blame Ortho Evra Birth Control Patch for Death of Their 14-Year-Old Daughter," NewsInferno.com, November 20, 2005.

[191] Associated Press, "Warning Issued for Birth-Control Patch," *USA Today*, November 11, 2005.

[192] J. Alexander Cole, et al., "Venous Thromboembolism, Myocardial Infarction, and Stroke Among Transdermal Contraceptive System Users," *Obstetrics & Gynecology* 109 (February 2007), 339–346.

[193] "Warning Issued for Birth-Control Patch."

[194] Patient Information Sheet: Norelgestromin/ethinyl estradiol (marketed as Ortho Evra), www.fda.gov (September 20, 2006).

[195] Johnson & Johnson, "2005 Annual Report," 31.

[196] "Women Sue Birth Control Patch Maker," CNNmoney.com (July 25, 2005).

[197] Associated Press, "Birth Control Patch Linked to Higher Fatality Rate," MSNBC (July 17, 2005).

[198] "Birth Control Patch Linked to Higher Fatality Rate."

[199] Evelyn Pringle, "500 Ortho Evra Birth Control Patch Victims Sue Johnson & Johnson," lawyersandsettlements.com (September 17, 2006).

[200] "Lawsuit Filed Against Johnson & Johnson in Los Angeles Over Ortho Evra Birth Control Patch," PRWeb Press Release Newswire (February 15, 2007).

[201] Linda A. Johnson, "Johnson & Johnson Exec Claims He Was Fired for Raising Safety Concerns," Associated Press (December 20, 2006).

[202] Johnson & Johnson, SEC Filing, Quarterly Report for Period Ending 7/2/2006.

[203] Johnson & Johnson, SEC Filing, Quarterly Report for Period Ending 10/1/2006.

[204] Johnson & Johnson, SEC Filing, Annual Report for Period Ending

12/31/2007.

[205] Johnson & Johnson, SEC Filing, 12/31/2007.

[206] Johnson & Johnson, SEC Filing, 12/31/2007.

[207] "Warning Issued for Birth-Control Patch."

[208] "Top 200 Drugs for 2004 by U.S. Sales," idrugs.com data from ND-CHealth (March 2005).

[209] Johnson & Johnson, 2004 Annual Report (March 2005), 30–31.

[210] "Systemic Hormonal Contraceptives: Schering Goes from Strength to Strength," imshealth.com (August 23, 2006).

[211] Daniel J. Kevles, "The Secret History of Birth Control," *The New York Times*, July 22, 2001.

[212] Mifeprex (mifepristone) Tablets, 200mg. Danco Laboratories, LLC (July 19, 2005), 8.

[213] Mifeprex, Medication Guide. Danco Laboratories, LLC (July 19, 2005) 1.

[214] Mifeprex (mifepristone) Tablets, 200mg. Danco Laboratories, LLC (July 19, 2005), 9–10.

[215] Sabin Russell, "Taker of Abortion Pill Died Due to Infection," *San Francisco Chronicle*, November 1, 2003, A:19.

[216] Brewer, "Family Blames RU-486 in Woman's Death," *Contra Costa Times* (September 20, 2003).

[217] Monty and Helen Patterson, "An Open Letter from the Parents of Holly Patterson—Death by RU-486," November 6, 2003.

[218] Danco Laboratories, "Dear Health Care Provider," July 19, 2005.

[219] "Planned Parenthood Kills Two More Mothers," Wednesday STOPP report, March 22, 2006.

[220] " 'Holly's Law' Still Necessary to Protect Women From RU-486," USCCB Office of Media Relations (May 12, 2006).

[221] "Mifepristone Questions and Answers," FDA, November 16, 2004.

[222] Danco Laboratories, "Dear Health Care Provider," July 19, 2005.

[223] Susan Wills, "Statistics and Complications Who Were Someone's Daughter," USCCB Life Issues Forum (November 19, 2004).

[224] Christine Hall, "Lawsuit Alleges Medical Malpractice in RU-486-Related Death" CNSNews.com (September 3, 2002).

[225] "Smith Urges Passage of Holly's Law After RU-486 Is Linked to Additional Deaths of Women," Washington, D.C., March 16, 2006.

[226] "Smith Urges Passage of Holly's Law."

[227] Michael Greene, "Fatal Infections Associated with Mifepristone-Induced Abortion," *The New England Journal of Medicine* 353:22 (December 1, 2005), 2317–2318.

[228] Mifeprex (mifepristone) Tablets, 10.

[229] Anonymous, M.D., *Unprotected*, 87–89.

[230] Baylor, "Evolution and Revolution," 15.

[231] Baylor, "Evolution and Revolution," 15.

[232] Andrea Tone, "Contraceptive Consumers: Gender and the Political Economy of Birth Control in the 1930s," *Journal of Social History* (Spring 1996).

[233] K. M. Wittkowski, "The Protective Effect of Condoms and Nonoxynol-9 Against HIV Infection," *American Journal of Public Health* 88:4 (April 1998), 590–596.

[234] FDA press release, "FDA Proposes New Warning for Over-the-Counter Contraceptive Drugs Containing Nonoxynol-9," (January 16, 2003); Centers for Disease Control, "Nonoxynol-9 Spermicide Contraception Use—United States, 1999," *MMWR Weekly* 51:18 (May 10, 2002), 389–392.

[235] Press release, "Dr. Coburn Says New FDA Condom Regulations Make Inconclusive, Exaggerated Claims About Condom Effectiveness," Washington, D.C. (November 10, 2005).

[236] Hatcher, et al., *Contraceptive Technology, Nineteenth Revised Edition*.

[237] "Condoms: Extra Protection," *Consumer Reports* (February 2005).

[238] Microbicides, World Health Organization (2006).

[239] http://dontfixit.org/.

[240] R. A. Kronmal, et al., "Vasectomy and Urolithiasis," *The Lancet* 331 (1988), 22–23.

[241] Jon Knowles, "Tubal Sterilization," Planned Parenthood (April 1, 2005).

[242] Mercedes Mclughlin, "Tubal Ligation," *Encyclopedia of Medicine*.

[243] Centers for Disease Control and Prevention, "Unintended Pregnancy Prevention: Female Sterilization," Department of Health and Human Services (April 26, 2006); United Nations, "World Contraceptive Use—2005."

[244] United Nations, "World Contraceptive Use—2005."

[245] National Institutes of Health, "Facts about Vasectomy Safety" (August 17, 2006); "World Contraceptive Use, 2005."

[246] Mosher, et al., *Advance Data From Vital and Health Statistics* 350, (CDC) 10.

[247] Essure Patient Information Booklet, Conceptus (October 31, 2006), 13.

[248] Essure Patient Information Booklet, 12.

[249] Essure Prescribing Information, Conceptus (September 8, 2005).

[250] Essure Patient Information Booklet, 12.

[251] Essure Instructions for Use, Conceptus (June 12, 2002), 4.

[252] Malcolm Gladwell, "John Rock's Error," *The New Yorker* (March 13, 2000), 52–63.

253 Sue Ellin Browder, "Dirty Little Secret: Why Condoms Will Never Stop AIDS in Africa," *Crisis* (June 1, 2006).

254 Tim Allen and Suzette Heald, "HIV/AIDS Policy in Africa: What Has Worked in Uganda and What Has Failed in Botswana?," *Journal of International Development* 16:8 (November 8, 2004), 1141–1154; Michael Cassell, et al., "Risk Compensation: The Achilles' Heel of Innovations in HIV Prevention?" *British Medical Journal* 332 (March 11, 2006), 605–607.

255 Craig Timberg, "Speeding HIV's Deadly Spread," *Washington Post* Foreign Service (March 2, 2007), A01.

256 N. Hearst and S. Chen, "Condom Promotion for AIDS Prevention in the Developing World: Is It Working?" *Studies in Family Planning* 35:1 (March 2004), 39–47, emphasis added.

257 Allen and Heald, 1141.

258 Edward Green, et al., *Evidence That Demands Action* (Austin, Tex.: Medical Institute for Sexual Health, 2005), ii.

259 Yoweri Museveni, 11th International Conference of People Living with HIV, as reported by Panafrican News Agency Daily Newswire (October 29, 2003).

260 Joseph Loconte, "The White House Initiative to Combat AIDS: Learning from Uganda," The Heritage Foundation: Backgrounder 1692 (September 29, 2003).

261 Allen and Heald, 1141, emphasis added.

262 Arthur Allen, "Sex Change: Uganda v. Condoms," *The New Republic* (May 27, 2002).

263 Allen and Heald, 1149.

264 D. Low-Beer and R. Stoneburner, "Behavior and Communication Change in Reducing HIV: Is Uganda Unique?" African Journal of AIDS Research 2 (2004), 2.

265 Edward Green, "Testimony before the Subcommittee on African Affairs," Committee on Foreign Relations, U.S. Senate (May 19, 2003) 2.

266 Edward Green, "The New AIDS Fight: A Plan as Simple as ABC," *The New York Times* (March 1, 2003).

267 Edward C. Green and Wilfred May, "Let Africans Decide How to Fight AIDS," *The Washington Post* (November 29, 2003), A23.

268 S. Gregson, et al., "HIV Decline Associated with Behavior Change in Eastern Zimbabwe," Science 311:5761 (February 3, 2006), 620–621; Richard Hayes and Helen Weiss, "Understanding HIV Epidemic Trends in Africa," Science 311:5761 (February 3, 2006), 620–621.

269 Testimony of Edward C. Green, Ph.D., before the Committee on Energy and Commerce, U.S. House of Representatives (March 20, 2003), 3.

270 Green and May, A23.

[271] Allen.

[272] Rand Stoneburner, quoted in Allen.

[273] Low-Beer R. Stoneburner, 1.

[274] Anna Wald et al., "Effect of Condoms on Reducing the Transmission of Herpes Simplex Virus Type 2 from Men to Women," *Journal of the American Medical Association* 285 (June 27, 2001), 3103.

[275] J. Thomas Fitch, "Are Condoms Effective in Reducing the Risk of Sexually Transmitted Disease?" *The Annals of Pharmacotherapy* 35:9 (September 2001), 1137; A. Saracco, et al., "Man-to-Woman Sexual Transmission of HIV: Longitudinal Study of 343 Steady Partners of Infected Men," *Journal of Acquired Immune Deficiency Syndromes* 6:5 (May 1993), 497–502; I. de Vincenzi, "A Longitudinal Study of Human Immunodeficiency Virus Transmission by Heterosexual Partners," *The New England Journal of Medicine* 3331 (August 11, 1994), 341–346, as quoted in Fitch.

[276] S. Ahmed, et al., "HIV Incidence and Sexually Transmitted Disease Prevalence Associated with Condom Use: A Population Study in Rakai, Uganda," *AIDS* 15:16 (November 9, 2001), 2171–2179.

[277] "New Research Confirms Condoms Not Effective in HIV Prevention," LifeSiteNews.com (January 14, 2004).

[278] Joshua Mann, et al., "The Role of Disease-Specific Infectivity and Number of Disease Exposures on Long-Term Effectiveness of the Latex Condom," *Sexually Transmitted Diseases* 29:6 (June 2002), 344–349.

[279] R. E. Bunnell, et al., "High Prevalence and Incidence of Sexually Transmitted Diseases in Urban Adolescent Females Despite Moderate Risk Behaviors," *Journal of Infectious Diseases* 180:65 (November 1999), 1624–1631.

[280] Fitch, 1137.

[281] "New Research Shows Dangers of Condoms in HIV Prevention," *Culture & Cosmos* 1:23 (January 13, 2004), emphasis added.

[282] Fleming and Wasserheit, 3–17.

[283] Peter Greenhead, et al., "Parameters of Human Immunodeficiency Virus Infection of Human Cervical Tissue and Inhibition by Vaginal Virucides," *Journal of Virology* 74:12 (June 2000), 5577–5586.

[284] Nancy Padian, et al., "Heterosexual Transmission of Human Immunodeficiency Virus (HIV) in Northern California: Results from a Ten-Year Study," *American Journal of Epidemiology* 146:4 (August 15, 1997), 350–357.

[285] Dr. Daniel Low-Beer, as quoted by Alisa Colquhoun, "Ugandan Lessons?" *Public Health News*, February 6, 2004.

[286] Fitch, 1137; Ronald Gray, et al., "Probability of HIV-1 Transmission Per Coital Act in Monogamous, Heterosexual, HIV-1 Discordant Couples in Rakai, Uganda," *Lancet* 357 (2001), 1149–1153; I. de Vincenzi, "A Longitudinal Study of Human Immunodeficiency, 341–346; Medical Institute for

Sexual Health, *Sex, Condoms, and STDs: What We Now Know* (Austin, Tex.: Medical Institute for Sexual Health, 2002), 13.

[287] Bluma Brenner, et al., "High Rates of Forward Transmission Events After Acute/Early HIV-1 Infection," *The Journal of Infectious Diseases* 195 (April 1, 2007), 951–959; M.J. Wawer, et al., "Rates of HIV-1 Transmission Per Coital Act, by Stage of HIV-1 Infection, in Rakai, Uganda," *The Journal of Infectious Diseases* 191:9 (May 1, 2005), 1403–1409.

[288] Harvey Elder, "Human Immunodeficiency Virus (HIV)," a presentation at Health on the Horizon, sponsored by The Medical Institute for Sexual Health (June 13, 2002).

[289] Seth Mydans, "Low Rate Of AIDS Virus In Philippines Is a Puzzle," *The New York Times* (April 20, 2003).

[290] Human Life International, "Condom Exposé" hli.org, 16.

[291] UNAIDS "Report on the Global AIDS Epidemic," 2006, Annex 2, 511, 514.

[292] Mydans.

[293] Cecile Balgos, "Philippines Proud of its Low Infection Rate, Number of Cases," *San Francisco Chronicle* (May 21, 2003).

[294] Amin Abboud, "Searching for Papal Scapegoats Is Pointless," *British Medical Journal* 331 (July 30, 2005), 294.

[295] Bureau of Democracy, Human Rights, and Labor, "International Religious Freedom Report 2004," U.S. Department of State (September 15, 2004); UNAIDS "Philippines" Country Situation Analysis (unaids.org).

[296] "Doubts About Condoms: Science Questioning Their Efficacy in Halting HIV/AIDS," Zenit Daily Dispatch, Nairobi, Kenya (June 26, 2004).

[297] Commonly attributed to Arthur Schopenhauer.

[298] Archbishop Charles J. Chaput, O.F.M. Cap., "Of Human Life: A Pastoral Letter to the People of God of Northern Colorado on the Truth and Meaning of Married Love," July 22, 1998, 16.

[299] Pope John Paul II, remarks to President George W. Bush, July 23, 2001.

[300] Jim Hopkins, "Egg-Donor Business Booms on Campuses," *USA Today* (March 15, 2006).

[301] Dr. Janet Smith, *Sexual Common Sense*, "Reproductive Technologies: Why Not?"

[302] "Marriage of Unwitting Twins Sparks IVF Debate," bioedge.org, January 16, 2008.

[303] Panos Ioannou, "Free Consanguinity Testing for All," *Nature* 419 (September 19, 2002), 247–248; Amy Harmon, "Hello, I'm Your Sister. Our Father Is Donor 150," *The New York Times* (November 20, 2005).

[304] Sabrina Paradis, "Frozen," babble.com.

## 8. SEXUALLY TRANSMITTED DISEASES

[1] National Institutes of Health, "Scientific Evidence on Condom Effectiveness for Sexually Transmitted Disease (STD) Prevention" (June 2000).

[2] John Diggs, M.D., "NIH [National Institutes of Health] Report Collapses Foundation of Comprehensive Sex Education," Abstinence Clearinghouse, August 6, 2001.

[3] NIH, "Scientific Evidence on Condom Effectiveness for Sexually Transmitted Disease (STD) Prevention," 26.

[4] U.S. Department of Health and Human Services. "Scientific Review Panel Confirms Condoms Are Effective Against HIV/AIDS, But Epidemiological Studies Are Insufficient for Other STDs," by HHS News, press release, July 20, 2001.

[5] L. Manhart, L. Koutsky, "Do Condoms Prevent Genital HPV Infection, External Genital Warts, or Cervical Neoplasia? A Meta-Analysis," Sexually Transmitted Diseases 29:11 (2002), 725–735; S. Vaccarella, et al., "Sexual Behavior, Condom Use, and Human Papillomavirus: Pooled Analysis of the IARC Human Papillomavirus Prevalence Surveys," Cancer Epidemiology Biomarkers & Prevention 15:2 (2006), 326–333; R. Winer, et al., "Condom Use and the Risk of Genital Human Papillomavirus Infection in Young Women," The New England Journal of Medicine 354:25 (2006), 2645–2654; S. Ahmed S, et al., "HIV Incidence and Sexually Transmitted Disease Prevalence Associated with Condom Use: A Population Study in Rakai, Uganda," AIDS 15:16 (2001), 2171–2179; J. Baeten, et al., "Hormonal Contraception and Risk of Sexually Transmitted Disease Acquisition: Results from a Prospective Study," American Journal of Obstetrics & Gynecology 185:2 (2001), 380–385; J. Shlay, et al., "Comparison of Sexually Transmitted Disease Prevalence by Reported Level of Condom Use Among Patients Attending an Urban Sexually Transmitted Disease Clinic," Sexually Transmitted Diseases 31:3 (2004), 154–160; A. Wald, et al., "Effect of Condoms on Reducing the Transmission of Herpes Simplex Virus Type 2 from Men to Women," Journal of the American Medical Association 285:24 (2001), 3100–3106.

[6] Nancy Pelosi et al., "Pelosi and House Colleagues Criticize Administration Report for Undermining Condom Effectiveness: Members Request Study Guided by Science Not Ideology," press release, Washington, D.C. (July 24, 2001) as referenced in note 10, "The NIH Condom Report: The Glass is 90% Full," by Willard Cates, Jr., Family Planning Perspectives 33:5 (September/October 2001), 232.

[7] Fitch, 1137.

[8] Haishan Fu, et al., 60.

[9] Joe McIlhaney, M.D., Safe Sex (Grand Rapids, Mich.: Baker House

Books, 1992), 23.

[10] *Sex is a Choice: Be Informed* (Grand Rapids, Mich.: The Core-Alliance Group, Inc., 2000).

[11] Medical Institute for Sexual Health, *Sex, Condoms, and STDs*, 28; B. Dillon, "Primary HIV Infections Associated with Oral Transmission," CDC's 7th Conference on Retroviruses and Opportunistic Infections, Abstract 473, (San Francisco, February 2000); Centers for Disease Control, "Transmission of Primary and Secondary Syphilis by Oral Sex—Chicago, Illinois, 1998–2002," *Morbidity and Mortality Weekly Report* 51:41 (October 22, 2004), 966–968.

[12] Rachel Winer, et al., "Genital Human Papillomavirus Infection: Incidence and Risk Factors in a Cohort of Female University Students," *American Journal of Epidemiology* 157:3 (2003), 218–226; Sepehr Tabrizi, et al., "Prevalence of Gardnerella Vaginalis and Atopobium Vaginae in Virginal Women," *Sexually Transmitted Diseases* 33:11 (November 2006), 663–665; C. Sonnex, et al., "Detection of Human Papillomavirus DNA on the Fingers of Patients with Genital Warts," *Sexually Transmitted Infections* 75 (1999), 317–319.

[13] A. Frega, et al., "Human Papillomavirus in Virgins and Behaviour at Risk," *Cancer Letters* 194:1 (May 8, 2003), 21–24; Gypsyamber D'Souza, et al., 1944–1956; Hammarstedt, et al., 2620–2623; Justine Ritchie, et al., 336–344; Herrero, et al., 1772–1783.

[14] F. Martinon-Torres, et al., "[Human Papillomavirus Vaccines: A New Challenge for Pediatricians]," *Anales de Pediatría* 65:5 (November 2006), 461–469; Helen Trottier and Eduardo L. Franco, "The Epidemiology of Genital Human Papillomavirus Infection," *Vaccine* 24:S1 (March 30, 2006): S4; Division of STD Prevention, "Prevention of Genital HPV Infection and Sequelae: Report of an External Consultants' Meeting," Department of Health and Human Services (Atlanta: Centers for Disease Control and Prevention, December, 1999), 1; Janet Torpy, "Human Papillomavirus Infection," *Journal of the American Medical Association* 297:8 (February 28, 2007), 912.

[15] M. A. Van Ranst et al., "Taxonomy of the Human Papillomaviruses," *Papillomavirus Report* 3 (1993), 61–65. As reported by NIH, "Scientific Evidence on Condom Effectiveness for Sexually Transmitted Disease (STD) Prevention," 23.

[16] World Health Organization, "Cervical Cancer," International Agency for Research on Cancer, 2005 (iarc.fr).

[17] "Genital Skin Cancer More Deadly for Women," HealthDay News (February 5, 2007).

[18] L. Koutsky, "Epidemiology of Genital Human Papillomavirus Infection," *American Journal of Medicine* 102:5A (May 5, 1997), 3–8.

[19] Eloise M. Harman, "Recurrent Respiratory Papillomatosis,"

eglobalmed.com/opt/MedicalStudentdotcom/www.emedicine.com/med/top
ic2535.htm (June 2, 2006).

[20] Harman.

[21] Tarkowski, et al., 46–50.

[22] Eileen F. Dunne, et al., "Prevalence of HPV Infection Among Females
in the United States," *Journal of the American Medical Association* 297:8 (February 28, 2007), 813–819.

[23] F. Xavier Bosch, et al., "Male Sexual Behavior and Human Papillomavirus DNA: Key Risk Factors for Cervical Cancer in Spain," *Journal of the National Cancer Institute* 88:15 (August 1996), 1060–1067.

[24] S. Collins, et al., "High Incidence of Cervical Human Papillomavirus
Infection in Women During Their First Sexual Relationship," *BJOG: An International Journal of Obstetrics and Gynaecology* 109:1 (January 2002), 96–98.

[25] L. E. Manhart and L. A. Koutsky, "Do Condoms Prevent Genital HPV
Infection, External Genital Warts, or Cervical Neoplasia?: A Meta-Analysis,"
*Sexually Transmitted Diseases* 29:11 (November 2002), 725–735; Division of
STD Prevention, "Prevention of Genital HPV Infection and Sequelae: Report
of an External Consultants' Meeting," Department of Health and Human
Services, 7.

[26] A. B. Moscicki, et al., "The Natural History of Human Papillomavirus
Infection As Measured by Repeated DNA Testing in Adolescent and Young
Women," *The Journal of Pediatrics* 132:2 (February 1998), 277–284; E. L.
Franco, et al., "Epidemiology of Acquisition and Clearance of Cervical Human Papillomavirus Infection in Women from a High-Risk Area for Cervical Cancer," *The Journal of Infectious Diseases* 180:5 (November 1999), 1415–1423; Ho G. Y., R. Bierman, et al., "Natural History of Cervicovaginal Papillomavirus Infection in Young Women," *The New England Journal of Medicine*
338:7 (February 12, 1998), 423–428.

[27] L. Koutsky, "Epidemiology of Genital Human Papillomavirus Infection," *The American Journal of Medicine* 102:5A (May 5, 1997), 3–8, as cited
in Centers for Disease Control, "Tracking the Hidden Epidemics, Trends
in STDs in the United States 2000" (April 6, 2001), 18.

[28] Dunne, et al., 815.

[29] Dunne, et al., 816.

[30] Dunne, et al., 813–819.

[31] Medical Institute for Sexual Health, Sex, Condoms, and STDs, 28; C.
Sonnex, et al., 317–319; Winer, et al., 218–226; Hammarstedt, et al., 2620–2623.

[32] NIH, "Scientific Evidence on Condom Effectiveness for Sexually Transmitted Disease (STD) Prevention," 26; House of Representatives, "Breast

and Cervical Cancer Prevention and Treatment Act of 1999" (November 22, 1999), 10.

[33] R. Winer, et al., "Genital Human Papillomavirus Infection: Incidence and Risk Factors in a Cohort of Female University Students," *American Journal of Epidemiology* 157:3 (February 1, 2003), 218.

[34] R. Winer, et al., "Condom Use and the Risk of Genital Human Paillomavirus Infection in Young Women," *The New England Journal of Medicine* 354:25 (2006), 2645-2654.

[35] Public Law 106-554, 106th Congress, 114 Stat. 2763 (December 21, 2000).

[36] Julie Louise Gerberding, "Report to Congress: Prevention of Genital Human Papillomavirus Infection," Centers for Disease Control and Prevention, Department of Health and Human Services (June 2004), 4-5.

[37] Division of STD Prevention, "Prevention of Genital HPV Infection and Sequelae: Report of an External Consultants' Meeting," Department of Health and Human Services, 14.

[38] "Rep. Souder Asks FDA for Action on Condom & HPV Information Law," abstinence.net (February 12, 2004), emphasis added; Manhart and Koutsky, 725-735.

[39] Tom Coburn, "Cervical Cancer and Human Papillomavirus," Hearing before the Subcommittee on Criminal Justice, Drug Policy and Human Resources, U.S. House of Representatives (March 11, 2004), 4.

[40] Ilka Couto and Cynthia Dailard, "Wanted: A Balanced Policy and Program Response to HPV and Cervical Cancer," *The Guttmacher Report on Public Policy* 2:6 (December 1999).

[41] Lara Jakes Jordan, "Condom Warning Labels Mulled," cbsnews.com, *Associated Press*, Washington (March 12, 2004).

[42] Audio transcript, "Scientific Evidence on Condom Effectiveness and STD Prevention," National Institute of Allergy and Infectious Diseases (June 12-13, 2000).

[43] Tamara Kerinin, as quoted by Cheryl Wetzstein, "Agencies Rapped for Shirking HPV Law," *Washington Times* (December 23, 2003).

[44] Sylvia Smith, "Condom Labels Called Inadequate," *The Journal Gazette* (March 12, 2004) 5-A.

[45] Statement of Daniel G. Schultz, M.D., before the Subcommittee on Criminal Justice, Drug Policy, and Human Resources Committee on Government Reform United States House of Representatives, March 11, 2004.

[46] LifeStyles Condoms, press release, Ansell Healthcare, Inc. (July 31, 2000).

[47] Letter from Kerry A. Hoffman, Regional Director, Ansell Healthcare, Inc. (September 8, 2000).

[48] "Latest News: Andrew C. Von Eschenbach, M.D., Confirmation, Questions for the Record," Abstinence Clearinghouse E-mail Update (September 9, 2006), reply to Question 14.

[49] R. Eng and W. T. Butler, *The Hidden Epidemic: Confronting Sexually Transmitted Diseases* (Washington, D.C.: National Academy Press, 1997), 1.

[50] Joe McIlhaney, M.D., *Safe Sex* (Grand Rapids, Mich.: Baker House Books, 1992), 23.

[51] Hillard Weinstock et al., "Sexually Transmitted Diseases Among American Youth: Incidence and Prevalence Estimates, 2000," *Perspectives on Sexual and Reproductive Health* 36:1 (January/February 2004), 6–10.

[52] Centers for Disease Control, "Trends in Reportable Sexually Transmitted Diseases in the United States, 2005," Division of STD Prevention (December 2006), 1.

[53] "Trends in Reportable Sexually Transmitted Diseases in the United States, 2005," 1.

[54] "Trends in Reportable Sexually Transmitted Diseases," 2.

[55] McIlhaney, 103.

[56] Medical Institute for Sexual Health, "Sexual Health Update," 7:2 (Summer 1999), 1.

[57] S. Edwards and C. Carne, "Oral Sex and Transmission of Non-Viral STIs," *Sexually Transmitted Infections* 74:2 (April 1998), 95–100.

[58] S. S. Witkin, et al., "Relationship Between an Asymptomatic Male Genital Tract Exposure to Chlamydia Trachomatis and an Autoimmune Response to Spermatozoa," *Human Reproduction* 11 (November 10, 1995), 2952–2955; R. Gdoura, et al., "Chlamydia Trachomatis and Male Infertility in Tunisia," *The European Journal of Contraception & Reproductive Health Care* 6:2 (June 2002), 102–107; A. A. Pacey and A. Eley, "Chlamydia Trachomatis and Male Fertility," *Human Fertility* 7:4 (December 2004), 271–276.

[59] Tatiana Goldner, et al., "Surveillance for Ectopic Pregnancy—United States, 1970–1989," *MMWR Weekly* 42:SS-6 (December 17, 1993) 73–85; "Current Trends Ectopic Pregnancy—United States, 1990–1992," Centers for Disease Control, *MMWR Weekly* 44:3 (January 27, 1995), 46–48.

[60] Centers for Disease Control, "Pelvic Inflammatory Disease," Fact Sheet (May 2004).

[61] "Trends in Reportable Sexually Transmitted Diseases, 2005," 1.

[62] "Tracking the Hidden Epidemics, Trends in STDs in the United States 2000," CDC, 6.

[63] Jolande Land, et al., "Chlamydia Trachomatis in Subfertile Women Undergoing Uterine Instrumentation," *Human Reproduction* 17:3 (March 2002), 526.

[64] Land, et al., 525–527; S. D. Spandorfer, "Previously Undetected Chla-

mydia Trachomatis Infection, Immunity to Heat Shock Proteins and Tubal Occlusion in Women Undergoing In-Vitro Fertilization," *Human Reproduction* 14:1 (January 1999), 60–64; J. Debattista, et al., "Immunopathogenesis of Chlamydia Trachomatis Infections in Women," *Fertility and Sterility* 79:6 (June 2003), 1273–1287.

[65] S.S. Witkin, et al., "Unsuspected Chlamydia Trachomatis Infection and In Vitro Fertilization Outcome," *American Journal of Obstetrics and Gynecology* 171:5 (November 1994), 1208–1214; A. Neuer, et al., "The Role of Heat Shock Proteins in Reproduction," *Human Reproduction Update* 6:2 (2000), 149–159; S.S. Witkin, et al., "Immune Recognition of the 60kD Heat Shock Protein: Implications for Subsequent Fertility," *Infectious Diseases in Obstetrics and Gynecology* 4 (1996), 152–158; A. Neuer, et al., "Humoral Immune Response to Membrane Components of Chlamydia Trachomatis and Expression of Human 60 kDa Heat Shock Protein in Follicular Fluid of In-Vitro Fertilization Patients," *Human Reproduction* 12:5 (1997), 925–929; A. Neuer, et al., "Heat Shock Protein Expression during Gametogenesis and Embryogenesis," *Infectious Diseases in Obstetrics and Gynecology* 7 (1999), 10–16.

[66] A. Neuer, et al., "The Role of Heat Shock Proteins in Reproduction," *Human Reproduction Update* 6:2 (March/April 2000), 149–159.

[67] Land, et al., 525–527; C.M.J. Mol, et al., "The Accuracy of Serum Chlamydial Antibodies in the Diagnosis of Tubal Pathology: A Meta-Analysis," *Fertility and Sterility* 67:6 (June 1997), 1031–1037.

[68] Thomas Lickona, "The Neglected Heart: The Emotional Dangers of Premature Sexual Involvement" (January 2007), 11.

[69] "Tracking the Hidden Epidemics," 4.

[70] Centers for Disease Control, "2006 Sexually Transmitted Diseases Treatment Guidelines" (September 2006).

[71] "Chlamydia," fact sheet, CDC.

[72] F.X. Bosch, et al., "Chlamydia Trachomatis and Invasive Cervical Cancer: A Pooled Analysis of the IARC Multicentric Case-Control," *International Journal of Cancer* 111:3 (September 1, 2004), 431–439.

[73] National Institutes of Health, "Workshop Summary: Scientific Evidence on Condom Effectiveness for Sexually Transmitted Disease (STD) Prevention," 17.

[74] Ahmed, et al., 2171–2179; Baeten, et al., 380–385.

[75] Fujie Xu, et al., "Trends in Herpes Simplex Virus Type 1 and Type 2 Seroprevalence in the United States," *Journal of the American Medical Association* 296:8 (August 2006), 964–973.

[76] C.M. Roberts, et al., "Increasing Proportion of Herpes Simplex Virus Type 1 as a Cause of Genital Herpes Infection in College Students," *Sexually*

*Transmitted Diseases* 30:10 (October 2003), 797–800; G. B. Lowhagen, et al., "First Episodes of Genital Herpes in a Swedish STD Population: A Study of Epidemiology and Transmission by the Use of Herpes Simplex Virus (HSV) Typing and Specific Serology," *Sexually Transmitted Infections* 76 (2000), 179–182; Mary Jo Groves, "Transmission of Herpes Simplex Virus Via Oral Sex," *American Family Physician* 73:7 (April 2006), 1527–1534.

[77] Fujie Xu, et al., 964–973.

[78] McIlhaney, 100.

[79] D. T. Fleming, et al., "Herpes Simplex Virus Type 2 in the United States, 1976 to 1994," *The New England Journal of Medicine* 337 (October 16, 1997), 1105–1111; P. Leone, "Type-specific Serologic Testing for Herpes Simplex Virus-2," *Current Infectious Disease Reports* 5:2 (April 2003): 159–165.

[80] Fujie Xu, et al., 964–973.

[81] J. S. Smith, et al., "Herpes Simplex Virus-2 as a Human Papillomavirus Cofactor in the Etiology of Invasive Cervical Cancer," *Journal of the National Cancer Institute* 94:21 (November 6, 2002), 1604–1613.

[82] Centers for Disease Control, "Genital Herpes," Fact Sheet (May 2004).

[83] J. C. Shlay, et al., "Comparison of Sexually Transmitted Disease Prevalence by Reported Level of Condom Use Among Patients Attending an Urban Sexually Transmitted Disease Clinic," *Sexually Transmitted Diseases* 31:3 (March 2004), 154–160; Anna Wald, et al., "The Relationship Between Condom Use and Herpes Simplex Virus Acquisition," *Annals of Internal Medicine* 143:10 (2005), 707–713.

[84] "Trends in Reportable Sexually Transmitted Diseases," 3.

[85] "Trends in Reportable Sexually Transmitted Diseases," 3.

[86] National Institutes of Health, "Workshop Summary: Scientific Evidence on Condom Effectiveness for Sexually Transmitted Disease (STD) Prevention."

[87] National Institutes of Health, "Workshop Summary."

[88] Fleming and Wasserheit, 3–17.

[89] D. S. Michaud, et al., "Gonorrhoea and Male Bladder Cancer in a Prospective Study," *British Journal of Cancer* 96 (2007), 169–171.

[90] National Institutes of Health, "Workshop Summary: Scientific Evidence on Condom Effectiveness for Sexually Transmitted Disease (STD) Prevention."

[91] Rob Stein, "Drugs Losing Efficacy Against Gonorrhea," *Washington Post* (April 13, 2007), A03.

[92] "Trends in Reportable Sexually Transmitted Diseases," 4.

[93] National Institutes of Health, "Workshop Summary," 16.

[94] Ahmed, et al., 2171–2179; Baeten, et al., 380–385.

[95] Ahmed, et al., 2177.

[96] T. K. Young, et al., "Factors Associated with Human Papillomavirus Infection Detected by Polymerase Chain Reaction Among Urban Canadian Aboriginal and Non-Aboriginal Women," *Sexually Transmitted Diseases* 24:5 (May 1997), 293–298; Manhart Koutsky, 725–735.

[97] Robert E. Rector, Heritage Foundation, in Avram Goldstein, "District to Offer Condoms for Free," *Washington Post* (December 2, 2003), B01.

[98] Centers for Disease Control, "Trichomoniasis," fact sheet (May 2004).

[99] F. Sorvillo, et al., "Trichomonas Vaginalis, HIV, and African-Americans," *Emerging Infectious Diseases* 7:6 (November/December 2001), 927–932; J. R. Schwebke, "Update of Trichomoniasis," *Sexually Transmitted Infections* 78:5 (2002), 378–379; Centers for Disease Control, "Trichomoniasis," fact sheet.

[100] National Institutes of Health, "Workshop Summary."

[101] C. Everett Koop, M. D., as quoted by *Safe Sex?* (Boise, Id.: Grapevine Publications, 1993).

[102] *How at Risk Are You?* (Chattanooga, Tenn.: AAA Women's Services, Inc., 1997).

[103] Eng Butler, 71–73; Centers for Disease Control, "Pelvic Inflammatory Disease," fact sheet; Moscicki, et al., "Differences in Biologic Maturation, Sexual Behavior, and Sexually Transmitted Disease Between Adolescents with and without Cervical Intraepithelial Neoplasia," *Journal of Pediatrics*, 487–493; A. B. Moscicki, et al., "The Significance of Squamous Metaplasia in the Development of Low Grade Squamous Intraepithelial Lesions in Young Women," *Cancer* 85:5 (March 1, 1999), 1139–44; M. L. Shew, et al., "Interval Between Menarche and First Sexual Intercourse, Related to Risk of Human Papillomavirus Infection," *Journal of Pediatrics* 125:4 (October 1994), 661–666; Vincent Lee, et al., "Relationship of Cervical Ectopy to Chlamydia Infection in Young Women," *Journal of Family Planning and Reproductive Health Care* 32:2 (April 2006), 104–106.

[104] G. Yovel, et al., "The Effects of Sex, Menstrual Cycle, and Oral Contraceptives on the Number and Activity of Natural Killer Cells," *Gynecologic Oncology* 81:2 (May 2001), 254–262; M. Blum, et al., "Antisperm Antibodies in Young Oral Contraceptive Users," *Advances in Contraception* 5 (1989), 41–46; C. W. Critchlow, et al., "Determinants of Cervical Ectopia and of Cervicitis: Age, Oral Contraception, Specific Cervical Infection, Smoking, and Douching," *American Journal of Obstetrics and Gynecology* 173:2 (August 1995), 534–43; Baeten, et al., 380–385; Catherine Ley, et al., "Determinants of Genital Human Papillomavirus Infection in Young Women," *Journal of the National Cancer Institute* 83:14 (July 1991), 997–1003; M. Prakash, et al., "Oral Contraceptive Use Induces Upregulation of the CCR5 Chemokine Receptor on CD4(+) T Cells in the Cervical Epithelium of Healthy Women," *Journal*

*of Reproductive Immunology* 54:1–2 (March 2002), 117–131; C. C. Wang, et al., "Risk of HIV Infection in Oral Contraceptive Pill Users: A Meta-Analysis," *Journal of Acquired Immune Deficiency Syndromes* 21:1 (May 1999), 51–58; L. Lavreys, et al., "Hormonal Contraception and Risk of HIV-1 Acquisition: Results From a 10-Year Prospective Study," *AIDS* 18:4 (March 2004), 695–697; W. C. Louv, et al., "Oral Contraceptive Use and the Risk of Chlamydial and Gonococcal Infections," *American Journal of Obstetrics and Gynecology* 160:2 (February 1989), 396–402; J. A. McGregor and H. A. Hammill, "Contraception and Sexually Transmitted Diseases: Interactions and Opportunities," *American Journal of Obstetrics and Gynecology* 168:6:2 (June 1993), 2033–2041.

[105] Wilks, *A Consumer's Guide to the Pill and Other Drugs*, 30.


## 9. PURITY RENEWED

[1] Christopher West, *The Love That Satisfies* (West Chester, Pa.: Ascension Press, 2007), 14.

[2] McDowell, *Why Wait?*, 159–160.

[3] M. Lasswell and T. Lasswell, *Marriage and the Family* (Lexington, Mass.: Health, 1982), as reported by Parrott, *Saving Your Marriage Before It Starts*, 156.

[4] Shalit, 150.

[5] Sister Lucy Vertrusc, letter to religious superior, as reported by "Going the Distance," *Envoy*, January–February 2000, 7.

[6] D. M. Fergusson, et al., "Abortion in Young Women and Subsequent Mental Health," *Journal of Child Psychology and Psychiatry* 47:1 (January 2006), 16–24; Mika Gissler, et al., "Suicides After Pregnancy in Finland, 1987–94: Register Linkage Study," *British Medical Journal* 313 (December 1996), 1431–1434.

[7] Pope John Paul II, homily, 17th World Youth Day, Toronto (July 28, 2002).

[8] McDowell, *Why Wait?*, 17.

[9] *Catechism of the Catholic Church* 2843.

[10] Hannah Arendt, *The Human Condition* (Chicago: University of Chicago Press, 1958), 237.

[11] Gresh, *And the Bride Wore White*, 150.


## 10. HOW TO STAY PURE

[1] Mother Teresa, foreword to *A Plea for Purity*, by Johann Christoph Arnold (Farmington, Pa.: Plough Publishing House, 1996).

[2] Parrott, *Saving Your Marriage Before It Starts*, 145.

[3] Shalit, *A Return to Modesty*, 57.

[4] Josemaría Escrivá, *The Way* (New York: Scepter, 2002), 40.

[5] Wojtyla (Pope John Paul II), *Love and Responsibility*, 172.

[6] Michael Collopy, *Works of Love Are Works of Peace* (San Francisco: Ignatius Press, 1996), 30.

[7] Pope John Paul II, general audience, July 30, 1980, as quoted in *Man and Woman He Created Them*, 261.

[8] The National Center on Addiction and Substance Abuse, "National Survey of American Attitudes on Substance Abuse IX: Teen Dating Practices and Sexual Activity," Columbia University (August 2004), 6.

[9] The Australian Family Association 7:1 (February 2001), as reported by *Abstinence Network* 5:1 (Spring 2001), 9.

[10] Paul M. Quay, S.J., *The Christian Meaning of Human Sexuality* (San Francisco: Ignatius Press, 1985), 106.

[11] Shalit, *A Return to Modesty*, 157.

[12] Mike Mathews, "Sexy Fashions? What Do Men Think?" *Lovematters.com* (newspaper supplement), 4:2001:10.

[13] Pope John Paul II, *Mulieris Dignitatem* 1.

[14] Mary Beth Bonacci, "Expressing Love: How to Speak the Language of Permanence," *Be*, May–June 2000, 10.

[15] "Digest of Education Statistics Tables and Figures, 2005," The National Center for Education Statistics, U.S. Department of Education.

[16] Pope John Paul II, *L'Osservatore Romano* 41 (October 8, 1997), 7.

[17] Shalit, *A Return to Modesty*, 229.

[18] St. Catherine of Siena, letter 368, as referenced by Pope John Paul II, address, 15th World Youth Day, Rome (August 2000).

## 11. VOCATIONS

[1] Pope John Paul II, address, May 31, 1982, Edinburgh, Scotland, as quoted by López, ed., *The Meaning of Vocation*, 10.

[2] Pope John Paul II, address, May 18, 1988, Asuncion, Paraguay, as quoted by López, ed., *The Meaning of Vocation*, 22.

[3] Pope John Paul II, address, January 13, 1996, Manila, Philippines, as quoted by López, ed., *The Meaning of Vocation*, 23.

[4] Pope John Paul II, address, October 16, 1987, Rome, Italy, as quoted by López, ed., *The Meaning of Vocation*, 33.

[5] Pope John Paul II, *Crossing the Threshold of Hope* (New York: Alfred A. Knopf, Inc., 1994), 121.

[6] "A Letter to the Entire Order," 29 in Regis J. Armstrong and Ignatius C. Brady, trans. *Francis and Clare: The Complete Works* (New York: Paulist Press, 1982), 58.

[7] Dossier, "Church Experiencing Unprecedented 'Boom' of Seminarians," Zenit News Agency, June 4, 1999.

[8] John Thavis, "Vatican Stats Confirm Growth of Church, Especially in Asia, Africa," Catholic News Service, February 12, 2007.

[9] John Thavis, "The Numbers Game: Stats Give Picture of Pope John Paul's Pontificate," Catholic News Service, May 5, 2006.

[10] Dossier, "Church Experiencing Unprecedented 'Boom.'"

[11] Doug Tattershall, "Dear Bishop: If You Really Want More Vocations . . ." *New Oxford Review* (April 2001), 25–28; *The Official Catholic Directory* (New Providence, N.J.: P.J. Kenedy & Sons, 2006).

[12] Pontifical Council for the Family, *The Truth and Meaning of Human Sexuality* (Boston: Pauline Books & Media, 1996), 33.

BRING THESE POWERFUL DISPLAYS TO YOUR CHURCH, SCHOOL, BUSINESS OR RETREAT CENTER, AND GIVE OTHERS THE CHANCE TO OBTAIN CHASTITY RESOURCES AND OTHER INSPIRATIONAL PRODUCTS BY VISITING

CHASTITYPROJECT.COM

# GOT QUESTIONS? GET ANSWERS.

WATCH VIDEOS
GET RELATIONSHIP ADVICE
LAUNCH A PROJECT
READ ANSWERS TO TOUGH QUESTIONS
FIND HELP TO HEAL FROM THE PAST
LISTEN TO POWERFUL TESTIMONIES
SHOP FOR GREAT RESOURCES
SCHEDULE A SPEAKER

# FOR $2 OR LESS, WHO WOULD YOU GIVE THESE BOOKS AND CDS TO?

In order to reach as many people as possible, more than 20 chastity CDs and books (including the one you're reading) are available in bulk orders for $2 or less! Therefore, share this book and others like it with the people in your life who need it right now. For example:

### YOUR COLLEGE DORM
### YOUR HIGH SCHOOL
### YOUR YOUTH OR YOUNG ADULT GROUP AT CHURCH
### YOUR ALMA MATER

Buy a case of books and donate them as gifts at graduation, freshman orientation, retreats, conferences, confirmation, as a missionary effort through campus ministry, or to people you meet anywhere. You never know whose life you could change.

## TO ORDER, VISIT

CHASTITY PROJECT.COM